Language in use

UPPER-INTERMEDIATE

Teacher's Book

ADRIAN DOFF & CHRISTOPHER JONES

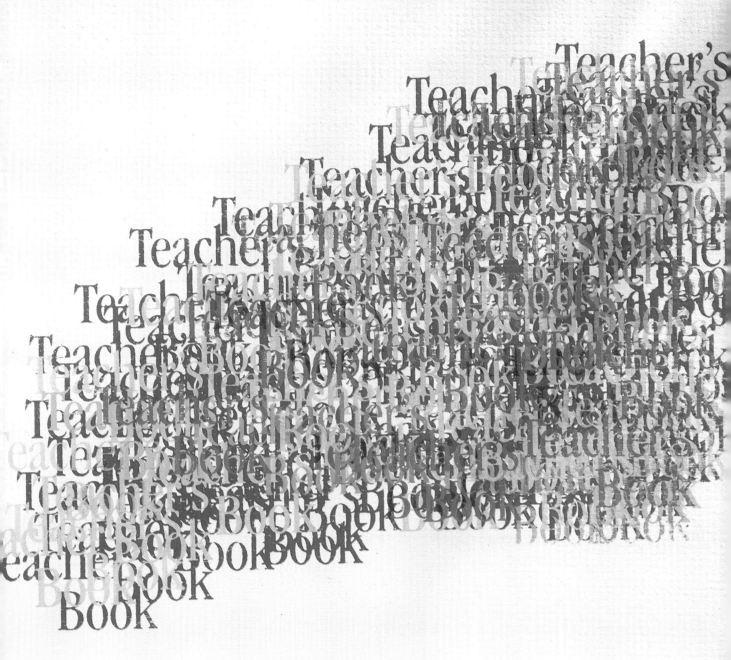

CAMBRIDGE
UNIVERSITY PRESS

PUBLISHED BY THE PRESS SYNDICATE OF THE UNIVERSITY OF CAMBRIDGE
The Pitt Building, Trumpington Street, Cambridge CB2 1RP, United Kingdom

CAMBRIDGE UNIVERSITY PRESS
The Edinburgh Building, Cambridge CB2 2RU, United Kingdom
40 West 20th Street, New York, NY 10011–4211, USA
10 Stamford Road, Oakleigh, Melbourne 3166, Australia

© Cambridge University Press 1997

First published 1997
Reprinted 1998

Printed in the United Kingdom at the University Press, Cambridge

ISBN 0 521 55547 7 Teacher's Book
ISBN 0 521 55550 7 Classroom Book
ISBN 0 521 55548 5 Self-study Workbook
ISBN 0 521 55549 3 Self-study Workbook with Answer Key
ISBN 0 521 55546 9 Class Cassette Set
ISBN 0 521 55545 0 Self-study Cassette

Contents

Introduction

How the course is organised

Who the course is for

Language in Use Upper Intermediate is a one-year course at upper intermediate level. It can be used by students who have completed *Language in Use Intermediate*, or who have studied English using another course at intermediate level.

The components of the course

The course contains 16 units, each designed to last for about three classroom hours, plus six double-page spreads of Study Pages. The students' materials are divided into two major components: a Classroom Book, for use in class by students working with a teacher; and a Self-study Workbook, for use by students working alone at home or in a self-access session. The Classroom Book is accompanied by a set of two cassettes and the Self-study Workbook is accompanied by a cassette or CD.

The syllabus

The course has a dual syllabus: a grammatical syllabus, which deals with the main structures of English that are important at upper intermediate level, and a topic syllabus, which deals with vocabulary. These two strands are reflected in Grammar units and Vocabulary units, which alternate through the course. For example:

Unit 1	Present, past and future	*Grammar unit*
Unit 2	Communicating	*Vocabulary unit*
Unit 3	Making things clear	*Grammar unit*
Unit 4	Sports and games	*Vocabulary unit*

This alternation of Grammar and Vocabulary units allows systematic coverage of the two major content areas of English. It also allows a natural recycling of language through the course: structures are recycled in Vocabulary units and vocabulary is recycled in Grammar units.

The Classroom Book

The Classroom Book contains the main presentation and practice material of the course, as well as activities in speaking, writing, reading and listening.

Grammar

The Grammar units cover the main grammatical areas that are essential at this level. These include verb tenses, the passive, modal and conditional structures, relative clauses, and structures that are useful in organising writing.

Our aim in *Language in Use* is to help students use grammar actively in communication, so the main activities in the unit are open-ended and give opportunities for communicative use of language.

Each Grammar unit also has a section called *Focus on Form*, which provides more controlled practice of the main structures of the unit. These exercises are optional, and can be used for extra accuracy and remedial work.

A typical Grammar unit is shown on page 3e.

Vocabulary

The Vocabulary units cover a number of topic areas that are relevant to students at this level (e.g. sports, ways of communicating, careers and business, science and politics). Each unit introduces a range of key vocabulary, including not only individual words but also phrases, items of lexical grammar and common collocations.

As in the Grammar units, the aim is to help students to activate vocabulary and use it in communication, so many of the activities are open-ended, and involve discussion and exchange of information.

Vocabulary work is also included in some exercises in the Grammar units. Examples are:

– astronomy (Unit 7, Exercise 1)
– population (Unit 9, Exercise 1)
– crime and the law (Unit 13, Exercise 1).

A typical Vocabulary unit is shown on page 3f.

Study Pages

After Units 2, 4, 6, 10, 12 and 14, the Classroom Book contains a double-page spread of *Study Pages*. Each of these contains:

– a set of across-the-board *Grammar study* exercises dealing with general areas of grammar such as infinitives, gerunds, time and articles.
– a *Language awareness* exercise, on topics such as homophones and homonyms, conversational fillers, and formal/informal English.
– an exercise on *Pronunciation*. These exercises focus on stress and intonation.

Other features

After Units 8 and 16, there is a *Review* section, which revises the main language dealt with so far.

There is also a *Reference Section*, which includes a full summary of each unit.

The Self-study Workbook

The Self-study Workbook contains a variety of exercises which provide back-up for work done in class and give opportunities for further self-study:

– *homework exercises* focusing on grammar and vocabulary; these include some reading tasks
– *listening tasks*, in every unit
– exercises dealing with *common idioms*, in every unit
– exercises focusing on particular *common verbs* (e.g. *do, make, get, take*), in each Grammar unit
– exercises on *word building*, in each Vocabulary unit
– exercises developing *study skills*, such as understanding new words, note-taking, preparing and organising writing, and reading for implication; these exercises occur after Units 2, 4, 6, 10, 12 and 14.

(For more information about these exercise types, see *To the Student* in the Self-study Workbook, and the boxes at the end of each unit of teaching notes.)

After every eight units there is a *Review* section, which follows the format of the Cambridge First Certificate *Use of English* paper.

Skills development

Speaking skills

Because *Language in Use* is concerned with active use of grammar and vocabulary, oral fluency is developed through many of the exercises in the Classroom Book, and especially through the freer activities in each unit.

Writing skills

Writing is developed through both the Classroom Book and the Self-study Workbook.

In the Classroom Book, there is an exercise in each Grammar unit specifically designed to develop writing skills; these exercises focus on such areas as linking events in a story, weighing up alternatives, balancing an argument, and talking about reason, purpose and causes and results.

Elsewhere in the Classroom Book, writing is either a follow-up to oral work or an integrated part of the classroom activity; it takes the form of note-making, writing sentences and paragraph writing.

The Self-study Workbook includes guided paragraph writing; it also provides exercises on making and expanding notes and summary writing. These exercises form part of an independent Study Skills syllabus which runs through the course.

Listening and reading skills

There are two types of reading and listening activities: those which are designed for use in class with interaction between students and help from the teacher (which appear in the Classroom Book), and those which are designed for students working alone (which appear in the Self-study Workbook).

In the Classroom Book, listening and reading are used in each unit as a basis for presentation or as a stimulus for a speaking or writing activity. In addition, each Vocabulary unit contains an extended activity which integrates reading and listening.

In the Self-study Workbook, there are short tasks designed to develop particular listening and reading strategies.

Pronunciation

The Pronunciation exercises in the Study Pages form an independent Pronunciation syllabus that runs through the course.

Functions

Functions are included in parts of the Grammar and Vocabulary units, and also in some of the Language awareness exercises in the Study Pages. Examples are:

– correcting (Unit 7)
– emphasising (Unit 7)
– conversational fillers (Study Pages D)
– evaluating (Unit 11)
– showing annoyance (Unit 13).

Other more general functions are linked to broader grammatical areas, and these form part of the grammar syllabus of the course. Examples are:

– clarifying (Unit 3)
– making deductions (Unit 7)
– speculating (Unit 9).

Underlying principles

Flexibility

Language in Use takes account of the fact that no two language classes are alike: students vary in level, age and interests, and may have different cultural and learning backgrounds; classes vary in size, physical layout and formality; teachers have different teaching styles; and learners may have widely differing ideas about what and how they need to learn. The course caters for some of these variations by:

– providing open-ended activities, so that classes can find their own level, and so that both weaker and stronger students have something to contribute
– encouraging students to contribute their own ideas, and draw on their own knowledge and experience
– providing activities that can be adapted to a variety of different teaching styles and types of class.

Clarity

In any language course, it is important that students understand clearly what they are doing and why they are doing it, and have a clear idea of what they have learnt. In writing *Language in Use*, clarity (for both learners and teachers) has been a major consideration, particularly in the following areas:

– the organisation and design of the units
– instructions, explanations and examples
– the Reference Section at the end of the book
– the design of the teaching notes.

Classwork and self-study

Activities in class are only one part of the language learning process; also important is individual work done by students in their own time, which gives them a chance to consolidate and build on what they have learnt. There are also certain kinds of activity that can sometimes be done more efficiently by students working alone than in class. These include, in particular:

– activities which students often prefer to do at their own pace (e.g. some listening and reading tasks)
– activities which some students may need more than others (e.g. Word building and Common verbs).

For these reasons, the Self-study Workbook is not just a homework book accompanying the Classroom Book. Rather, there is a careful division of material between the two books so that each contains appropriate activities.

Learning and acquisition

We believe that both 'learning' and 'acquisition' are important elements in learning a language. In other words, it is useful to spend time consciously focusing on particular language items, and it is also important to provide opportunities for natural language acquisition through fluency activities.

Both these elements are therefore incorporated in *Language in Use*. Some activities involve careful use of language and focus mainly on accuracy; in others, students develop fluency through freer, more creative use of language. Similarly, some reading and listening tasks focus on specific language items, while others are concerned with fluency and skills development.

In addition, the dual syllabus gives opportunity for acquisition of both grammar and vocabulary. In Grammar units, the focus is on learning grammatical structures, and this allows vocabulary to be acquired naturally. In Vocabulary units, the focus is on learning vocabulary, and this allows the natural acquisition of grammatical structures.

Using the course

The teaching notes

The teaching notes are designed to help you to make the most appropriate use of the Classroom activities with your students. They are in two columns.

The main notes for each activity (in the left-hand column) give a simple and straightforward route through the material, and include explanations for students and ideas for blackboard presentations.

In the right-hand column are a variety of options and alternatives which include:

- suggestions for homework both before and after the lesson
- optional phases within the lesson such as sentence writing, comprehension checks, vocabulary work, role-play and extra practice
- alternative procedures suitable for
  – classes which are better/weaker than average
  – larger/smaller classes
  – monolingual/mixed-nationality classes
  – more formal/less formal teaching situations
- notes giving explanations and examples of further language points arising from the main presentation.

The teaching notes for each unit also contain a summary of the exercises in the Self-study Workbook, and suggestions for suitable homework exercises are included in the notes for individual activities.

Working in pairs and groups

Many of the classroom activities are designed to be done in pairs or small groups. Most of these activities naturally fall into three phases:

- *Preparation.* Introduce the activity and make sure everyone knows what to do. It is often helpful to give a model or a demonstration yourself first.
- *Pair-/Groupwork.* During the activity, move around the class, listening and giving help when necessary.
- *Round-up.* Ask a few students to report back to the rest of the class on what they've done.

If you have a large class, or students who are not used to working in pairs, it may be better to introduce pairwork gradually, using it at first only for clearly defined tasks such as filling tables and controlled grammar practice. Other activities can be done with the whole class together.

Correcting errors

In some kinds of classroom activity, it is important to monitor students' language and correct errors: otherwise the point of the activity is lost. These can be spoken or written, and include:

- the presentation phase of activities in Grammar and Vocabulary units
- Focus on Form exercises in Grammar units
- homework exercises, including those in the Self-study Workbook.

In freer, more communicative activities, especially those involving pair- and groupwork, students should be involved in using language fluently, and you should avoid interrupting the flow of the activity by correcting mistakes too often. If you notice particular errors that you consider important, it is usually better to wait till the end of the activity before dealing with them.

Many of the activities in the course include a short writing phase, often involving sentence-writing as a preparation for a speaking activity. This gives an opportunity for students to monitor their own language more carefully, and for you to move round the class giving help and correcting errors.

Listening

Some listening activities involve fairly short pieces of listening which form part of the presentation and are used to introduce new structures or vocabulary. With these, you should aim for students to understand almost everything they hear. If necessary, you can help them to do this by:

- giving extra preparation for the listening (e.g. pre-teaching vocabulary, talking about the topic)
- playing the tape several times, and perhaps repeating difficult phrases yourself more slowly
- at the end, letting students listen and follow the tapescript at the back of the book.

Other listening activities are concerned with more general skills development. These usually involve longer pieces of listening, with accompanying tasks. Here the aim is that students should understand enough to complete the tasks, but not that they should attempt to understand every word they hear. However, as students often want to know exactly what was said, it may sometimes be a good idea to play the tape through again at the end and let students follow the tapescript.

Reading

As far as possible, get students to read texts silently (rather than reading aloud or following as the teacher reads). This allows them to read at their own speed, and in a more natural way.

As with listening, it is often unnecessary for students to understand every word they read. Often, the task only involves grasping the main points, or reading for particular information. It is also possible in many cases for students to guess the meanings of unfamiliar words from their contexts. Strategies for dealing with unknown words are developed in Study Skills sections (Self-study Workbook) and also in many of the combined reading and listening activities (Classroom Book).

Using the Focus on Form pages

Each Grammar unit ends with a page of Focus on Form exercises. These exercises give simple intensive practice of the main structures that are covered in the unit. They are intended as optional back-up material, and you do not need to do them all or do them in any particular order.

The Focus on Form exercises can be used in a variety of ways. Here are some suggestions:

- *Pre-presentation check*

Focus on Form exercise → Main exercise

  Begin with a Focus on Form exercise, to focus on the structure that you are teaching and to check that students can form it correctly. Then go on to the main exercise in the unit.

- *Basic structure practice*

Main exercise → Focus on Form exercise

  Do one of the exercises in the unit. If there are no problems, go on to the next exercise. But if students are having difficulty, do a Focus on Form exercise to give quick extra practice of the structure.

- *Extra remedial practice*

Whole unit → Focus on Form exercise

  Do Exercises 1–4 in the unit, then do selected Focus on Form exercises at the end, choosing areas that students have had problems with or which you think need more practice. You could also do individual Focus on Form exercises for five or ten minutes at the end of a lesson, to give variety and a change of pace.

- *Revision*

Series of units → Focus on Form exercise

  Leave out the Focus on Form exercises, then use them as a way of revising the main grammar points that you have covered over a number of weeks.

- *Self-access/homework*

  Some of the Focus on Form exercises can be done in writing. Students could do these in a self-access session or as homework, as an addition to the Self-study Workbook.

Using the Self-study Workbook

There are three ways of using the exercises in the Self-study Workbook. You will probably want to adopt a mixture of these approaches.

Homework
In the teaching notes for each classroom activity, there are cross-references to Grammar, Vocabulary and Listening exercises which are suitable for homework. The other exercise types (Idioms, Word building, Common verbs and Study Skills) can also be set for homework. If you use the Workbook extensively for this purpose, you might prefer students to have the version without the Answer Key.

Independent self-study
Allow students to work independently, choosing exercises that suit their individual needs. Students can either use the Answer Key to check their answers, or give in their books periodically to be marked.

Classwork
Some Workbook exercises are also suitable for use in class. Some possibilities are:
- Listening exercises, which are often closely linked to classroom activities
- Study Skills exercises, which lend themselves to classroom discussion.

Short cuts through the course

Language in Use is designed to provide plenty of material, and it is quite possible to cover the course without doing every single exercise. If you are short of time, or if you wish to move through the units quickly with a good class, there are various short cuts you can take through the book:

- With a good class, leave out the Focus on Form exercises.
- With a weaker class, leave out some of the freer, more demanding activities, and use the Focus on Form exercises instead.
- In the combined reading and listening activities, you could give the reading for homework, and do the listening only in class.
- Limit the time you spend in class on material from the Self-study Workbook. If students have no time to work outside class, you could leave out the Workbook altogether and use only the Classroom Book.

Grammar units

Grammar units contain:

– three activities that introduce key structures.
– one activity focusing on writing skills.
– optional exercises for controlled practice (Focus on Form).

Main presentation of *must*, *might* and *can't* for making deductions. Students read short texts about aliens, and use the structures to give their opinion.

Shows how we use unreal conditionals to justify deductions. A simple sentence-making exercise, focusing on meaning.

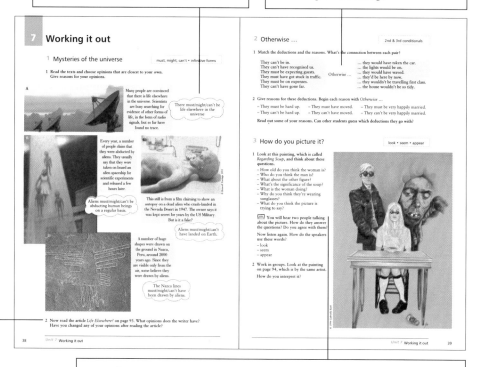

Part 2 – students read an article in the back of the book, and say whether their opinions have changed as a result.

Introduces structures with *look*, *seem* and *appear*. Students hear two interpretations of a painting. In Part 2, they give their own interpretation of another painting by the same artist at the back of the book.

Vocabulary units

Vocabulary units contain:

– three activities linked by topic. Each activity focuses on a different area of vocabulary.
– an integrated reading and listening activity, for skills development.

Common vocabulary related to running a business. Students read authentic facts about a successful business, and put them in order. They then hear the story of what happened.

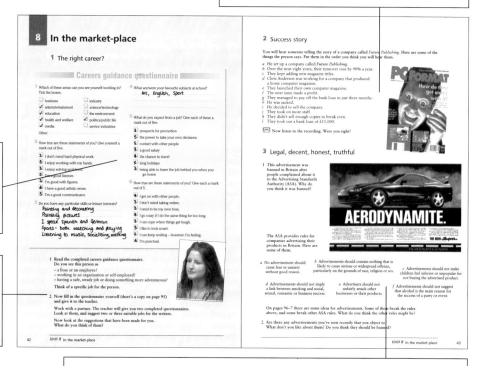

Introduces a range of vocabulary about jobs and careers, via a filled-in questionnaire. Students evaluate the answers, and suggest a suitable career for the person.

Part 2 – a chance for students to fill in the questionnaire for themselves. Other students evaluate their answers, and suggest suitable careers.

A discussion of the rights and wrongs of advertising. Students read some of the rules of the Advertising Standards Authority, then look at some draft advertisements in the back of the book and decide if they should be banned.

A writing skills activity focusing on reason and purpose. In Part 1, students read texts which suggest reasons why people gamble.

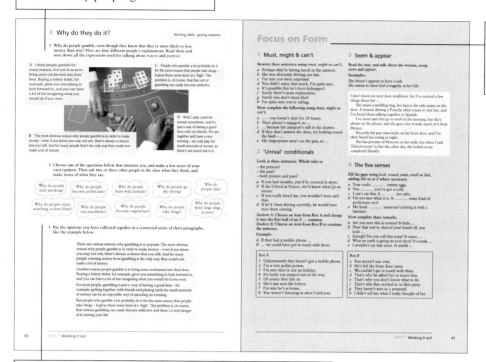

Focus on Form exercises. These are optional, and give extra controlled practice of key structures.

Part 2 – students choose a topic that interests them, and collect opinions from other people in the class. They then write a connected series of paragraphs, based on a model.

Integrated reading and listening activity.

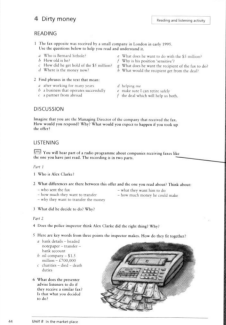

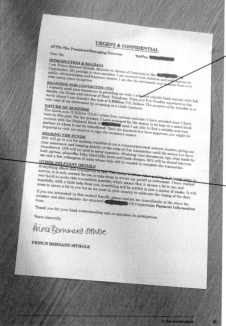

Part 1 – Reading.
Students read an authentic fax offering businesses large sums of money, and decide how they would react if they received it.

Part 2 – Listening.
Students hear a radio discussion, and discover whether their decision was the right one.

Guide to units

Classroom Book	Self-study Workbook

1 Present, past and future

Talking about the present; talking about the past; making predictions

Grammar: revision of present, past and future tenses

Writing skills: writing a job application

Grammar exercises
Idioms: *Common idioms with nouns*
Listening: *Gossip*
Common verbs: *do and make*

2 Communicating

Vocabulary: types of written and spoken English; personal communication; learning a language

Reading and listening activity: *The truth about lying*

Vocabulary exercises
Idioms: *Common idioms with prepositions*
Listening: *Varieties of English*
Word building: *Nouns and verbs (1)*

Study pages A

Grammar study: *Infinitives*
Language awareness: *Double meanings*
Pronunciation: *Intonation and meaning*

Study skills A

Using reference books
A *Using a dictionary*
B *Finding your way around a book*

3 Making things clear

Defining; correcting wrong statements; emphasising

Grammar: defining relative clauses; cleft sentences with 'It ...'; cleft sentences with 'What ...'; participle phrases

Writing skills: describing a scene

Grammar exercises
Idioms: *Colours*
Listening: *Radio news*
Common verbs: *get*

4 Sports and games

Vocabulary: dangerous pastimes; how to play sports and games; issues in spectator sports

Reading and listening activity: *Problems, problems ...*

Vocabulary exercises
Idioms: *Animals*
Listening: *Cricket*
Word building: *Adjectives and nouns (1)*

Study pages B

Grammar study: *Articles*
Language awareness: *Conversational remarks*
Pronunciation: *Where's the stress?*

Study skills B

Dealing with vocabulary
A *Guessing unknown words*
B *Learning new vocabulary*

Classroom Book	Self-study Workbook

5 Set in the past

Talking about past events and actions; reporting; giving extra information

Grammar: Past and Past perfect simple and continuous; reporting verbs; non-defining relative clauses

Writing skills: linking events in a story

Grammar exercises
Idioms: *Numbers*
Listening: *Holiday incident*
Common verbs: *go*

6 Do it yourself

Vocabulary: instructions for common products and appliances; damage and repairing damage; cooking

Reading and listening activity: *They did it themselves*

Vocabulary exercises
Idioms: *Parts of the body (1)*
Listening: *How to do it*
Word building: *Prefixes (1)*

Study pages C

Grammar study: *-ing forms*
Language awareness: *British and US English*
Pronunciation: *Rising and falling tones*

Study skills C

Approaching a reading text
A *Predicting what you will read*
B *Reading for the main idea*
C *Finding specific information*

7 Working it out

Drawing logical conclusions; giving reasons for deductions; interpreting things you see

Grammar: must/might/can't; second and third conditionals; look/seem/appear

Writing skills: giving reasons

Grammar exercises
Idioms: *Parts of the body (2)*
Listening: *Life elsewhere?*
Common verbs: *come*

8 In the market-place

Vocabulary: jobs and what they involve; careers; success and failure in business; advertising

Reading and listening activity: *Dirty money*

Vocabulary exercises
Idioms: *Describing feelings*
Listening: *The new design manager*
Word building: *Nouns and verbs (2)*

Review Units 1–8

Classroom Book	Self-study Workbook

9 Possibilities

Discussing alternative possibilities; saying what things depend on; saying how likely things are

Grammar: will and would; depends (on); indirect questions; probability expressions

Writing skills: weighing up alternatives

Grammar exercises
Idioms: *Streets and roads*
Listening: *Return from Berlin*
Common verbs: *see*

10 Life, the universe and everything

Vocabulary: branches of science; science and the environment; beliefs

Reading and listening activity: *Science fiction*

Vocabulary exercises
Idioms: *Things people say*
Listening: *Reading the tarot*
Word building: *Adjectives and nouns (2)*

Study pages D / Study skills D

Grammar study: *Time*
Language awareness: *Conversational fillers*
Pronunciation: *High key*

Summarising information
A *Taking notes*
B *Writing a summary*

11 Evaluating

Comparing past and present; saying if things are worth doing; talking about advantages and disadvantages

Grammar: time comparison structures; evaluation structures; causative verbs

Writing skills: organising information

Grammar exercises
Idioms: *Other people*
Listening: *Panel discussion*
Common verbs: *take*

12 Yourself and others

Vocabulary: adjectives describing personality; relationships with partners; other relationships

Reading and listening activity: *Skin deep*

Vocabulary exercises
Idioms: *Reactions*
Listening: *Two jokes*
Word building: *Prefixes (2)*

Study pages E / Study skills E

Grammar study: *Pronouns and determiners*
Language awareness: *Regional accents*
Pronunciation: *Low key*

Developing a piece of writing
A *Jotting down ideas*
B *Making a draft and making improvements*

Classroom Book	Self-study Workbook

13 Right and wrong

Criticising and justifying past actions; talking about mistakes

Grammar: should(n't) have done / been doing; could/needn't/might have done

Writing skills: balancing an argument

Grammar exercises
Idioms: *All in the mind*
Listening: *Mistakes*
Common verbs: *put*

14 Body and mind

Vocabulary: diseases – symptoms, causes and cures; forms of medical treatment; alternative forms of medicine

Reading and listening activity: *All the perfumes of Arabia*

Vocabulary exercises
Idioms: *Money*
Listening: *The limits of medicine*
Word building: *Nouns and verbs (3)*

Study pages F

Grammar study: *Degree and comparison*
Language awareness: *Formal and informal*
Pronunciation: *Disagreeing politely*

Study skills F

Reading between the lines
A *Understanding implied meaning*
B *Reading a poem*

15 Using the passive

Choosing between active and passive; reporting using the passive; talking about experiences

Grammar: passive forms; passive reporting verbs; the *have* passive

Writing skills: causes and results

Grammar exercises
Idioms: *Sports and games*
Listening: *Oriental spices*
Common verbs: *set*

16 World affairs

Vocabulary: war and peace; politics and politicians; election issues

Reading and listening activity: *On the front line*

Vocabulary exercises
Idioms: *All at sea*
Listening: *A minimum wage?*
Word building: *Adjectives and nouns (3)*

Review Units 9–16

Present, past and future

1 Images

1 Which of these statements do you agree with more?

A Everyone has an 'image', which is the way we present ourselves to other people. So you can tell a lot about people from the way they look.

B You can't tell what people are like from their appearance. In fact, appearances are often deceptive.

Now do this test. Can you tell which of these people wrote the sets of sentences below?

1 I cycle a lot, and I go jogging regularly. These days I'm cooking quite a lot, especially for dinner parties with friends.

I've just come back from a skiing holiday in France – my third one this year!

I've travelled widely in Europe and the USA, but I've never been to the Far East.

I enjoy dancing, especially ballroom dancing, and I've been doing quite a lot of it recently.

I've been playing the flute for quite a few years now, but I still don't play it very well.

2 I don't do any sports, but I like flying kites. At the moment, I'm attending a course on jazz singing.

I speak fluent German, and I've just come back from a trip to Germany.

I love live jazz, and I've been to Chicago on my own a couple of times, just to visit their blues and jazz bars.

I've been eating out a lot with friends recently.

I've been playing the piano since I was eight.

I haven't been to a dentist for about ten years.

2 What different tenses do the two people use? What is each tense used for?

Write a set of similar sentences about yourself, and give it to the teacher. The teacher will read some of them out. Can you tell who wrote them?

This is an introductory unit which has two parallel aims: to revise the tense systems of English, and at the same time to get students using the language and interacting with each other. The first three activities cover the three 'time frames' which underlie tense usage in English:
– the present (Present and Present perfect tenses)
– the past (Past and Past perfect tenses)
– the future (Future and Future perfect tenses).

The fourth activity develops writing skills. It deals with the language of job applications, and focuses on ways of writing about experience and qualifications.

1 Images

This exercise is about whether you can judge people from their appearance. The two sets of sentences give personal information about two of the people in the photos, and students see if it is possible to identify them. The sentences are all set in the present (i.e. they are about 'now' or the period 'up to now') and they use the Present and Present perfect tenses. In the last part of the activity, students write sentences about themselves. With a new class, this is a chance for students to begin to get to know each other.

1 Reading & discussion

● Look at the two statements, and find out from a show of hands how many students agree with A and how many with B. If you like, ask students to say why they agree with one statement rather than the other.

● Read through the sets of sentences, explaining any unknown vocabulary (e.g. *ballroom dancing*, *flute*, *kites*). Then divide the class into pairs, and ask them to decide who wrote each set of sentences.

● Discuss with the whole class what conclusions they came to and why. Then tell them the answers:

Person 1: F   Person 2: C

2 Presentation & writing activity

● Write the names of the four tenses used on the board:

> **Present simple**
> **Present continuous**
> **Present perfect simple**
> **Present perfect continuous**

Ask students to find examples of each tense, and establish what the tenses are used for:
– *Present simple*: for talking in general, saying what you do often, sometimes, etc. (*I cycle a lot*)
– *Present continuous*: for saying what you're doing at the moment or 'around now' (*I'm attending a course on jazz singing*)
– *Present perfect simple*: for talking about recent events (*I've just come back from a skiing holiday*), and for talking about experience (*I've travelled widely in Europe and the USA*)
– *Present perfect continuous*: for talking about recent activities (*I've been eating out a lot with friends recently*)
– *Present perfect continuous + for/since*: for things that started in the past and are still going on (*I've been playing the piano since I was eight*)

● Working alone, students write a few true sentences about themselves on a piece of paper, using the tenses you have focused on.

● Collect the papers, and then read out some of the sets of sentences. The class tries to guess which students wrote them.

● As a round-up, refer again to the two statements you considered at the beginning. Ask students if they have changed their mind about them, and if so why.

➤ Focus on Form: Exercises 1, 2 & 3
➤ Workbook: Exercises A & B

Discussion option
Prompt further discussion by asking specific questions, e.g.
If you saw a man wearing a suit and tie, what would you think about him?
What about a woman with lots of make-up?
Is this just prejudice, or can you really tell something about them?

Option
Students choose one or two of the other four people, and imagine the kind of things they spend their time doing.
Information about them can be found on page T25.

Presentation option
If necessary, give other examples of your own to show how the tenses are used and the differences between them.

Language note
We use the Present perfect simple instead of continuous
1 with stative verbs (*be*, *have*, *know*, etc.), e.g.
I've been away a lot recently.
We've known each other since June. (not ~~have been knowing~~)
2 with negative expressions (saying how long since something happened), e.g.
I haven't seen them for a year.

Note
This will work best in classes where students do not know each other very well. If they already know each other fairly well, they should write things about themselves that are not too well known to the others in the class.

2 Past experiences

In this exercise students hear someone describe a real encounter with a polar bear in the Arctic, and this is used as a basis for personal anecdotes of their own. The language the speaker uses is set in the past (i.e. it is about an experience at a particular time in the past) and uses Past and Past perfect tenses.

▶ Focus on Form: Exercise 4
▶ Workbook: Exercises A & B

1 Listening & presentation

- ▣ Play the recording once without pausing. Ask which of the topics the speaker is talking about. Answer:

  The most terrifying experience he's ever had.

- ▣ Play the recording again, pausing if necessary, and get answers to the questions. Answers:
  a He was in the Arctic, with an Inuit guide.
  b Photographing seals under water.
  c The weather had turned bad.
  d They'd decided to spend the night on the ice.
  e He was just waking up when he felt a polar bear playing with his feet.
  f He kept as still as he could; he woke his Inuit guide.
  g The guide stuck his head out of the tent, and the bear went away.

- Use the answers to focus on the tenses used in the story:
  – Past simple for giving the main events of the story (*I felt something …, I woke my Inuit guide*)
  – Past continuous for giving the background (*I was camping, I was lying in the tent*)
  – Past perfect for going back to events that had happened earlier (*the weather had turned bad (the evening before), we'd decided to spend the night on the ice*).

2 Speaking activity

- Divide the class into groups of four or five. In turn, students choose a topic and tell the others in the group what happened.

- A student in each group tells the group's best story to the rest of the class.

Optional lead-in
Ask one of the questions in the bubbles, getting brief responses from two or three students, e.g.

What's the luckiest thing that's ever happened to you?
It was last April. I won $500 on the lottery.

Use this to establish that
– the question uses the Present perfect tense because it means 'at any time up to now'
– in answering the question, we use the Past tense, because we're thinking about a particular occasion in the past.

Note: This is similar to the better-known sequence 'Have you ever been to London?' 'Yes. I went there last year'.

▣ The tapescript is on page 104.

3 They got it wrong

This exercise presents real predictions made in the 1950s and 1960s about developments in technology, as a basis for discussion and for students to make similar predictions of their own. The language used in the predictions is set in the future, and revises the three future tenses: the Future simple, Future continuous and Future perfect.

▶ Focus on Form: Exercise 5
▶ Workbook: Exercises A & B

1 Reading & presentation

- Give time for students to read through the predictions and decide whether they think they will ever come true. Then discuss each prediction in turn with the whole class. Encourage students to give reasons for what they say.

  will + infinitive
  will be -ing
  will have -ed

- Write these structures on the board and ask students to find examples of each in the text.

  Show how *will be -ing* and *will have -ed* are 'future versions' of the Present continuous and Present perfect:
  – Now everyone *is living* on Earth, but by 2010 some people *will be living* in space stations.
  – Buses *haven't disappeared* from cities yet, but by 2010 they *will have disappeared*.

2 Writing & speaking activity

- Working alone or with a partner, students write a few predictions of their own.

- In turn, students read out their predictions. Ask the class to comment on them.

Vocabulary option
Students read through the predictions and note down any words or expressions they don't understand (e.g. *package tour, cabin, rotor, habitable, ray, harvest (v.)*). Go through these together before you discuss the predictions.

Language note
In talking about why predictions won't come true, it is natural to change from *will* to *would*, because we are talking about things we see as 'unreal', e.g. 'There will never be package tours to the moon. They would be too expensive, and no one would want to go on them.'
This is focused on in Unit 9.

Alternative
Students move freely round the class. They read out their predictions to other students and ask them for comments.

2 Past experiences

Revision of past tenses

1 🔲 **You will hear someone talking about one of the topics in the bubbles. Which topic do you think he's talking about? Answer these questions:**

a Where was he? Who was he with?
b How had he spent the previous day?
c What had happened?
d What had they done?
e What happened in the morning?
f How did he react?
g How did they solve the problem?

> What's the biggest surprise you've ever had?

> What's the silliest thing you've ever done?

> What's the most unusual thing you've ever eaten?

> What's the most terrifying experience you've ever had?

> What's the luckiest thing that's ever happened to you?

> What's the unluckiest thing that's ever happened to you?

2 **Work in groups. Choose one of the topics that you find interesting, and tell the others what happened.**

Now choose the most interesting experience, and tell the rest of the class about it.

3 They got it wrong

Revision of future tenses

1 The first package tour to the Moon will take place on 15 March 1975.
New York travel agent Jack Garvoy, 1950

2 The last buses will have disappeared from cities by the early 1990s. They will have been replaced by a system of individual computer-operated cabins on rails.
Batelle Institute, Geneva, 1968

3 People will be able to fly through the air in a standing position, using small rotors attached to their backs. This will solve transport problems in cities.
C H Zimmermann, National Advisory Committee of Aeronautics, 1951

4 In 15 to 20 years passenger aircraft will travel at six times the speed of sound (about 6,000 kph) and fly at a height of 30 km. It will be possible to cross the Atlantic in less than an hour.
H Hertel, Technical University of Berlin, 1961

5 We'll be able to provide the Sahara with so much rain that it will become habitable.
Hermann Oberth, physicist, 1960s

6 By 1980 at the latest, thousands of people will be living in giant space stations, thereby solving the problem of overpopulation.
G K O'Neill, physicist, 1955

7 By using radioactive rays, we'll be able to grow cherries as big as apples.
Nuclear biologists, Brookhaven National Laboratory, New York, 1958

8 Trained apes and birds will be used to harvest crops.
Sir George Thompson, psychologist, 1955

9 By the year 2000, the fight against world hunger will have been won, thanks to automation and developments in agricultural technology.
F Baade, Institute of World Economics,

1 **None of these nine predictions has come true.**

Do you think any of them will ever come true? If so, suggest a date. If not, say why you think it'll never happen.

2 **Think about the year 2100. What do you think**

– people will be able to do?
– people will be doing?
– people will have done?

Read your predictions out. What do other people think of them?

4 Just the job

1 Look at these sentences from letters of application.
Which advertisements are they replying to?

I have a good sense of rhythm.

I am a trained mechanic.

I am used to going without sleep for long periods.

I have visited Australia several times, so I have a good knowledge of spoken English.

I have three years' experience of working with young children.

I am a qualified nursery teacher.

I have worked as a model for an advertising agency.

I am a good cook.

A **WANTED** Responsible person to look after two children during summer holidays. Luxury villa in Southern Spain. Duties include some light housework.

B **WORK IN** a travel agency this summer. Help required during holiday period. Secretarial and travel experience an advantage.

C **YOUR CHANCE** to be a star. Film extra required for crowd scenes and small speaking parts.

D **JAZZ/SAMBA BAND** looking for singer (male or female) for weekend gigs. Cafés and private parties.

E **PRIVATE TUTOR** required to teach English to 10-year-old boy.

F **BUSINESSWOMAN** seeks personal assistant. Must have secretarial skills. Knowledge of French an advantage.

G **FIFTH MEMBER** wanted to join group travelling overland to West Africa, starting November.

2 Look at these notes for a letter of application. Which of the jobs is it for?

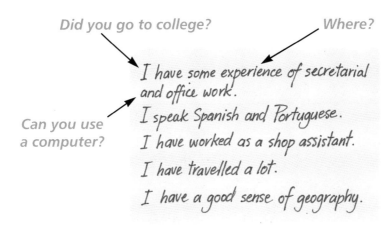

Did you go to college? *Where?*

Can you use a computer?

I have some experience of secretarial and office work.
I speak Spanish and Portuguese.
I have worked as a shop assistant.
I have travelled a lot.
I have a good sense of geography.

What else do you think an employer might want to know?
Think of some more questions like the ones above.

Now look at the letter on page 88. Did the writer answer your questions?

3 Choose one of the jobs, and make notes about your qualifications and experience.
Either write real things or make things up. Then exchange notes with your partner.

Look at your partner's notes, and write questions asking for other information.

Using your notes, write a letter of application. Try to include details your
partner has asked for.

4 Just the job

Writing skills: *writing an application for a job; expanding outline notes in response to feedback.*
Language focus: *describing experience, qualifications and knowledge; letter formulae.*

This activity helps students to write a non-specialist letter of application. It follows these three stages:
1 Presentation. Students study examples of language that may be useful in talking about experience and qualifications.
2 Reading and discussion. Students look at examples of outline notes and a model letter of application.
3 Writing. Students write their own notes, get feedback from other students, and write their own letter of application.

➤ Workbook: Exercise C

1 Presentation

- Read through the advertisements and explain any new vocabulary, e.g. *duties* (= what you have to do), *secretarial experience*, *film extra* (= appearing in crowd scenes), *gig* (= concert), *tutor* (= individual teacher). Ask students to match the sentences with the advertisements. Possible answers:

mechanic: G
sense of rhythm: D
going without sleep: G (F)
good knowledge of spoken English: E (B)
young children: A, E
nursery teacher: A
model for advertising agency: C
good cook: A (G)

> **Presentation option**
> From the sentences, build up useful expressions on the board for talking about knowledge, experience and qualifications:
>
> | a trained … | |
> | a qualified … | |
> | have a good | sense of knowledge of |
> | have experience of | |
> | be used to -ing | |

2 Reading & discussion

- Look at the notes, and establish which job the person is applying for. (Answer: the travel agency.)

> **Language note**
> The notes and the letter of application use the *Present perfect tense* to talk about experience (things you have done at some time in your life).

- Ask students to suggest other questions. If you like, build them up on the board, e.g.

> **I speak Spanish and Portuguese:**
> *How well? Do you have any qualifications?*
> **I have worked as a shop assistant:**
> *Where? What kind of shop? How long for?*
> **I have travelled a lot:**
> *Where to? Have you been to any holiday areas?*
> *Do you have any training as a secretary?*

> **Alternative: professional English courses**
> With classes that are learning English for particular professions (e.g. business English, English for tourism), you could add advertisements that are connected with students' own field of interest.

- Give time for students to read the letter. Discuss which of the students' questions it answers.

3 Writing

- Working alone, students write notes for a letter of application for one of the jobs.
- Students exchange notes with someone else. They write questions on the notes they have received, then give them back.
- Students expand their notes into a complete letter of application, using the letter on page 88 as a rough model.

> **Optional extension**
> Taking each job in turn, ask all the students who applied for it to read out their letters. The rest of the class vote on who should get the job.

> **Homework option**
> Students write the notes and questions in class, and write the letter itself for homework.

Focus on Form

1 Present simple & continuous

Uses of the Present simple and continuous

- Give time for students to study the sentences.
- Look at the sentences together, and focus on these differences:
  - *The sun sets* = always, in general. *The sun's setting* = at this moment.
  - *He works in a bank* = it's his job. *I'm working in a bank* = it's what I'm doing at the moment, during the present period (probably temporarily).
  - *She often watches TV* = she watches quite a lot (a neutral remark). *She's always watching TV* = she watches too much, she never seems to do anything else (a critical remark).
  - *The plane leaves at ten:* Present simple because it's a scheduled time, it's the same every day. *We're leaving at ten:* Present continuous with future meaning = it's definitely arranged.

2 Recent events & activities

Present perfect simple and continuous

- Use the examples to establish that
  - the sentences in A are about *completed* actions, things the person has achieved (*the ironing's finished, I've finished three books*)
  - the sentences in B are about *continuous activities* with no 'end-point' (*he's been ironing for a time, I've been spending time reading*).
- Students do the exercise alone or in pairs. Then go through the answers together. Answers:

  a I've been trying
  b I've been preparing, I've been going
  c I've washed, I've done
  d Have you been crying, I've been peeling

3 Duration

Present perfect continuous and simple + *for/since*

- Give time for students to study the sentences, then go through the answers together. Answers:

  a lived *or* been living   *b* been watching   *c* had
  d had *or* been having   *e* eaten

- Point out the difference between *c* and *d*: in *c*, *have* = own, possess (it has no continuous form); in *d*, *have* = do an activity (play the piano), so it can have a continuous form.
- Students expand the phrases into true sentences about themselves.

4 Past events

Past simple, Past continuous and Past perfect

- Look at the example, and ask students to use the paragraph to answer the questions. Answers:
  What was happening? I was walking home.
  What had already happened? I'd missed the last bus.
  What happened next? I started running.
- Students write the two other paragraphs. Expected answers:

  a I'd left work early, and I was just opening the front door of my flat when I heard a noise in the living room. So I closed the door quietly, went to a phone box and rang the police.
  b I'd forgotten to bring a map with me and I'd taken a wrong turning. I was driving past a field when I saw a woman sitting on the gate. (So) I stopped the car and asked the way.

5 Talking about the future

Future simple, Future continuous and Future perfect

- Read through what the fortune-teller says. If necessary, focus on the three future tenses used.
- Pairwork. Students discuss which predictions will be true of them, and what they think will really happen to them.
- As a round-up, ask a few students what they think their future will be like.

Self-study Workbook

Exercise A: Tenses
Revision of present, past and future tenses. Students fill gaps with suitable verb forms.

Exercise B: Your present, your past and your future
Revision of present, past and future tenses. Students write short paragraphs about themselves.

Exercise C: Selling yourself
Experience, knowledge and ability. Students rewrite sentences using key words.

Idioms: Common idioms with nouns
Idioms with noun phrases (e.g. *a piece of cake*).

Listening: Gossip
Three people gossip about other people they know. Students listen for the general idea, and for examples of exaggeration.

Common verbs: do and make
Difference between *do* and *make*. Idiomatic expressions with *do* and *make*.

Focus on Form

1 Present simple & continuous

Look at these sentences. What are the differences between the Present simple and the Present continuous?

Present simple	*Present continuous*
The sun sets in the west.	The sun's setting.
He works in a bank.	I'm working in a bank.
She often watches TV.	He's always watching TV.
The plane leaves at ten tomorrow morning.	We're leaving at ten tomorrow morning.

2 Recent events & activities

A	He's done the ironing. I've read three books in the last week.
B	He's been doing the ironing. I've been reading a lot recently.

What is the difference between the sentences in A and those in B?

Rewrite these sentences, putting the verbs in brackets into either the Present perfect simple or the Present perfect continuous.

a I'm fed up with living in chaos, so I (try) to get my life a bit more organised.
b I (prepare) for my exams all this week, so I (go) to bed really early.
c I (wash) all the dishes and I (do) the washing. What would you like me to do next?
d – Why are your eyes all red? (You cry)?
  – No. I (peel) onions.

3 Duration

Choose the correct forms of the verbs in italics. Which must be simple? Which must be continuous? And which can be either?

a She's *lived / been living* there for 70 years.
b They've *watched / been watching* TV ever since they came home.
c I've *had / been having* this photo album since my grandfather died.
d He's *had / been having* piano lessons for six months.
e I haven't *eaten / been eating* since breakfast.

Expand these phrases into sentences that are true of you.

a ... for several years.
b ... since I was a child.
c I've been playing ...
d I've had ...
e I haven't been to ...

4 Past events

Look at the sentences in italics. What was happening at the time? What had already happened? What happened next? Write short paragraphs, and add a sentence of your own.

Example:

> *A car stopped and a voice said 'Get in'*
> start running   miss the last bus
> walk home   be frightened

I'd just missed the last bus, and I was walking home when a car stopped and a voice said 'Get in'. I was frightened, and I started running. The car followed me slowly down the street.

a *I heard a noise in the living room*
  open the front door   go to a phone box
  ring the police   close the door quietly
  leave work early

b *I saw a woman sitting on the gate*
  forget to bring a map   ask the way
  stop the car   drive past a field
  take a wrong turning

5 Talking about the future

Imagine that a fortune-teller says these things about your future.

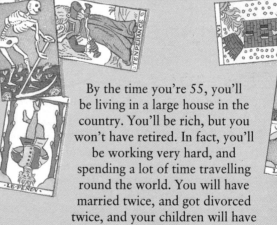

By the time you're 55, you'll be living in a large house in the country. You'll be rich, but you won't have retired. In fact, you'll be working very hard, and spending a lot of time travelling round the world. You will have married twice, and got divorced twice, and your children will have grown up and left home, so you'll be quite lonely. You will have given up eating meat, but you'll be smoking very heavily.

Which of the predictions do you believe? What do you think your life will really be like?

2 Communicating

1 Lines of communication

1 Here are some examples of different kinds of written and spoken English. Which pictures do they go with? How can you tell?

A
It means being open, it means telling it as it is, not opposing everything every other party does for the sake of it. People look to politicians for leadership. And leadership is about having the courage to say no as well as yes.

B
From: cdk@demon.co.uk
To: dave@cityscape.co.uk
Are we playing table tennis tonight? What time?
Philippe

C
Now if we look at the next picture, we can see how fashions gradually changed over the next 20 years. By 1850, women's skirts had become fuller, and waists much narrower.

D
Would the owner of a white Ford Escort registration number P452 JTE please move it, as it is blocking the entrance to the car park.

E
Here's your train fare. Sandwiches in fridge. Have a good time. See you tonight. C.

F
Dangerous Currents
Do not swim when the red flag is flying

G
The Author hereby assigns to the Publisher the full copyright in the Work throughout the world on the understanding that the Publisher shall not at any time assign the said copyright to any other party without the prior written consent of the Author.

H
These days there's so much to read, so much to see, so much to do that our lives are busier than ever before. So where does God fit in to all this? For many people, the answer is, sadly, that He doesn't.

I
Equipment Fair. 9–12 Oct. Berlin. Helen and Mike.
Ken to organise tickets/accommodation, and check availability of samples.
Meeting with FKR, 10 Oct 12.30.
Helen to submit report by 19th.

2 Work in pairs. Make up an example of written or spoken English, following instructions your teacher will give you.

Read out your example. Can other students identify what it is?

This unit is about the way people speak and write to each other. It focuses on the following vocabulary areas:
– types of written and spoken English, and verbs associated with them
   (e.g. *leave a note, send a message, give a lecture*)
– phrases connected with communication (e.g. *keep in touch, make small talk, not be on speaking terms*)
– expressions for talking about language and language learning
   (e.g. *pronunciation, fluent, make a mistake*).

The Reading and Listening activity is about lying: when people tell lies, what kind of lies they tell, and who they lie to.

1 Writing and speaking

This exercise presents real examples of written and spoken English. These are used as a basis for recognition and discussion of where they can be found, who they are for, what they are about, etc. They also introduce two kinds of vocabulary: types of written and spoken English (e.g. note, lecture, instructions) *and verbs associated with them (e.g.* leave a note, give a lecture).

1 Reading & presentation

- Give time for students to look at the samples of written and spoken English and match them with the pictures. Then go through the answers together. As you do so, build up on the board a list of key words with the phrases they commonly appear in (e.g. *leave a note for someone, give a lecture*). Answers:

  A 3: part of a political *speech* (in the picture, someone is *giving a speech*)
  B 8: an *e-mail message* (you *send someone a message*)
  C 9: part of a *lecture* about the history of fashion (in the picture, someone is *giving a lecture*)
  D 4: an public *announcement* (someone is *making an announcement* over the loudspeaker)
  E 1: a *note* (someone has *written/left a note*, perhaps for his/her son/daughter)
  F 7: a *notice* (on the other side of the *notice board*)
  G 2: part of a *contract* for a book (the author has *signed a contract*)
  H 5: part of a *sermon* (in the picture, a *priest/minister* is *giving a sermon*)
  I 6: *notes* (or *minutes*) from a business meeting (the person on the left is *taking notes*)

2 Writing & speaking activity

- In pairs, students choose one of the types of written or spoken English listed on the board, and make up an example of their own. Ask them to think of a particular situation, so that it is possible to say who wrote/said it and why.
- Write these questions on the board:

  > **What type of writing/speaking?**
  > **Who wrote/said it? Who to?**
  > **What's it about?**

  Students read out their examples. Other students identify the type of writing/speech it is, and try to answer the other questions on the board.

➤ Workbook: Exercise A, Listening

Presentation option
Write the key words on the board (in random order) and ask students to match them with the examples.

Language note
A *note* is a short piece of writing, usually to ask or remind someone to do something. You can also *make a note of* something, to remind yourself (e.g. *Phone Peter*). You *take* or *make notes* from a book, a lecture or a meeting.

Message is mainly used for telephone, answerphone and e-mail, or for occasions when you cannot communicate normally (e.g. a secret message). You *send* a message *to* someone, or *leave* a message *for* them.

Option
Prepare different types of writing or speech on slips of paper, and give one to each pair, e.g.

Instructions for using a fire extinguisher
An office memo from the boss asking staff to dress more smartly
A notice on a beach saying what you can and can't do.

2 Person to person

This exercise focuses on idiomatic expressions used to describe how people communicate or fail to communicate. It covers three main areas: keeping in touch with people, getting on well/badly, and speaking/not speaking to people.

➤ Workbook: Exercise B

1 Presentation

- Ask students to match the bubbles. Answers:

  We used to get on very well, but now we aren't on speaking terms.
  We've known each other since childhood and we still keep in touch.
  We've really got nothing to say to each other, so we tend to just make small talk most of the time.
  I used to write to them regularly but now we've lost touch.
  We had a terrible argument last week but now we've made it up.

- Write a table on the board to show expressions with *(in) touch with*:

be get	*in*	
keep		touch with someone
lose be out of		

2 Speaking activity

- To introduce the activity, tell the class about someone you know, using one of the expressions from the exercise.

- Groupwork. In turn, students talk about someone they know that one of the phrases applies to.

- Each group chooses its most interesting story to tell to the rest of the class.

Presentation option
Before doing the exercise, elicit key expressions and write them on the board. Do this by giving simple situations, e.g.
I've got an old schoolfriend, and we still write to each other and ring each other up from time to time. (= We still keep in touch, we haven't lost touch with each other)

Language note
You can also say *be in contact with*, *get in contact with*, etc. This means the same, but is more formal.

3 In a manner of speaking

This activity is about different aspects of learning a language. The first part focuses on different ways in which learners speak English, and introduces key vocabulary (e.g. pronunciation, accent, fluent). The second part develops into a discussion of how we learn a language and what 'knowing a language' means.

➤ Workbook: Exercise C

1 Listening, presentation & discussion

- ⬜ Play the recording, pausing after each speaker. Quickly establish what each speaker is talking about, and then discuss:
  – where students think he/she comes from, and how they can tell
  – what his/her strengths and weaknesses seem to be in English.
  Use the checklist in the exercise as a basis for discussion.

  Answers, and points that might emerge:

  1 Russian. Talking about his job. Not very fluent, hesitant but clear, problems with articles (*the*, *a*), pronunciation of /r/, /h/.

  2 Palestinian (first language: Arabic). Talking about the family she's staying with in Britain. Typical features: /r/, /h/, intonation. Very fluent, wide range of vocabulary, occasional grammar mistakes.

  3 Italian. Saying what she does at the weekend. Not very fluent, strong Italian accent, problems with verb tenses.

  4 Japanese. Talking about the family he's staying with in Britain. Typical features: consonants, especially /l/, /r/, intonation.

- Ask students to write a 'profile' of their own ability in English, in note form.

- Pairwork. Students use their notes to tell each other about what they think their strengths and weaknesses are in English.

Vocabulary option
As you discuss the four speakers, build up other useful words and expressions on the board, e.g.
have a strong/slight (Italian) accent
hesitate/hesitant
have problems with …

⬜ The tapescript is on page 104.

Optional extension
Build up a 'class profile' on the board in the form of two lists: things students feel they can do well, and things they feel they have problems with or need to improve.

2 Discussion

- Ask students whether they agree or disagree with the opinions. If you like, ask them to give a score from 0 to 5 for each, and see how much agreement there is in the class.

- Ask students to choose one of the opinions and to think of arguments for or against it.

Groupwork option
Students discuss the opinions in groups. They choose the most interesting one, and note down reasons to support their opinion. Then ask each group to report back to the class.

2 Person to person

1 Match the bubbles on the left with those on the right, to make five complete sentences.

We used to get on very well …

We've known each other since childhood …

… but now we've lost touch.

… but now we've made it up.

We've really got nothing to say to each other …

… but now we aren't on speaking terms.

… and we still keep in touch.

I used to write to them regularly …

We had a terrible argument last week …

… so we tend to just make small talk most of the time.

2 Work in groups. Think of someone you know (or used to know) that one of the phrases could apply to. Tell the others about it.

3 Learning a language

1  You will hear four foreign learners speaking English. What countries do you think they come from?

How would you describe their English? What do they seem to be good at? What do they seem to have problems with? Think about these things:

– fluency: how fluently do they express themselves? how well can they make themselves understood?
– pronunciation: vowels, consonants, complete words
– intonation, stress and rhythm
– grammar: how accurate? particular mistakes?
– vocabulary: how wide a range? specialised words?

Think about yourself. What are your own strengths and weaknesses in English?
Make some notes, and show them to your partner.

2 Here are some opinions about learning English. To what extent do you agree with them?

It doesn't matter how many mistakes you make provided people understand you.

You haven't learnt English properly unless you sound just like a native speaker.

If you want to learn English successfully, you have to be familiar with British or American culture.

Choose one of the opinions that interests you.
What arguments can you think of either for or against it?

4 The truth about lying

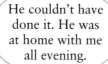

INTRODUCTION

All these people are lying.
Why are they lying?
What do you think the truth
might be?

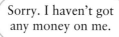

Which of the lies do you think is the most serious? Which is the least serious? Why?

READING

The article opposite describes a survey which examined how much people lie and who they lie to.

1 *Before you read*
  Who do you think people tell the most lies to? Put the categories in order (from 1 to 5).

  – mothers   – best friends   – romantic partners
  – strangers   – acquaintances

  Now read the text and check your answer.

2 Choose the best synonyms for the words in italics.
  a their children don't *appreciate* them   obey/value
  b their *offspring* are lying to them   children/friends
  c mums *fare better* than total strangers   have a better result / are more patient
  d and *jot down* whether they lied   describe / make a note of
  e your *hideous* taste in sweaters   terrible/unusual
  f on the dishonesty *spectrum*   list/scale
  g the researchers *grilled* them   selected/questioned
  h mothers can *take heart from* one other finding feel proud of / be encouraged by

3 Is there anything in the article that you find particularly interesting or surprising?
  Do you think the study's conclusions are generally valid?

4 The truth about lying

This combined Reading and Listening activity is about when people tell lies, why they lie and who they lie to. The reading text is an article from the New Scientist *describing a survey carried out by the University of Virginia into people's lying behaviour. In the listening activity, various people talk about occasions when they have told lies.*

Reading skills: *making predictions about the content of a text; reading to check assumptions.*
Vocabulary: *matching words with synonyms.*
Listening skills: *matching what you hear with your own experience.*

Introduction

● Give time for students to look at the captions and think about them. Then discuss together what each lie is about, and what kind of lie it is. Possible answers:

A A woman lying to protect her son or husband/partner (and also herself). In fact he wasn't at home, and has probably committed a crime (e.g. a burglary).
B A woman lying so as not to hurt the man's feelings (or possibly in order to get something from him, e.g. money). In fact she either dislikes him or she's indifferent to him.
C A government minister denying accusations of corruption, to protect himself. In fact he has used his position to make money, or perhaps has accepted bribes.
D Someone making an excuse not to give a beggar money, perhaps because he's too embarrassed simply to say 'No'.
E Someone lying so as not to offend a friend. In fact she thinks the outfit looks terrible.
F A parent lying to scare a child into not biting his nails.
G A sign making a false claim about food, so that people will buy it. In fact the ingredients are probably frozen or from a packet.
H A daughter lying to avoid her parents' disapproval, or perhaps just because she doesn't want them to know what she was doing.
I Someone making an excuse to get away, so as not to offend the other person. In fact she's probably bored with the conversation, or wants to talk to someone else.

● Discuss which of the lies students think are the most serious, and why.

> **Note**
> This could develop into a more general discussion of what makes a lie serious, and whether lying is ever justified.
>
> If you want to extend this part of the activity, you could also ask students to write down other examples of common lies and discuss them together.

Reading

● Ask students to cover the text. Discuss who they think people tell most lies to, and write the categories in Question 1 on the board in the order that most students agree on.

● Give time for students to read the text. Then ask what order the categories should be in according to the survey. Answers:

> 1 Strangers (77%)   2 Acquaintances (48%)   3 Mothers (46%)
> 4 Romantic partners (33%)   5 Best friends (28%)

● Give time for students to read the text again and find answers to Question 2. Then go through the answers:

> *a* value   *b* children   *c* have a better result   *d* make a note of   *e* terrible
> *f* scale   *g* questioned   *h* be encouraged by

> **Note**
> The title of the reading text is based on a well-known quotation from British statesman Benjamin Disraeli, who said 'There are lies, there are damned lies, and there are statistics' (in other words, statistics are the worst kind of lie).

● Discuss Question 3 with the class. If necessary, ask particular questions to help the discussion, e.g.
  – Do you think 70 is a big enough sample?
  – What do you think of the method they used? If you keep a record of your lies, does it affect how often you lie?
  – If you were taking part in the survey, would you tell the truth about your lies?
  – Do you think a survey in your own country would have similar results? What factors might be different?

Listening

- Look at the items in the list, and ask students to suggest what the lies might be. Try to get a variety of suggestions for each item.

- ☐ Play the recording, pausing after each item. Check comprehension by asking a few questions, e.g.

  Speaker 1: Who did she lie to? What did she tell him? How much was the frame really worth? Who was it for?

  Answers:

  1 She lied to her husband about how much the photo frame cost.
  2 He pretended he liked the plate when in fact he didn't.
  3 She lied to her parents by saying she was in the orchestra.
  4 She pretended to like the curtain fabric an acquaintance had chosen.
  5 He told the pupil who made the bike that it was good, when in fact it wasn't.
  6 She didn't admit to her mother that she had taken a banana.

- Look at the reasons and discuss which lies they apply to. Possible answers:

  To avoid being criticised: 1, (3), 6
  To avoid doing something unpleasant: 3
  In order not to hurt someone's feelings: 2, 4, (5)
  To make someone feel good: 5

- Ask students to give each lie a score out of five. If there is disagreement, ask them to say why they think the lie is or isn't serious.

☐ The tapescript is on page 104.

Self-study Workbook

Exercise A: Communicative phrases
Common phrases (e.g. *give a lecture, take notes*). Students fill gaps with words from boxes.

Exercise B: Small talk
Idioms for describing communication. Students write short anecdotes.

Exercise C: Language for talking about language
Vocabulary of language learning. A crossword.

Idioms: Common idioms with prepositions
Common idioms with prepositional phrases (e.g. *in a nutshell*).

Listening: Varieties of English
Four pieces of spoken English. Students identify the genre, then listen for details.

Word building: Nouns and verbs (1)
Nouns ending in *-tion* and *-sion*.

Lies, damned lies, and here are the statistics

MOTHERS who feel their children don't appreciate them can add another grievance to the list: half the time, their offspring are lying to them. A study designed to reveal the truth about lying shows that undergraduates lie to their mothers in 46 per cent of their conversations. Still, mums fare better than total strangers, who are told lies an astonishing 77 per cent of the time.

Bella DePaulo and a team of psychologists from the University of Virginia, Charlottesville, asked 77 undergraduates and 70 local townspeople to keep a record of all their conversations for a week, and jot down whether they lied at any time. DePaulo defined lying as 'when you intentionally try to mislead someone', so she would catch the smallest of lies.

The students told an average of two lies a day, while the others lied once a day. They said they had been studying when they had been out with friends. One told his parents that a textbook cost $50 rather than $20 – so that they would send him extra money. Female students constantly told their plain-looking room-mates that they were pretty. 'They're everyday lies,' says DePaulo.

DePaulo and her colleagues conclude that people tend to tell fewer lies to those they feel closest to. College students lied to their best friends 28 per cent of the time but lied to acquaintances 48 per cent of the time. In close relationships, people were more likely to tell 'kind-hearted' lies, designed to protect feelings, rather than self-serving lies. 'In short, don't expect even

your closest friend to tell you about your hideous taste in sweaters,' says DePaulo.

Romantic partners fall somewhere between close friends and acquaintances on the dishonesty spectrum. Both students and people outside university lied to romantic partners about a third of the time. DePaulo thinks that unmarried lovers can expect less honesty than best friends because of the insecurity that comes with romance.

DePaulo thinks the results are representative of society as a whole because the two groups had such similar patterns of lying behaviour. She also believes those taking part were telling the truth about lying. The researchers grilled them vigorously to check whether they had written misleading reports.

Mothers can take heart from one other finding. They may have been lied to, but at least their children talked to them. The students recorded telling few lies to their fathers – because they had virtually no interaction with them.

Vincent Kiernan, Washington

LISTENING

1 You will hear six people talking about times they told a lie. The lies are about:

– a silver photo frame
– a decorative plate engraved with a horse and carriage
– a school orchestra
– a sample of curtain fabric
– a young child's push-along bike
– a banana.

Try to imagine what lie each person told.

🔲 Now listen and see if you were right.

2 Match the lies you heard with these reasons:

– to avoid being criticised
– to avoid doing something unpleasant
– in order not to hurt someone's feelings
– to make someone feel good.

How bad do you think the lies are?
Give each one a score from 0 (= completely harmless) to 5 (= extremely serious).

Grammar study: infinitives

1 The infinitive

Can you find the ten infinitives in these sentences? When do we use the infinitive without *to*?

a   When I grow up, I want to be an airline pilot.
b   There were so many good things to eat, I couldn't decide what to have first.
c   You must be careful not to let anyone see you leave.
d   He made me wait for an hour, then he said I could go.

2 Verbs followed by the infinitive

Here are two typical verb patterns with the infinitive:

A They decided to …   B They asked me to …

Look at the verbs in the box. Which of the patterns do they follow?

agree	encourage	pretend	refuse
remind	bother	forget	warn
recommend	remember		

Complete the sentences, using suitable verbs.

a   I strongly .... see the Picasso exhibition.
b   I phoned six times, and finally he .... see me.
c   Why do I always have to .... switch the light off?
d   I don't know why you .... read rubbish like that.
e   I .... go any further without having a rest.
f   Don't .... cleverer than you really are.

Which verbs haven't you used yet? Include one or two in sentences of your own.

3 Seeing and hearing

Look at the sentences in the box. Why do those in A use an infinitive, and those in B use an *-ing* form?

A	I saw them *come* in. I heard them *switch* on the television.
B	I saw some people *coming* towards the house. I could hear them *talking* in whispers.

Read the paragraph below. What did the person see and hear?

As I passed the door, I stopped. A woman was crying. I tiptoed to the door and listened. A man said, 'Give me the keys'. I bent down and looked through the keyhole. A man was kneeling in front of an open safe. Suddenly, the woman pulled a gun from her handbag and pointed it at the man. A shot rang out, and the man fell to the floor.

4 Indirect questions

Notice how we use *to* + infinitive after question words:

– I don't know how to get to the station.
– Can you show me what to do?
– I'm not sure how long to cook it for.

Complete these sentences using an infinitive.

a   Shall I call him Bert? Dad? Mr Smith?
    I'm never quite sure …
b   Should I invite Maria? Fernando? José?
    I can't decide …
c   Shall I read a book? go for a walk? watch TV?
    I don't know …
d   Should I leave the waiter 50p? £1? £2?
    I have no idea …
e   Shall I talk about cars? the weather? politics?
    I don't know …

Do any of these remind you of something that has happened to you recently? Write a similar sentence connected with your own life. Show it to your partner and talk about it.

5 Forms of the infinitive

The infinitive can have various forms: present and past, simple and continuous. There are also two passive forms.

Find all the forms of the verb *tell* in these sentences, and write them in the table.

a   They might be telling lies.
b   I want to be told immediately if anything happens.
c   He seems to have been telling the truth.
d   She should have been told the news.
e   I would have told you, but there wasn't time.
f   You must tell me all about it.

	ACTIVE		PASSIVE
	Simple	*Continuous*	*Simple*
Pres		be telling	
Past			

Fill the gaps with an appropriate form of the verb in brackets.

a   It's their own fault. They shouldn't .... in the middle of the road. (stand)
b   I don't know where they are. They might .... lunch. (have)
c   That jumper needs to .... very carefully. (wash)
d   They seem to .... each other before. (meet)
e   That was a stupid thing to do. You might .... ! (electrocute)

Grammar study A: infinitives

1 The infinitive

> Infinitives with and without *to*

- Answers:

  a be   c be, let, see, leave
  b eat, decide, have   d wait, go

- Use this exercise to establish that
  – the infinitive is the basic form of the verb – it doesn't have endings (e.g. *-ed* or *-s*)
  – it can follow a verb + *to* (*want to be*)
  – it can follow *to* after a noun phrase or a question word (*good things to eat, what to have first*)
  – after modal verbs, and after *make* and *let*, *see* and *hear*, we use the infinitive without *to* (*must be, could go, let anyone see, see you leave*).

2 Verbs followed by the infinitive

> Intransitive and transitive verbs + infinitive

- Build up two tables of verbs on the board, and focus on any that students find difficult or whose form they are likely to confuse (e.g. the difference between *remember* and *remind*, and that we can't say 'refused me to'). Answers:

  A agreed to, bothered to, forgot to, pretended to, refused to, remembered to
  B encouraged me to, recommended me to, reminded me to, warned me (not) to

- Ask students to do the second part of the exercise in pairs, and then go through the answers together. Expected answers:

  a recommend you to   d bother to
  b agreed to   e refuse to
  c remind you to   f pretend to be

- Students write sentences using the other verbs. As a round-up, ask a few students what they wrote.

3 Seeing & hearing

> *see/hear* + infinitive vs *see/hear* + *-ing*

- Use the examples to establish that
  – we use *see/hear* + infinitive when we see or hear a complete action (*They came in – I saw the whole of it*)
  – we use *see/hear* + *-ing* when we see or hear part of an action (*When I looked, they were coming towards the house – I saw that bit of it*)
  – the difference is the same as between the Past simple (*they came*) and the Past continuous (*they were coming*).

- Ask students to change the paragraph using *see* and *hear*. Answers:

  I heard a woman crying ... I heard a man say ... I saw a man kneeling ... I saw the woman pull ... I saw her point ... I heard a shot ring out ... I saw the man fall ...

4 Indirect questions

> Question words + *to* + infinitive in indirect questions

- Show how *to* + infinitive replaces other structures in English:

> **I don't know how ~~I can~~ get to the station.**
> **to**
> **Can you show me how ~~I should~~ do it?**
> **to**
> **I'm not sure how long ~~I should~~ cook it for.**
> **to**

- Complete the sentences round the class or in pairs. Answers:

  a I'm never quite sure what to call him.
  b I can't decide who to invite.
  c I don't know what to do.
  d I have no idea how much / how big a tip to leave the waiter.
  e I don't know what to talk (to him) about.

- Students write similar sentences, then show them to their partner and talk about them. As a round-up, ask a few students what they wrote.

5 Forms of the infinitive

> Forms of the infinitive: active/passive, present/past, simple/continuous

- Ask students to complete the table. If you like, build up a table on the board, showing the structures in the abstract:

	Simple	ACTIVE Continuous	PASSIVE Simple
Pres	(verb)	be -ing	be -ed
Past	have -ed	have been -ing	have been -ed

- Ask students to do the second part of the exercise in pairs, and then go through the answers together. Answers:

  a have been standing   d have met
  b be having   e have been electrocuted
  c be washed

Language awareness A: double meanings

In English, many words have the same spelling but different meanings (homonyms), or the same sound but different spellings and meanings (homophones). Because of this, the English language easily lends itself to 'playing with words', and double meanings are often used in jokes.

1 Presentation: homonyms

- Ask students to find different meanings for the words and give examples. Possible answers:
  - you light a fire with a *match*; she's playing in the tennis *match*; his socks don't *match*.
  - *Miss* Mary Smith; they *missed* the train; I *miss* my parents when I'm away; he *missed* the goal.
  - a *light* blue carpet; switch the *light* on; it's *light* enough to carry; let's *light* a fire.
  - in the wrong *order*; I *ordered* a meal; she *ordered* us to sit down.
  - the *past* tense; we went *past* the house; half *past* two.
  - the *present* tense; is everyone *present*?; I gave him a *present*; they *presented* her with a bouquet of flowers.

2 Presentation: homophones

- Ask students to find words with the same sounds but different spellings. Answers:

  bored; know; whether; passed; bean; threw

- Look at the crossword, and establish the answers to 1 Across (*type*) and 1 Down (*tale*). Make sure students understand the idea of the double meanings:
  - *1 Across*: to write with a keyboard is to *type* (e.g. a letter); a *type* of cheese = a kind of cheese.
  - *1 Down*: a *tale* is a story; an animal has a *tail* (sounds the same, but is spelt differently).

- Give time for students to do the crossword, working alone or in pairs, then go through the answers. Alternatively, let students do it for homework. Answers:

  Across: 1 type 3 watt 7 lie 8 utter 9 weights 13 altar 15 ape 16 knew 17 knot

  Down: 1 tale 2 piece 4 act 5 turn 6 Hungary 10 train 11 park 12 cent 14 tie

3 Listening: children's jokes

- 🔲 Play the recording. Pause after each joke, and establish what double meaning the joke depends on. Answers:

  1 horse (little horse = pony); hoarse (= with a rough voice)
  2 match (= tennis match / match for lighting a cigarette)
  3 a Thai (= person from Thailand); a tie (= they were equal)
  4 spotted (= with spots / noticed)
  5 pasteurised (= treated by heat); past your eyes!
  6 claws (= nails on a cat's feet); clause (= part of a sentence); paws (= a cat's feet); pause (= a short break)

> 🔲 The tapescript is on page 104.

Pronunciation A: intonation and meaning

This activity focuses on different ways of saying the single sound Mmm, to show how meaning can be expressed directly through intonation. It introduces the main intonation patterns of English: falling, rising, and falling–rising.

1 Introduction

- As a lead-in, ask students to try out saying *Mmm* in their own language in a few different ways. (If students don't say *Mmm* in their own language, use an equivalent sound.)

2 Listening, presentation & practice

- 🔲 Play the conversations. Pause after each one, establish what it is about, and ask students to match the *Mmm* with one of the meanings in the list. Answers:

  1 *b*   2 *e*   3 *f*   4 *d*   5 *c*   6 *a*

- 🔲 Play the conversations again, pausing after each *Mmm*. Establish the intonation pattern, and get students to try imitating it. The patterns are:

  1 Falling tone, starting from the middle
  2 Falling tone, starting low
  3 Falling tone, starting high
  4 Rising tone, starting in the middle
  5 Falling, then rising
  6 Rising, then falling

3 Prediction task & listening

- Pairwork. Students imagine what meaning the *Mmm* might express and how it might be said.

- Discuss ideas together. In some cases, more than one answer is possible:

  2 Last *Mmm* could be *mid rise* (= go on) or *mid fall* (= I agree).
  3 Could be *mid fall* (= yes) or *fall–rise* (= I'm not sure).
  4 Could be *rise–fall* (= yes, delicious!) or *mid fall* (= yes).
  6 Could be *mid fall* (= yes) or *fall–rise* (= I'm not sure).

- 🔲 Play the conversations, and establish what patterns the speakers actually use. Answers:

  1 high fall   2 mid rise, then mid rise, then mid fall or high fall   3 mid fall   4 rise–fall   5 low fall   6 fall–rise

> 🔲 The tapescript is on page 105.

Self-study Workbook

Study Skills A: Using reference books   *See notes on page 129.*

Language awareness: double meanings

1 In English, a lot of words have more than one meaning. What different meanings do you know for the following?

match	light	past
miss	order	present

2 Many other words have the same sound, but a different spelling and meaning: e.g. *horse* (an animal) and *hoarse* (having a rough voice, when you've got a cold).

Look at these words. For each one, write down another word that sounds the same but is spelt differently.

board	weather	been
no	past	through

Now try the crossword. Each answer either has two meanings, or sounds like another word.

3 English speakers make use of double meanings for making puns and jokes.

[cassette] You will hear six jokes. What double meaning does each depend on?

Across

1 Kind, sort – write with a keyboard (4)
3 Unit of electricity – sounds like a question word (4)
7 Be on your back – say something untrue (3)
8 Make a sound with your mouth – total, complete (5)
9 Heavy things – sounds like 'stands in a queue' (7)
13 Change – sounds like a table in a church (5)
15 Intelligent animal – copy (3)
16 Was aware – sounds like the opposite of 'old' (4)
17 You make this in a piece of string – sounds negative (4)

Down

1 Story – sounds like what an animal has at the back (4)
2 Bit, part – sounds like the opposite of 'war' (5)
4 Behave – part of a play (3)
5 Revolve – 'Now it's my ....' (4)
6 Central European country – sounds short of food (7)
10 Form of transport – teach someone a skill (5)
11 Leave your car – green area in a town (4)
12 A very small amount of money – sounds like 'posted' (4)
14 You .... a knot – sounds like someone from Bangkok (3)

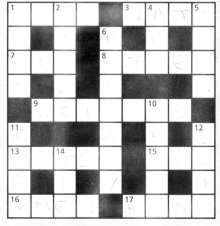

Pronunciation: intonation and meaning

1 When we say *Mmm*, it can mean different things depending on how we say it. Think of different ways of saying *Mmm*. How does the way you say it change the meaning?

2 [cassette] You will hear six short conversations. Listen to the way the people say *Mmm* each time. Which of these meanings do they express?

a Delicious!   *d* Go on – I'm listening
b I agree   *e* I'm changing the subject
c Yes and no   *f* Surprisingly, yes

Listen again, and each time notice what the *Mmm* sounds like. Does it

– *fall* or *rise*?
– start *high*, *low* or in the *middle*?

Try saying it in the same way.

3 Look at these conversations. How do you think the *Mmm* might sound each time? Could it be said in more than one way?

1 A You never did like living in London much, did you?
   B Mmm. I had a very good time there.

2 A I spoke to my father about it.
   B Mmm.
   A And he thought about it for a bit.
   B Mmm.
   A And he said he thought I should take the job.
   B Mmm.

3 A You know Jane quite well, don't you?
   B Mmm. Why do you ask?

4 A Is the soup all right?
   B Mmm. Wonderful.

5 A What does 'mutton' mean?
   B It's meat that comes from a sheep. OK?
   A Thank you.
   B Mmm. Now let's look at Question 3.

6 A Do you like José?
   B Mmm. He's all right.

[cassette] Now listen to the recording. Did the speakers say *Mmm* in the way you expected?

1 Definitions

Defining relative clauses

1 Do this quiz, and then check your answers. How many did you get right?

Watch your words

Here are eight simple sentences. But can you guess what the words in italics mean?

1 'Oh Charles,' she sobbed. 'They say you're an *embezzler*.'
a someone who snores
b a man who has more than one wife
c someone who steals money from the company they work for

2 'Don't touch that *toadstool*,' he warned.
a a frog whose bite is poisonous
b a sharp-edged tool that is used for cutting stone
c a mushroom that you can't eat

3 'I spent three years in that *orphanage*,' he said, 'and I hated every moment.'
a accommodation for people whose houses have been destroyed in war
b a home for children whose parents have died
c a prison for young people who have committed serious crimes

4 'I've had enough of this *drudgery*!' she screamed.
a work that is difficult and boring to do
b food that has a very plain taste
c conversations that are really about nothing

5 'Over the years,' he said, 'that *couch* has had some very strange people on it.'
a a bed you lie on while visiting a psychiatrist
b a table you lie on while having an operation
c a chair you sit on while having dental treatment

6 'Nobody seems to use *thimbles* these days,' she said.
a stone bottles you fill with hot water and place in your bed
b metal cups you wear on your finger while sewing
c scissors you use to trim the hairs in your nose

7 We spent the afternoon playing *tag*.
a a children's game in which one player has to try to touch the others
b a card game in which players try to be first to get rid of all their cards
c a party game in which players pin cards on each other's backs

8 'Don't go there in August,' she advised. 'There are *midges* everywhere!'
a young boys who pick people's pockets and snatch handbags
b badly behaved tourists who spoil other people's holidays
c small flying insects that bite

Add relative pronouns to these definitions where necessary. Use the quiz answers to help you.
a A bouncer is a person .... throws troublemakers out of nightclubs.
b Slush is snow .... has started to melt.
c A colleague is someone .... you work with.
d Slippers are soft shoes .... you wear indoors.
e A widow is a woman .... husband has died.
f A crèche is a place .... parents can leave small children while they are at work.

2 Work in groups of three. The teacher will give you a word and its true definition. In your group, make up two other definitions.

Read out your three definitions. Can the rest of the class guess which is correct?

This unit covers language used for identifying and defining. It focuses on three main grammar areas:
– defining relative clauses
– cleft sentences with *It*
– cleft sentences with *What*.

The fourth activity develops writing skills. It deals with the language of explaining reason and purpose.

1 Definitions

This exercise introduces defining relative clauses in the context of giving definitions of unknown words. It focuses on subject and object clauses, clauses with prepositions, and clauses with whose *and* where.

➤ Focus on Form: Exercises 1, 2
➤ Workbook: Exercise A

1 *Reading & presentation*

- In pairs, students work through the quiz, noting down the answers they think are correct.
- Go through the quiz together or let students check the answers in a dictionary. Students score one point for each correct answer. Answers:

  1 *c* 2 *c* 3 *b* 4 *a* 5 *a* 6 *b* 7 *a* 8 *c*

- Go through the six sentences below the quiz, asking students what relative pronouns should go in the gaps. Answers:

  a *who* or *that*
  b *which* or *that*
  c *who*, *that* or no pronoun
  d *which, that* or no pronoun
  e *whose*
  f *where*

  Point out that
  – *a* and *b*: *person* and *snow* are the subject of the relative clause (*he throws …, the snow has started …*). We use *who* or *that* for people, *which* or *that* for things.
  – *c* and *d*: *someone* and *shoes* are the object of the relative clause (*you work with him, you wear shoes*). We can use *who* or *that* for people, *which* or *that* for things, or we can leave out the pronoun altogether.

  Ask students to find other examples of each type in the quiz itself, and build up a summary of relative pronouns on the board:

	PERSON	THING
Subject	who/that	which/that
Object	(who/that)	(which/that)
Possessive	whose	–
Place		where

2 *Writing & speaking activity*

- Photocopy the words and definitions on page 128 of the Teacher's Book, and cut them up.
- Divide students into groups of three and give one item to each group. Together, they think of two other likely definitions using relative clauses, and write them down.
- The students in each group in turn write their word on the board, and read out their three definitions. The others try to guess which definition is correct.

Note
Emphasise that students are not expected to know what the words mean (although they may happen to know one or two of them) – the point of the quiz is simply to guess the answer.

Language note
Sentence *c* has a 'hanging preposition' at the end (*… you work* with). This is normal in modern English. We could also say *A colleague is someone with whom you work*, but this would sound more formal.

Practice option
Do some simple transformation practice of relative clauses, e.g.

She married my brother.
→ That's the woman who married my brother.

I share a room with him.
→ That's the person I share a room with.

Homework idea
Ask students to find some unusual English words in a dictionary which could be defined using a relative clause. They bring them into class and see if other students can guess what they mean.

2 Getting your facts right

This exercise shows how we can use cleft sentences with It was/wasn't ... *to focus on a particular part of a sentence. A common use of this type of cleft sentence, as in this exercise, is for correcting what other people say.*

➤ Focus on Form: Exercise 3
➤ Workbook: Exercise B

1 Presentation

- Look at the first sentence, and ask students how to correct it using *It wasn't ...* and *It was ...* . Answers:

  It wasn't Paul McCartney who/that married Yoko Ono. It was John Lennon.
  It was John Lennon who/that married Yoko Ono, not Paul McCartney.

- Give time for students to look at the other sentences, and correct them in the same way. Answers:

  It wasn't Italy who/that won the 1994 World Cup. It was Brazil.
  It was Brazil who/that won the 1994 World Cup, not Italy.
  (It wasn't in 1994 that Italy won the World Cup. It was in 1990.
  It was in 1990 that Italy won the World Cup, not in 1994.)

  It wasn't her grandmother (that) she saw. It was the big bad wolf.
  It was the big bad wolf (that) she saw, not her grandmother.

  It wasn't in China that Buddhism originated. It was in India.
  It was in India that Buddhism originated, not in China.

- Write a table on the board, showing the basic structure:

  It wasn't X that ..., it was Y.
  It was Y that ..., not X.

> *Language note*
> The pronouns in cleft sentences follow the same rules as in relative clauses (see 3.1). It is nearly always correct to use *that*:
> John was the person that gave me the money.
> John was the person (that) I met.
> John was the person (that) I went there with.
> York was the place (that) I went to.

2 Writing & speaking activity

- Working alone or in pairs, students write a sentence containing one factual error. It can be in the past, like the examples, or in the present (e.g. *Volvos, which are produced in Italy, are a very reliable make of car*).

- Students show their sentence to others in the class, who try to correct it.

> *Game option*
> Divide the class into two teams. In turn, students from each team read out a sentence, and the other team tries to correct it. Give one point for each successful correction which uses the structure correctly.

3 Emphasising the point

This exercise introduces cleft sentences with What ..., *and shows how they can be used to give special emphasis to feelings, attitudes and reactions.*

➤ Focus on Form: Exercise 4
➤ Workbook: Exercise B

1 Listening & presentation

- 🔲 Look at the remarks on the page, and then play the recording. Establish what the speakers actually say:

  What I enjoy doing at weekends is reading the Sunday papers in bed.
  What I find really difficult is phrasal verbs.
  What really surprised me in New York was the way the shops stay open all night.
  The thing that really annoyed me was that he didn't answer my letters.

  Point out that the speakers use these structures to give special emphasis to how they feel.

> 🔲 The tapescript is on page 105.

> *Language note*
> We can also use similar structures with *The person ...*, *The place ...*, etc., e.g. *The person I admire most is my father. The place I enjoyed was Amsterdam.*
>
> But we cannot say 'Who I admire most ...', 'Where I found really interesting ...'.

2 Writing & speaking activity

- Working alone, students write a few true sentences based on the table.
- Students show their sentences to their partner. They talk a bit about each one, and find out if their partner agrees.
- As a round-up, ask a few students to read out their sentences.

> *Optional lead-in*
> To show how the activity works, write a sentence of your own on the board, e.g. *The thing that really annoys me about TV newsreaders is the clothes they wear.*
>
> Then say a bit more about what you wrote, and see if the class agrees with you.

2 Getting your facts right

Cleft sentences with 'It'

It wasn't … Paul McCartney married Yoko Ono in 1968. It was …

1 The sentence above isn't true.
Correct it, beginning with the words
in the bubbles.

There's one factual error in each of these
sentences. Correct it in the same way.

Italy won the 1994 football World Cup,
which was played in America.

When Little Red Riding Hood went into the cottage,
she saw her grandmother sitting in the bed.

Buddhism originated in China in the
6th century BC.

2 Write a similar sentence with one factual
error. Show it to other students, and see
whether they can correct it.

3 Emphasising the point

Cleft sentences with 'What'

1 Listen to the recording.
How do the speakers express these ideas?

I enjoy reading the
Sunday papers in bed.

I find phrasal verbs
really difficult.

In New York the shops
stay open all night. That
really surprised me.

He never answered
my letters – that
really annoyed me.

2 Write two or three true sentences using the table.

	I enjoy		
	I admire		
What	I can't stand		
	I find difficult	about …	is …
The thing (that)	surprises me		
	annoys me		
	fascinates me		

Show your sentences to other students, and
answer any questions they may have.

4 In the frame

1 Here are some descriptions of famous works of art.
Do you recognise any of them?
How could you join the sentences together to make better descriptions of them?

a This picture shows two men. They are sitting by a river. They are wearing formal evening dress. Between them is a woman. She is wearing nothing at all. There is a picnic. It is spread on the grass beside them.

b This is a self-portrait. It shows the artist. His ear is missing. His face is wrapped in a bandage.

c This is a fresco. It portrays God. His arm is stretched out. He is creating Adam.

d This is a sculpture of a man. He is sitting. His forehead is supported by his fist. He is lost in thought.

2 Here is a brief description of Edvard Munch's painting *The Sick Child*.
How many of the ideas on the right could you incorporate into the three sentences?

The picture shows a child.
On the bedside table there is a bottle.
Beside her is a woman.

She has bright
red hair.

She's probably the
child's mother.

She's holding the
girl's hand.

It probably contains the
girl's medicine.

She has a very pale face.

Her head is bowed
in grief.

She's leaning against
a large pillow.

Her head is turned
towards the window.

She has grey hair.

3 Look at your own picture in the back of the book and write a description of it.
Include enough details so that someone else could visualise the picture.

Read your partner's description, and try to visualise the picture.

Now look at the picture. How good was your partner's description?

4 In the frame

Writing skills: *describing a scene; writing to convey information to another person.*
Language focus: *participle phrases with* -ing *and* -ed.

➤ Workbook: Exercise C

This activity develops the skill of writing a coherent description of a scene. It follows these stages:

1 *Presentation. Focus on joining sentences using participle phrases.*
2 *Discussion and collaborative writing. Students discuss how sentences can be incorporated into a single coherent description.*
3 *Communicative writing. Students write a description of a picture. Another student reads the description and tries to visualise the picture.*

1 Presentation

- Look at the descriptions of works of art and see if students recognise any of them. Discuss how the sentences could be joined together. Possible answers:

  a (Edouard Manet: *Le Déjeuner sur l'Herbe*, 1863) This picture shows two men sitting by a river, wearing formal evening dress. Between them is a woman wearing nothing at all. There is a picnic spread on the grass beside them.

  b (Vincent van Gogh: *Self-portrait with Bandaged Ear*, 1889) This is a self-portrait, showing the artist with his ear missing and his face wrapped in a bandage.

  c (Michelangelo: *The Creation of Adam*, 1508–12, Sistine Chapel, Rome) This is a fresco portraying God with his arm stretched out, creating Adam.

  d (Auguste Rodin: *The Thinker*, 1880) This is a sculpture of a man sitting with his forehead supported by his fist, lost in thought.

- On the board, write examples of the two types of participle phrase, with *-ing* and *-ed*, and show how we use *with* as a linking word:

  > **The picture shows two men <u>sitting</u> by a river.**
  > **There is a picnic <u>spread</u> on the grass beside them.**
  > **It shows the artist <u>with</u> his face <u>wrapped</u> in a bandage.**

> *Idea*
> Bring in reproductions of the works of art to show to the class.

2 Discussion & writing activity

- Look at the painting *The Sick Child*. Give students time to read through the ideas beside the picture, then discuss how they could be incorporated into the three sentences. Build up a possible answer on the board, e.g.

  The picture shows a child with a very pale face and bright red hair, leaning against a large pillow with her face turned towards the window. Beside her is a woman with grey hair, her head bowed in grief, holding the girl's hand. She's probably the child's mother. On the bedside table there is a bottle, probably containing the girl's medicine.

3 Writing activity

- Divide students into pairs, one A and one B, and ask them to look only at their own picture (A's picture is on page 89 and B's on page 90). Working alone, they write a description of their picture.

- Students exchange their descriptions and read them, still without looking at their partner's picture.

- Allow students to look at their partner's picture. As a round-up, discuss how clear the descriptions were.

> *Homework alternative*
> Students make brief notes, and then describe their picture orally. They get feedback from their partner, and then write the description for homework.

Focus on Form

1 Relative clauses

> Defining relative clauses

- Pairwork. One student reads out a sentence opening, and the other chooses a continuation from Box B, changing it into a relative clause.
- Go through the answers together. Answers:
  2 I've forgotten the name of that town where they hold the music festival.
  3 Did you hear the joke about the man whose wife bought him a Porsche?
  4 I'm afraid this is a decision (that/which) you can't put off any longer.
  5 There are some things that/which really make me angry.
  6 I really enjoyed that day (that/when) we went to the beach.
  7 What was the name of the Greek hero who/that killed the Minotaur?

2 Embedded relative clauses

> Defining relative clauses embedded within sentences

- Read through the examples. Then ask students to rewrite the sentences to include a relative clause.
- Go through the exercise with the class, asking students what ideas they had. Possible answers:
  a A man who jumped off a cliff wearing a pair of home-made wings died in hospital last night.
  b A woman whose husband attacked her has been awarded $500,000.
  c The house where Margaret Thatcher spent her childhood has been destroyed by fire.
  d From today, owners of vehicles that do not have rear seat belts can be fined up to £1,000.
  e And finally, a cat that was trapped up a chimney for three days was recovering at home …

3 Cleft sentences with 'It'

> Cleft sentences with It wasn't … and It was …

- Pairwork. One student turns to page 89 and the other to page 90. They choose the answers they think are correct, and check by asking their partner questions, as in the examples.
- Go through the answers together, asking questions and getting students to correct you, e.g.
  Was it in Portugal that Christopher Columbus was born? (No, it was in Spain).

4 Emphatic cleft sentences

> Cleft sentences with What … and The thing …

- Do the exercise round the class or in pairs. Possible answers:
  a What I didn't like about being at university was that I was always short of money.
  b What you need is a good night's sleep.
  c What I enjoy in the morning is a cold shower.
  d The thing that impressed everybody was her knowledge of African history.
  e The thing I admire about him is that he always tells the truth.
  f What fascinates me about ants is the way they always seem to know exactly where they're going.
  g What you don't seem to realise is that I work an 18-hour day.

Self-study Workbook

Exercise A: Relative clauses
Defining relative clauses. Students fill gaps in a text.

Exercise B: Cleft sentences
Students rewrite remarks as cleft sentences, using It …, What … or The thing ….

Exercise C: Descriptive phrases
Present and past participles. Students fill gaps in a text.

Idioms: Colours
Common idioms with colours (e.g. *a red herring*).

Listening: Radio news
Four short radio news items. Students predict what words they will hear, then listen for main points.

Common verbs: get
Idiomatic expressions and phrasal verbs with *get*.

Focus on Form

1 Relative clauses

Student A: **Read out a sentence beginning from Box A.**

Student B: **Complete the sentence with a suitable continuation from Box B, making any necessary changes.**

Example:

A Where did you get that coat ...
B ... (that) I saw you wearing last night?

Box A

1 Where did you get that coat ...
2 I've forgotten the name of that town ...
3 Did you hear the joke about the man ...
4 I'm afraid this is a decision ...
5 There are some things ...
6 I really enjoyed that day ...
7 What was the name of the Greek hero ...

Box B

a You can't put it off any longer.
b We went to the beach.
c I saw you wearing it last night.
d He killed the Minotaur.
e They really make me angry.
f His wife bought him a Porsche.
g They hold the music festival there.

---

2 Embedded relative clauses

Expand these sentences from news stories by inserting relative clauses.

Example:

An elephant has been destroyed.

– An elephant *that escaped from London Zoo and crushed six cars* has been destroyed.

– An elephant *whose teeth had worn away so badly that it could not eat* has been destroyed.

– An elephant *that was injured when it was hit by a train* has been destroyed.

a A man died in hospital last night.
b A woman has been awarded $500,000.
c The house has been destroyed by fire.
d From today, owners of vehicles can be fined up to £1,000.
e And finally, a cat was recovering at home after a six-hour rescue operation.

3 Cleft sentences with 'It'

Christopher Columbus   *Marco Polo*

Student A: **Look at the text about Christopher Columbus on page 89. Can you choose the correct version of the story? Check your answers with B.**

Student B: **Look at the text about Christopher Columbus on page 90, and check A's answers.**

Example:

Christopher Columbus was born in *Spain/Portugal/Italy* in 1451.

A I think it was Spain where Christopher Columbus was born.
B No, it wasn't Spain.
A OK. Was it ...?

Now do the same with the text about Marco Polo. It's B's turn to choose the correct version.

4 Emphatic cleft sentences

Make these sentences more emphatic by using *What ...* **or** *The thing ...*

Example:

This room's got big windows, and I like that.

What I like about this room is that it's got big windows.

a I was always short of money at university, and I didn't like that.
b You need a good night's sleep.
c I enjoy a cold shower in the morning.
d Her knowledge of African history impressed everybody.
e He always tells the truth, and I admire that about him.
f Ants always seem to know exactly where they're going – that fascinates me.
g You don't seem to realise that I work an 18-hour day.

4 | Sports and games

1 Dangerous pastimes

1 You will hear an interview with someone who is about to go on her first parachute jump. Imagine you were this person. How do you think you'd be feeling?

📼 Listen to the first part of the interview. How is she feeling? Does she seem to be prepared?

📼 Now listen to what she says after the jump. How does she feel about the experience? After hearing what she says, would you be prepared to try it yourself?

2 Divide these activities into three lists:
   – things you'd like to do (or have done)
   – things you'd be willing to try
   – things you'd never do.

Add one other activity to each list.

Compare lists with other students. Why did you answer as you did?

A Bungee jumping   B Rock climbing

C White water canoeing   D Potholing   E Off-piste skiing   F Scuba diving

This unit is about sports and games. It focuses on the following areas:
- 'dangerous' sports and what they involve
- language used to describe how games are played
- issues in sport (e.g. prize money, football violence, drugs).

The Reading and Listening activity is a series of logic problems with recorded solutions.

1 Dangerous pastimes

This exercise is concerned with sports that are usually considered 'dangerous'. In the first part, students hear an interview with a parachute jumper before and after her first jump. In the second part, they consider other dangerous sports and discuss how they feel about them.

1 Listening & discussion

- Ask students to imagine they are about to go parachute jumping. Ask them how they would be feeling, and build up a few key words on the board (e.g. *terrified, nervous, excited, calm*). Encourage students to say *why* they would feel these things (e.g. *The parachute might not open, I'm afraid of heights, I love taking risks*).

- 🔲 Play the first part of the recording. Establish what the woman is feeling and whether she's prepared. Answers:

  She's feeling very excited, a bit nervous, looking forward to it, not frightened.
  She's well prepared: she's trained for a whole weekend and knows what to do.

- 🔲 Play the second part of the recording, and again establish how she feels. Answer:

  She thought it was fantastic, she enjoyed it, she'll do it again.

  Find out how many students would go parachute jumping after hearing what the woman says.

2 Speaking activity

- Look at the activities in the pictures, and briefly check that students know what they involve (e.g. bungee jumping: you jump from a height tied to a long piece of elastic).

- Working alone, students write the activities in three lists, and add one activity to each list.

- Students sit in groups (or pairs) and compare their lists.

- As a round-up, draw three columns on the board and find out which column most of the class put each activity into. Then add activities that students thought of themselves – again find out what most students feel about them, and add them to the appropriate column.

➤ Workbook: Exercise A

Optional lead-in

Discuss what parachute jumping involves: what clothes and equipment you need, what you have to do, how you land, etc.

Alternative: discussion task

Students complete the sentence: *I would/wouldn't go parachute jumping because ...* Ask them to read out their sentences, and use this as a basis for discussion.

Optional comprehension check

Ask other questions to check comprehension, e.g.

Part 1: What kind of person is she? What does 'They sponsored me' mean? How many parachutes has she got? How do you land safely?

Part 2: What happens at first? What happens after the parachute opens? Did she land properly?

Optional lead-in

To show the idea of the activity, write the sports in three lists on the board to show how you feel about them yourself.

🔲 The tapescript is on page 105.

2 Play the game

This exercise introduces key verbs and nouns which are used in describing how to play sports and games. The vocabulary covers ball games with a net (like tennis), team games (like football), board games and card games.

➤ Workbook: Exercise B, Listening

1 Presentation

- Look at the pictures and establish what games they illustrate. Use this to introduce some of the key vocabulary (e.g. *piece, dice, board*).
- Give time for students to read the instructions and decide what games they describe. Then go through them together, and discuss what words should go in the gaps. Answers:
  - A *Table tennis:* serve, bounce, net, out, point
  - B *Draughts:* move, take, piece
  - C *Monopoly:* dice, move, board, land
  - D *Rugby football:* pass, tackle, pitch, score, points
  - E *A card game, e.g. whist:* shuffle, deal, suit

Presentation option

Using the pictures to help you, go through all the words in the box, giving your own presentation. Then ask students to fill the gaps in the instructions.

2 Writing & speaking activity

- Working alone or in pairs, students choose a sport or game they know something about. They write a few sentences describing how to play it.
- Students read out their sentences. The rest of the class tries to guess what game they are describing.

Homework option

Students write the sentences at home, and read them out in class the next day.

3 And now the sports news …

This is a general discussion activity which considers various issues in sport, e.g. illegal drugs, violence at football matches, sport and nationalism, the salaries earned by top sportsmen/women. As a basis for the discussion, students read four newspaper articles which describe events that took place in the mid-1990s.

➤ Workbook: Exercise C

1 Reading & presentation

- Look at each headline in turn, and ask students to guess what they think it might be about. If necessary, give help with interpreting some of the words (e.g. a swimmer is *suspended*, a footballer faces *suspension* = they aren't allowed to compete for a time; *strike it rich* = receive a large amount of money).
- Give time for students to read the stories. Then ask a few questions to check comprehension, e.g.
  - Who shot the footballer? Where? Why?
  - Where does tennis stars' money come from?
  - What did Cantona do? Why? What did he do the time before?
  - Why has Lu Bin been suspended?

  Establish how similar the stories are to what students expected.

Vocabulary option

Use the texts to focus on particular vocabulary connected with sport, e.g.

fans (= supporters), score a goal, defeat; prize money, champion; be suspended, spectator, send off; gold/silver medal, a world record, championship.

2 Discussion

- Working in groups, students look quickly through the questions. They choose one or two that interest them, and discuss what they think about them, trying to come to a conclusion within their group.
- Ask one student from each group to report back to the rest of the class. He/she should summarise their discussion and say what conclusion they came to.

Longer alternative

Students discuss each of the questions in turn in their group. As a round-up, take each question in turn and find out what conclusion different groups came to about it.

Alternative: class debate

Choose one of the topics, and ask some groups to prepare arguments for and other groups to prepare arguments against it. Then choose one speaker from each group, and organise a debate with the rest of the class as an audience.

2 Play the game

1 Here are some instructions relating to five different games.
What are the games? Fill the gaps with words from the box.

A

When you .... , the ball has to ....
twice, once on each side of the ....
... If your shot misses the table, it's .... ,
and you lose the ....

B

You can only .... diagonally, one
square at a time. You .... an
opponent's .... by jumping over it.

C

You throw the .... , and if you get a 3, for
example, you .... three squares around the
.... If you .... on a property owned
by another player, you have to pay rent.

board	net	score
bounce	out	serve
deal	pass	shuffle
dice	piece	suit
land	pitch	tackle
move	point	take

D

You can kick the ball forwards, but you can only
.... it backwards.
... The best way to .... a player who is
running with the ball is to grab him round the legs.
... If you can touch the ball down at the far end of
the .... , you .... five .... This is
called a try.

E

You .... the
cards, and ....
out 13 cards to each
player. Then the
players sort out their
cards into the four
different ....s.

2 Choose another sport or game and write a few sentences about how to play it.
Read out your sentences, and see if other people can guess what sport or game it is.

3 And now the sports news ...

1 Look at these newspaper headlines.
What would you expect to read in
the stories that accompany them?

**World champion swimmer
suspended after drugs test**

**FOOTBALLER FACES SUSPENSION
AFTER ATTACK ON SPECTATOR**

'Own-goal' defender shot
dead outside restaurant

**Tennis stars strike it rich
on and off the court**

Now read the stories on page 91.

2 Work in groups. Choose any of these questions that interest you, and try to reach
agreement about them.

   a Are we right to ban performance-enhancing drugs, or should they be made legal?
   b Why is it that there is so much violent behaviour at football matches?
   c Do top sportsmen and sportswomen earn too much money?
   d 'Sports personalities have a special responsibility to behave well because they
      have a tremendous influence over young people.' Do you agree?
   e How do you feel when your national team wins or loses? Is it just a game, or is it
      more than that?

Now report your conclusions to the rest of the class.

4 Problems, problems …

INTRODUCTION

1 Read Problem 1. If you can work out the answer, write it down.

Problem 1 In the post

Angela runs an antique shop. Last week she wanted to post a sword to a customer, so she wrapped it up and took it to the post office. Unfortunately, the sword was 100 cm long and the maximum length allowed for parcels is 95 cm, so the post office refused to accept it.

Not being one to give up easily, Angela repackaged the sword and took it back to the post office, who accepted it without argument.

How did she manage it?

2 🔲 You will hear two clues. After each clue, you will have another chance to work out the answer (or change your previous answer).

3 🔲 Now listen to the solution. Did you get the right answer? At what stage did you get it?

READING

Working with a partner, read Problems 2–8 and try to solve them together. If you are stuck, there is a clue for each Problem on page 92.

LISTENING

🔲 Listen to the answers. Score two points for each answer you got right without looking at a clue, and one point for each answer you got after looking at a clue. What is your total score?

Problem 2 Two boyfriends

Annie's flat is near an underground train station. She has two boyfriends, Bill and Mario, who live on the same train line, but in opposite directions. Every ten minutes, a train leaves in each direction.

Since she likes each of them equally, she lets the train decide which one of them she will visit. She turns up at the station, and catches whichever train comes first.

She is surprised to find that nine times out of ten she ends up visiting Mario. Can you explain?

Problem 3 An explosive mixture

The Professor has a problem. He has eight chemical bottles numbered 1 to 8, and they must be placed in a rack like that below. However, in order to avoid an explosion, bottles with consecutive numbers must not be placed next to one another diagonally, vertically or horizontally.

So if he puts bottle number 5 in space C, then neither bottle 4 nor bottle 6 can be placed in spaces A, D or G. What is your advice?

4 Problems, problems ...

This combined Reading and Listening activity consists of a series of logic problems (known as 'brainteasers'). In groups, students read each problem and try to solve it together, turning to the back of the book for a clue if they need one. The solutions to the problems are recorded on the cassette, and make up the listening part of the activity.

Reading skills: *reading for precise meaning.*
Listening skills: *matching what you hear with your own predictions, listening to check.*

Introduction

● Read Problem 1 together. Ask students to think silently about the answer, and to write down the solution if they think they know it, but not to suggest solutions aloud.

● ▭ Play the two clues, pausing to give students a chance to write down the solution. Again, don't allow students to suggest answers during this stage.

● ▭ Now ask students to suggest solutions. Then play the recording of the solution to the problem.

Reading

● Divide the class into pairs or small groups. Working together, students try to solve Problems 2–8. If they need help, they can turn to the clues on page 92.

Listening

● ▭ Go through the problems one by one. Find out if anyone can give you the answer, and then play the recorded solution. Students give themselves a score each time. If students still have difficulty understanding the solution to any of the problems, rephrase it in your own words.

Answers: see tapescript.

Optional lead-in
Write the word *brainteaser* on the board, and see if anyone knows or can guess what it means.

Vocabulary option
Focus on key words that appear in the problems by writing them on the board at the beginning, and seeing if students know what they mean:

maximum	**to alternate**
minimum	**to weigh**
diagonal	**a suspect**
vertical	**label**
horizontal	

▭ The tapescript is on page 105.

Homework option
Ask students to find other brainteasers, and to translate them into English. They can bring them in to a later class and try them out on other students.

Additional notes for Exercise 1.1: *Images*

Person A: Often goes to the theatre, the opera, museums and art galleries. Listens to classical music constantly. Reads novels and short stories. enjoys watching tennis. Has travelled widely. Has recently taken up gardening. Has never conducted an orchestra, but would like to.

Person B: Enjoys keeping fit, and teaches an evening class in aerobics. Often goes dancing in clubs with groups of friends. Is clothes-conscious, and tries to keep ahead of the fashion. Watches comedy and soaps on TV. Likes all kinds of music, reads music magazines, and buys several CDs a month.

Person D: Shares a house with friends, but very rarely spends a night in. Most evenings, meets friends in pubs or restaurants. Goes to at least one party a week. Doesn't watch much TV, doesn't go to the cinema, doesn't read much. Has recently taken up snowboarding. Plays computer games, but no other games.

Person E: Enjoys cooking, and socialising with small groups of friends. Main hobby is photography. Spends a lot of time walking in the hills, photographing the landscape. Doesn't read much or go to the theatre. Enjoys watching sumo wrestling and motor racing. Has recently restored an old car.

Self-study Workbook

Exercise A: Bungee jumping
A text about bungee jumping. Students read and find answers to questions.

Exercise B: Rules of the game
Verbs and nouns used to describe sports and games. Students find verb/noun pairs to fill gaps in sentences.

Exercise C: Football hooliganism
Guided writing. Students read a short newspaper article, and write a letter giving their opinion.

Idioms: Animals
Common idioms with animals (e.g. *a cat nap*).

Listening: Cricket
Someone explains how cricket is played. Students listen for key points.

Word building: Adjectives and nouns (1)
Adjectives ending in *-able, -al, -ous, -ful, -y*.

Problem 4 — Sweet revenge

Sick of the silly behaviour of his pupils, the maths teacher set them a brainteaser:

'If six sweet jars are arranged in a row, the first three full of sweets and the next three empty, what is the minimum number of jars that need to be moved so that they alternate full, empty, full, empty, full, empty?'

Since nobody got it right, he ate all the sweets himself. What do you think is the answer?

Problem 5 — One man and his dog

Farmer Bob, with his dog, Fang, is walking home at 5 kph. When he is 20 kilometres from home he lets Fang off its lead and the dog runs all the way home at 15 kph. As soon as it gets there it turns round and runs back to Bob, and keeps running back and forward at 15 kph until Bob gets home.

How far does Fang run?

Problem 6 — On balance

Smuggler Sam Crook has received nine 2 kg boxes of chocolates, in one of which is hidden 100 g of diamonds, giving the box a total weight of 2.1 kg. He wants to open that box as quickly as possible, and fortunately he has a balance handy.

What is the minimum number of weighings required for him to find the box containing the diamonds?

Problem 7 — Whodunnit?

Three people are suspects in a robbery case. They each make a statement to try and clear themselves:

I was miles from the house.   No he wasn't!   I'm innocent.

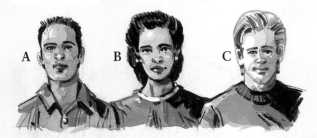

A   B   C

An informer has told the Chief Inspector that two of the suspects always lie, and one always tells the truth, though he didn't say which.

Which of the suspects is guilty?

Problem 8 — Wrong labels

The local greengrocer has just received three large sacks of potatoes. One contains white potatoes, one contains red potatoes and one contains a mixture of red and white.

Unfortunately, the suppliers have just rung to say that they have put all three labels on the wrong sacks.

Can the greengrocer, by taking one potato from one sack and not looking inside, work out which label should be on each sack?

Study pages

Grammar study: articles

1 The definite article

Look at the examples. Why is *the* used in B, but not in A?

A	*Money* makes the world go round. They sell second-hand *books*. Do you like *men* with beards?
B	Hand over *the money*! I've finished all *the books* you lent me. Do you recognise *the men* in this photo?

Make sentences using these expressions, with and without *the*.

a flowers
b silver knives and forks
c water

2 Article or not?

Here are six rules about the definite article, and one example of each rule. Match the rules with the examples.

1 We use *no article* before a noun followed by a number.
2 We use *no article* for talking 'in general'.
3 We often use *the + adjective* for talking about groups of people.
4 Names of countries, continents, cities and mountains usually have *no article*, but if they're plural we use *the*.
5 Names of rivers, seas and oceans have *the*.
6 Names of public buildings, hotels, cinemas, theatres and restaurants usually have *the*.

a The Nile flows into the Mediterranean.
b I'm staying in Room 420.
c More should be done to help the unemployed.
d Meet me outside the Sheraton.
e I love Albanian folk music.
f The Philippines are in East Asia.

Give one or two examples of your own for each rule.

3 School vs the school

Look at the examples. When do we say *hospital* and when do we say *the hospital*?

A	We live opposite the hospital. I went to the hospital to visit my sister. He works at the hospital as a porter.
B	She's been in hospital for six months now. I had to go into hospital for several days. When's he coming out of hospital?

In the sentences below, the words in italics are used in the same way as *hospital*. Add *the* where necessary.

a He was sent to .... *prison* for five years.
b A lot of tourists go to .... *church* to see the icons.
c I stayed in .... *bed* till eleven.
d She comes out of .... *school* at 3.30.
e I went to .... *college* to speak to the principal.
f She studied physics .... *university*.

4 Count and non-count nouns

Which of the words in italics are count and which are non-count? Fill the gaps with *a(n)* or *some*.

a Can I offer you .... *advice*?
.... *suggestion*?

b I've just heard .... interesting *news*.
.... interesting *announcement*.
.... interesting *information*.

c There's going to be .... *thunderstorm*.
.... bad *weather*.

d She's carrying .... *luggage*.
.... *suitcase*.

e We'll need .... *accommodation* for the night.
.... *room*

f He's got .... strange *equipment* in his
.... strange *machine* laboratory.

g Do you mind if I put on .... *music*?
.... *tape*?

Which of the non-count words can also be used with *a piece of …*?

5 Phrases with non-count nouns

We cannot say *a bread*, but we can say *a loaf of bread*. What other phrases can you make using words from the two boxes?

bag	jar	sheet
bar	loaf	slice
bottle	lump	tube
carton	piece	

bread	milk
chocolate	paper
flour	sugar
honey	toothpaste

Replace the words in italics with similar phrases.

a I think there's *some glue* in the cupboard.
b Could you bring *some charcoal* for the barbecue tonight?
c Would you like *some more toast*?
d We need to buy *some soap* and *some orange juice*.

Grammar study B: articles

1 The definite article

Nouns with *the* and with no article

- Use the examples to establish that
  - plural nouns (e.g. *men*) and non-count nouns (e.g. *money*) sometimes have *the* and sometimes have no article
  - we use no article if we are talking in general (e.g. *money in general, all kinds of second-hand books, bearded men in general*);
  - we use *the* if we are talking about something in particular or a particular group (e.g. *the money you owe me, the particular books you lent me, these particular men*).
- Ask students to make sentences using the expressions. Use this as a way of checking that they understand the difference between *the* and no article. Possible sentences:
  - *a* I love flowers. Thank you for the lovely flowers.
  - *b* The trouble with silver knives and forks is that you have to keep cleaning them. Help! The silver knives and forks are missing!
  - *c* Water is better for you than beer. Can we drink the water here?

2 Article or not?

Rules for using the definite article

- Students match the rules with the examples. Then go through the answers together, and ask students to think of other examples of each rule. Give more examples of your own if there are any points that students find difficult. Answers (other examples in brackets):
  - *a* 5 (the Atlantic, the Amazon)
  - *b* 1 (Turn to page 3, I'm in Class 2B)
  - *c* 3 (The government should tax the rich to help the poor)
  - *d* 6 (the Odeon Cinema, the National Gallery)
  - *e* 2 (Do you like Chinese food? Women live longer than men)
  - *f* 4 (England, the British Isles, South Africa, the USA)

3 School vs the school

the and no article with particular nouns

- Use the examples to make these points:
  - The sentences in A are about the hospital as a building. To be *in the hospital* means to be in the building, but not as a patient.
  - The sentences in B are about being ill or injured. To be *in hospital* means to be there as a patient.
- Do the exercise round the class. Answers:

a prison	*c* bed	*e* the college
b the church	*d* school	*f* university

4 Count & non-count nouns

Nouns which are non-count in English

- Answers:
  - *a* some advice, a suggestion
  - *b* some news, an announcement, some information
  - *c* a thunderstorm, some bad weather
  - *d* some luggage, a suitcase
  - *e* some accommodation, a room
  - *f* some equipment, a machine
  - *g* some music, a tape
- As you go through the exercise, build up a list of non-count nouns on the board:

advice	**accommodation**
news	**equipment**
information	**music**
luggage	

5 Phrases with non-count nouns

Making non-count nouns countable, using *a piece of, a bag of*, etc.

- Ask students to make phrases from the two boxes. Give other examples of any diffcult items. Expected answers:

  a bag of flour/sugar
  a bar of chocolate
  a bottle of milk
  a carton of milk
  a jar of honey
  a loaf of bread
  a lump of sugar
  a piece of bread/chocolate/paper
  a sheet of paper
  a slice of bread
  a tube of toothpaste

- Students do the second part of the exercise in pairs, then go through the answers together. Expected answers:
  - *a* a tube/(jar) of glue
  - *b* a bag of charcoal
  - *c* another slice/piece of toast
  - *d* a bar of soap and a carton/bottle of orange juice

Language awareness B: conversational remarks

In English, as in other languages, very simple conversational remarks are often hard for foreign learners to understand. This activity focuses on very brief phrases and remarks which are used as part of everyday conversation in English.

1 Listening

- 🔲 Read through the situations, then play the remarks. Pause after each one, and ask students which situation it goes with. Answers:

  1 e   2 c   3 f   4 b   5 a   6 d

2 Discussion & listening

- Look at each remark in turn, and ask students to suggest situations in which they might be said.

- 🔲 Play the recording, pausing after each item. Check that students understand what the remarks mean in context (for similar expressions, see 3).

3 Extension

- Ask students to suggest other ways of saying the remarks. Possible answers:

  2 It's just not on = It's not good enough, I don't accept it.
  3 Get on with it! = Hurry up, Get a move on.
  4 So what? = It doesn't impress me, It doesn't matter.
  5 It's up to you = It's your decision, It's for you to decide.
  6 What's up? = What's the matter? What's wrong (with you?)
  7 No idea = I don't know, I haven't any idea, I haven't a clue.
  8 Whoops! (No equivalent expressions: said when you trip, knock something over, bump into someone, etc.)
  9 Phew! = Thank goodness! Thank God! (expresses relief).

> 🔲 The tapescript is on page 106.

Pronunciation B: where's the stress?

This activity is concerned with which word in a sentence is given the main stress, and focuses particularly on two kinds of sentence: those where the last word is stressed, and those where the last word is unstressed.

1 Listening, presentation & practice

- 🔲 Play the conversations. Pause after each one, and ask students which of the underlined words is stressed. Answers:

1 one	4 minutes	7 there
2 got	5 me	8 been
3 here	6 see	

- Discuss why the last word is sometimes stressed and sometimes not. Establish that

  – normally, words like *me, one, here, there* are not stressed (as in 2, 4, 6 and 8)
  – in 1, 3, 5, and 7 they are stressed because they are contrasted with another possibility (I want *one*, not two; she lives *here*, not somewhere else; they chose *me*, not someone else; she's over *there*, not here).

- 🔲 Play the conversations again, pausing after each one and getting students to try to say it in the same way.

2 Prediction task & listening

- Pairwork. Students decide which of the underlined words will be stressed most.

- 🔲 Play the conversations, checking the answers as you go. Answers:

  1 me   2 ask   3 I   4 here   5 don't

- Ask students to practise the sentences, paying attention to sentence stress.

3 Extension

- Students choose one of the sentences, and try out different ways of saying it. Likely variations are:

  a It's time to *go* now (normal)
    It's time to go *now* (= this minute)
  b How do you *know* that? (= How can you be so sure?)
    How do you know *that*? (= that, of all things)
    How do *you* know that? (= you, of all people)
  c They *always* invite him (= every single time)
    They always invite *him* (= but not me!)
    They always invite him (= other people don't)
  d I *think* we've got one (= I'm not sure)
    I think we've got *one* (= but no more than that)
    I think *we've* got one (= but they haven't)

  If you like, ask students to write a few lines of dialogue including their remark, and read them out with appropriate stress.

Self-study Workbook

Study Skills B: Dealing with vocabulary   *See notes on page 129.*

Language awareness: conversational remarks

1  You will hear a number of short remarks. Listen and match them with the situations they go best with.

a You're having a drink with someone.
b You're checking if someone understands.
c You're saying goodbye to someone.
d You don't believe what someone says.
e A child's hurt himself.
f You want to start a new subject.

2 Here are some other short conversational remarks. Do you know what they mean? If not, can you guess?

Oh dear!
    It's just not on.
               Get on with it!

So what?
               What's up?
    It's up to you.

No idea.
    Whoops!
               Phew!

Now listen and check your answers.

3 Instead of *Oh dear*, we could also say

– What a pity!
– I'm sorry to hear that.
– What a shame!

Look at some of the other remarks. Can you think of other ways to say them?

Pronunciation: where's the stress?

1 Look at these sentences and listen to what B says. Which of the underlined words are stressed?

1 A You might as well take two.
  B But I only want one.

2 A Do you need an umbrella?
  B No, I've got one.

3 A Where does Beth live?
  B Well, in fact she lives here.

4 A Where are the nearest shops?
  B About five minutes from here.

5 A Who got the job?
  B Surprisingly, they chose me.

6 A Hello, Bill.
  B Hello. Thanks for coming to see me.

7 A Where's Jane?
  B She's over there.

8 A Do you like the new concert hall?
  B I've never been there.

The last word in B's replies is sometimes stressed and sometimes not. Why do you think this is?

Listen to the replies again and try saying them in the same way.

2 Look at these conversations. Which of the underlined words do you think will be stressed most?

1 A I asked John to help.
  B Why didn't you ask me?

2 A How old do you think he is?
  B Why don't you ask him?

3 A I really liked that film.
  B Did you? I didn't.

4 A Did you call me?
  B Yes. Could you come here a moment?

5 A Do you like cats?
  B No, I certainly don't!

Now listen and see if you were right.

3 Look at these remarks. Try saying them with the stress on different words. How does it change the meaning?

a It's time to go now.
b How do you know that?
c They always invite him.
d I think they've got one.

1 Whatever happened to Lord Lucan?

Tenses in narration

FOR SOME REASON, Lord Lucan was known to his friends as 'Lucky' Lucan. In the early 1970s, however, his luck was beginning to run out, and in 1974, at the age of 39, he found himself in serious financial difficulties. He had lost more than £250,000 at gambling tables around the world, and had been forced to sell the family silver to pay off some of his debts.

Lord Lucan in 1974 ...

He was also separated from his wife, and was fighting her in the courts for the custody of their three children.

But worse was to come. On 7 November 1974, Lady Lucan ran into a pub near her home in Belgravia, London. She was covered in blood and was screaming 'He's murdered my nanny!'

Apparently Lucan had gone to the house armed with a hammer, intending to murder his wife. He had been hiding in the kitchen when the children's nanny had walked in, and he had killed her by mistake. He had then panicked and run out of the house, attacking his wife on the way. A police search began.

But Lucan has never been found. On the day of the murder, he sent a note to an old schoolfriend saying that he was going to disappear for a time, and a car he had borrowed was found abandoned at the port of Newhaven, where police believed he had boarded a ferry for France.

Since then, Scotland Yard has followed up around 60 'sightings' a year in places as far apart as San Francisco, Brisbane, Madagascar, Botswana, Hong Kong and, more recently, South Africa. But they have led nowhere.

... and as he might look now

As recently as 1995, a woman claimed that she had been baby-sitting at the house of one of Lucan's friends on the day after the car was found (she was 16 at the time), and that Lucan had turned up at the door.

So what happened? Did he kill himself, perhaps by jumping off a cross-Channel ferry? His wife thinks so: he was a noble man, she says, and would behave in a noble way. Others point out that you need around 150 kilos of concrete to keep a body at the bottom of the sea – so if Lucan jumped into the sea, why has his body never been found?

Or did he leave the car at Newhaven and return to London (as the babysitter's evidence suggests)? Or is he living somewhere near you? If you happen to see him, Scotland Yard would like to hear from you.

---

1 Read the newspaper story.

a Here are some events in the order they appear in the story. What order did they actually happen in? Number them from 1 to 8.

Lady Lucan ran into a pub screaming.
Lord Lucan went to the house.
He was hiding in the kitchen when the nanny came in.
He killed the nanny.
He attacked his wife.
The police started a search for him.
A car was found at Newhaven.
Perhaps he boarded a ferry for France.

Which of the events are *flashbacks* (i.e. jump back to an earlier point of time)? What tenses are used for these parts of the story?

Find other examples of flashbacks in the story.

b Most of the story is set in the past, but some parts are about

– the present
– the period 'up to now'.

Which are they?

2 Imagine that you sighted Lord Lucan recently. Decide

– where it happened
– what you were doing
– what he was doing
– what happened next.

Complete this newspaper report about the sighting.

LORD LUCAN SIGHTED?

According to information received by Scotland Yard, Lord Lucan was sighted last Saturday in

This unit is concerned with the way we talk about events in the past. It focuses on three main areas:
– the use of verb tenses in narration
– particular verbs for reporting things people said (e.g. *admitted, offered, reminded*)
– use of non-defining relative clauses for adding extra information.

The fourth activity develops writing skills. It deals with ways of linking events in a story to show the time relationship between them.

1 Whatever happened to Lord Lucan?

This exercise shows how we use different tenses in telling a story which is set in the past. In particular, it shows how we use Past perfect tenses (simple and continuous) to go back from the story to fill in details of things that had happened earlier. The story is based on newspaper articles describing real events that took place in the 1970s.

➤ Focus on Form: Exercise 1
➤ Workbook: Exercise A

1 Reading & presentation

● Give students time to read through the text. If you like, quickly check comprehension by asking questions, e.g. *How did Lord Lucan get into debt? Was he living with his wife? What did he do to the nanny? What did he do to his wife?*

● Ask students to look at the events in the list. Establish what order they actually happened in. Answers:

1 He went into the house.	5 Lady Lucan ran into the pub.
2 He was hiding …	6 The police started a search for him.
3 He killed the nanny.	7 Perhaps he boarded a ferry …
4 He attacked his wife.	8 A car was found …

● Make these points:
  – This part of the story *starts* with 'Lady Lucan ran into a pub …'. The events that followed that are: The police started a search, they found a car at Newhaven.
  – The other events are *flashbacks* – they go back to things that had *already* happened earlier.

You could show this by means of a diagram on the board:

> 1, 2, 3, 4 ◄──── 5 Lady Lucan ran into a pub
>   ↓
>   6 The police started a search
>   ↓
> 7 ◄──── 8 They found a car at Newhaven

● Establish that for 'flashbacks' we use the Past perfect simple for single events, and the Past perfect continuous for activities:

> **Earlier events:** **He had killed her**
> **Earlier activities:** **He had been hiding**

Ask students to find other examples in the text. Answers:

He had lost more than £250,000; he had been forced to sell the family silver; he had panicked and run out of the house; a car he had borrowed; she had been babysitting; Lucan had turned up at the door.

● Focus briefly on the parts of the text which are about the present (*Is he living somewhere near you?*), and about the period 'up to now' (*Lucan has never been found; Since then, Scotland Yard …*).

2 Writing activity

● Students work in pairs or groups. Together, they think up a story about a sighting of Lord Lucan. One person acts as 'secretary' and writes the story.

● Ask a few pairs or groups to read out their story to the rest of the class.

Optional lead-in: pre-reading vocabulary activity

Write these key expressions on the board, and establish what they mean:

> **in financial difficulties**
> **gambling**
> **pay off his debts**
> **custody of the children**
> **a nanny**
> **a lead pipe**
> **a cross-channel ferry**

Ask students to guess how they might fit together in the story.

Presentation option

If necessary, give other examples of your own to show how the Past perfect continuous is used, e.g.

When I got home, I was absolutely exhausted – I'd been walking for five hours.

His face was bright red – he'd obviously been lying in the sun for too long.

Homework option

Students do the preparation stage in class, but write the newspaper report for homework.

2 Difficult situations

This exercise introduces particular verbs which are used in reporting things people said, and the structures associated with them. These verbs are often used when telling anecdotes, and this is the context in which they are introduced and practised in this exercise.

1 Discussion & listening

- Look at the sentences in turn, and ask students what they think the stories might be about.

- [cassette icon] Play the recording, and see how similar the stories were to what students expected. If you like, ask a few questions to check comprehension, e.g. (Story 1) *Where was the man going to? What did he really have with him? Why did the customs officers think it was cocaine? What happened to him in the end?*

2 Presentation & speaking activity

- Look at the verbs in the box. Either give examples yourself to show how each verb is used, or elicit examples from the class (e.g. *If I say 'You stole my watch', what am I doing? I'm … accusing you of stealing my watch*). Write the verbs in groups on the board, showing what structures they are used with:

> **admit -ing/that**
> **deny -ing/that**
> **accuse s.o. of -ing**
>
> **remind s.o. to/that**
> **warn s.o. not to / that**
>
> **offer to**
> **promise to**
> **refuse to**
> **threaten to**

- Give time for students to think of something that happened to them and write a sentence about it using one of the verbs.
- Pairwork. Using their sentence as a basis, students tell each other their story.
- As a round-up, ask students to read out their sentences. Then ask the class to choose two or three of the stories they would like to hear.

3 Background information

This exercise introduces non-defining relative clauses, used for adding background information to a story or a description.

1 Presentation

- Introduce the idea of non-defining relative clauses by writing a few simple examples on the board, e.g.

- Give time for students to work out how the story might fit together.

> | I visited my sister. | She lives in Canada. |
> | | I hadn't seen her for years. |
> | | Her husband is a doctor. |
> | | |
> | | who lives in Canada. |
> | I visited my sister, | who(m) I hadn't seen for years. |
> | | whose husband is a doctor. |

- Go through the answers together, building up a coherent story with relative clauses. Expected answer:

  … One was Mrs Mancini, who suffered from insomnia and (who) came every Thursday to get her week's supply of sleeping pills. Next to her was young Mickey Wilson, who I had treated for a knife wound six months before. This time he had a nasty cut on the eye, which he kept wiping with a handkerchief. And then there was my old friend Joseph, whose wife had died two years before and (who) had left him with three children to bring up single-handed. He had a job, which brought in a reasonable amount of money, but his landlord was threatening to evict him from his flat, where he'd been living since he had got married.

2 Writing & speaking activity

- Working alone or with a partner, students make up a continuation for the last sentence.
- In turn, students read out their sentences.

> ➤ Focus on Form: Exercise 2
> ➤ Workbook: Exercise B

> [cassette icon] The tapescript is on page 106.

> *Groupwork option*
> Groups discuss what the stories might be about. Then, before playing each story, ask each group to give their 'version' of it.

> *Language note*
> *admit* and *deny* can be used with -*ing* or *that*:
> He admitted taking the money.
> He admitted that he had taken the money.
> *warn* and *remind* can be used with *to* or *that*:
> She warned us not to go out.
> She warned us that the streets were dangerous at night.
> He reminded me to post the card.
> He reminded me that I still hadn't posted the card.

> ➤ Focus on Form: Exercise 3
> ➤ Workbook: Exercise C

> *Language note*
> Non-defining relative clauses are used to add extra information. They are different from defining relative clauses in several ways:
> Possible pronouns are *who(m)*, *which*, *whose* or *where*. We cannot use *that*, and we cannot leave the pronoun out.
> In writing we put a *comma* before the relative clause (and after it, if it comes in the middle of a sentence).
> Focus on Form Exercise 3 focuses specifically on these distinctions.
> For defining relative clauses, see Unit 3.

2 Difficult situations

Reporting verbs

1 Here are sentences from three separate stories.
What do you think the stories are about?

They kept accusing me
of bringing in almost five
pounds of cocaine.

A huge bloke emerged from behind the
door with a crowbar and threatened to
smash my windscreen unless I backed off.

The girl I had the argument with
finally admitted to me that she had
scratched my name in the table.

Now listen to the stories. How similar are they to what you thought?

2 *a* Look at the verbs in the box. Which are followed by *that*,
which by *to*, and which by *-ing*?

b Think of something real that happened to you,
and write a sentence about it using one of the verbs.

Tell your partner what happened. Include your sentence
in what you say.

accuse	offer	remind
admit	promise	threaten
deny	refuse	warn

3 Background information

Non-defining relative clauses

1 Here is an extract from a story.
How do you think the sentences in the box fit into it?

There were three patients in the waiting room that
evening.
One was Mrs Mancini …
Next to her was young Mickey Wilson …
And then there was my old friend Joseph …
… I pressed the buzzer, and wondered which of them
would come in first.

**Incorporate the extra information into the story, using
relative clauses where appropriate.**

2 Here is a later part of the story.
Continue it with a relative clause of your own.

At two minutes to six, I was just getting ready to lock up
the surgery when another patient walked in. It was Hannah
Roberts …

He kept wiping it with a
handkerchief.

His landlord was threatening to
evict him from his flat.

It wasn't enough to pay all his bills.

She suffered from insomnia.

It brought in a reasonable amount
of money.

He had a job.

I had treated him for a knife
wound six months before.

She had left him with three
children to bring up single-handed.

He'd been living there since he had
got married.

She came every Thursday to get her
week's supply of sleeping pills.

This time he had a nasty cut on the
eye.

His wife had died two years before.

4 One thing after another

1 Here are five similar sentences.
How do the underlined expressions affect the meaning?
Which ones have the same meaning?

A At first, everything seemed fine, but <u>when</u> we were in the air things started to go seriously wrong with the aircraft.

B At first, everything seemed fine, but <u>as soon as</u> we were in the air things started to go seriously wrong with the aircraft.

C At first, everything seemed fine, but <u>the moment</u> we were in the air things started to go seriously wrong with the aircraft.

D At first, everything seemed fine, and <u>it wasn't until</u> we were in the air <u>that</u> things started to go seriously wrong with the aircraft.

E At first, everything seemed fine, and <u>it was only when</u> we were in the air <u>that</u> things started to go seriously wrong with the aircraft.

2 How could you join these ideas together, using the underlined expressions above?

a got married – a year – discovered he had another wife
b arrived home – opened the kitchen door – saw there had been a burglary
c met at a party – started talking – knew we'd be lifelong friends
d went to teacher training college – started teaching – realised that it wasn't the right job for me
e absorbed in a book – turned round – realised there was a stranger in the room

3 Work in groups. Write the beginning of a story. Include one of the captions below, and one of the sequence expressions you have practised. Pass your paragraph to another group to continue.

Continue the story you have received, again including one of the captions and one sequence expression.

I didn't notice anything unusual about her at first.

I found an empty space and parked the car.

At first, he drove quite normally.

An old man in a straw hat was sitting in the café drinking whisky.

From the outside, the house looked deserted.

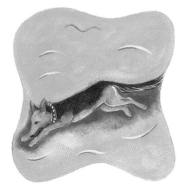

Stretched out on the floor was a large Alsatian dog.

4 One thing after another

Writing skills: *linking events in a story to show the time relationship between them; developing a coherent story.*
Language focus: *sequence expressions:* as soon as, the moment (that), not ... until, only when.

This activity helps students to write a story involving events in sequence. It follows these stages:
1 Presentation. Students study examples of language that are used to show time sequence.
2 Practice. Students expand notes into sentences showing time relationships.
3 Writing. Working together in groups, students develop part of a story. They then continue stories that other groups have started.

1 Presentation

- Look at the examples, and focus on the sequence expressions. Establish that they are of two types:
  - expressions that emphasise that one event followed another immediately: *as soon as ..., the moment (that) ...*
  - expressions that emphasise that there was a long interval between one event and the next: *it wasn't until ..., it was only when ...*

2 Practice

- Working alone or in pairs, students join together the ideas in each set of notes, incorporating the expressions you have presented.
- Discuss the answers together. Emphasise that there is more than one possible way of linking the ideas, and they can be expressed either in a single sentence or in more than one sentence. Possible answers:
  - *a* She got married and it was only a year later that she discovered he had another wife.
  - *b* I arrived home at about 8 o'clock. The moment I opened the kitchen door, I saw there had been a burglary.
  - *c* I met Alex at a party, and as soon we started talking we knew we'd be lifelong friends.
  - *d* I went to teacher training college and found it very interesting. It wasn't until I started teaching that I realised that it wasn't the right job for me.
  - *e* I was absorbed in a book, and didn't notice anything unusual. It was only when I turned round that I realised there was a stranger in the room.

3 Writing

- Divide the class into small groups. Working together, they choose one of the captions, and think of an opening to a story (a few sentences) that could incorporate their caption. They should also include one of the sequence expressions they have practised. A possible opening might be:

  The house I was interested in buying was outside the town, in the middle of a pine forest. I followed the route on the map and arrived at about nine. I got out of the car and walked through the garden to the front door. From the outside the house looked deserted, but as soon as I rang the bell, I heard someone move just behind the door ...

- Each group passes their paragraph to another group to continue. If you like, repeat this process a third time, so that each story contains three paragraphs.
- As a round-up, ask each group to read out their story.

Homework alternatives
Students write a story including three or more of the captions.

Focus on Form

1 Flashbacks

> Past perfect simple and continuous

- Give time for students to look at the story and work out what had happened.
- Go through the story together, and ask students to add the parts that are missing. Possible answers:

  1 … someone had thrown a javelin into his chest.
  2 … He'd been dead for nearly a week.
  3 … She'd been staying with her sister in Canada. She'd been there for a week and she'd only just got back.
  4 … had obviously been looking for something.
  5 … someone had been standing by the window.
  6 … Jay Roberts had been having an affair with someone called Alice, and his wife had agreed to a divorce. (He'd been in love with someone called Alice; his wife had known about the affair; he had been intending to leave his wife.)
  7 … she had left for Canada. The next day she'd bought a Chicago newspaper. On her return, she'd soaked the newspaper in chicken's blood and stuck the javelin through it.

2 Reporting verbs

> Reported speech using particular verbs

- Students do the exercise alone or in pairs. Then go through the answers together. Possible answers:

  a He threatened to call the police (if we didn't get off his land).
  b He admitted leaving the front door unlocked / that he had left the front door unlocked.
  c She accused me of breaking the window.
  d They warned us not to take much money with us (if we were going out at night).
  e She offered to pay for the damage.
  f He reminded her to take her key (with her).

3 Two kinds of relative clause

> Defining and non-defining relative clauses

- Look at the examples and establish these points:
  - In the first example, the relative clauses tell us *which person* and *which book* the speaker is talking about. In the second example, the relative clauses just give us *extra information*.
  - In the first example, after *book* we can use *that* or leave out the pronoun (*the book I'm reading*). In the second example, we must use *which*.
  - In the first example, there are *no commas* round the relative clauses. In the second example, the relative clauses are *separated by commas*.
- Students do the exercise alone or in pairs. Then go through the answers together. Answers:

  a My friend Laura, who I share a flat with, has just got a part in a film. (*or* …, with whom I share a flat, …)
  b Last night I met a man whose parents were trapeze artists.
  c The letter (that) you sent last week hasn't arrived yet.
  d They spend all their time playing with their new computer, which they keep in the kitchen.
  e Giant pandas, which are in danger of extinction, live entirely on bamboo shoots.

Self-study Workbook

Exercise A: Previous actions and activities
Past perfect simple and continuous. Students add sentences to make short paragraphs.

Exercise B: Reporting verbs
Reported speech with particular verbs. Students fill gaps in sentences, then write a paragraph.

Exercise C: Relative clauses
Students improve paragraphs by including relative clauses.

Idioms: Numbers
Common idioms with numbers (e.g. *put two and two together*).

Listening: Holiday incident
A story of a car crash. Students listen and answer questions, then focus on tenses and relative clauses.

Common verbs: go
Idiomatic expressions with the verb *go*.

Focus on Form

In cold blood

It was 11 am on 22 July, 1956. The phone rang. It was a Mrs Mary Roberts, reporting the murder of her husband Jay, in their remote lakeside cabin about two hours from Chicago.

I drove out.

It was clear what had happened. He had been reading the paper when …

The smell was dreadful. When I looked at the date on the newspaper, I knew why. …

The wife had a watertight alibi. …

The study was in a terrible mess. Someone …

Outside, there were two large footprints. It looked as if …

There was a letter in the dead man's pocket. Suddenly I realised a lot of things. …

I phoned the lab. An hour later, my suspicions were confirmed. It wasn't Jay Roberts' blood on the newspaper. I drove out and arrested Mary Roberts for murder.

She had been fiendishly clever. She had, of course, killed her husband before …

The next day, …

On her return, she …

Then she had phoned the police.

1 Flashbacks

Read the story, and use the information in the pictures to fill in the missing parts.

Can you solve the mystery?

2 Reporting verbs

> Don't take too much money with you if you're going out at night.

> I'll pay for the damage.

> If you don't get off my land immediately, I'll call the police.

> Well actually, it was me who left the front door unlocked.

> It was you who broke the window, wasn't it?

> Don't forget to take the key with you will you?

Match these remarks with the sentence beginnings below. Complete the sentences, to report what the people said.

a He threatened …
b He admitted …
c She accused …
d They warned …
e She offered …
f He reminded …

3 Two kinds of relative clause

> **Defining relative clauses**
> The man *who lives next door to me* is a novelist. He wrote the book *(that) I'm reading at the moment*.
>
> **Non-defining relative clauses**
> James Knott, *who lives next door to me*, is a novelist. He wrote 'Under the Stars', *which I'm reading at the moment*.

Look at the examples. What's the difference between defining and non-defining relative clauses? Think about

– meaning
– relative pronouns
– commas.

Now combine these pairs of sentences, using a suitable relative clause.

a My friend Laura has just got a part in a film. I share a flat with her.
b Last night I met a man. His parents were trapeze artists.
c The letter hasn't arrived yet. You sent it last week.
d They spend all their time playing with their new computer. They keep it in the kitchen.
e Giant pandas live entirely on bamboo shoots. They're in danger of extinction.

6 Do it yourself

1 Instructions

1 Here are some instructions for using a variety of products.
What kind of products do you think they are?

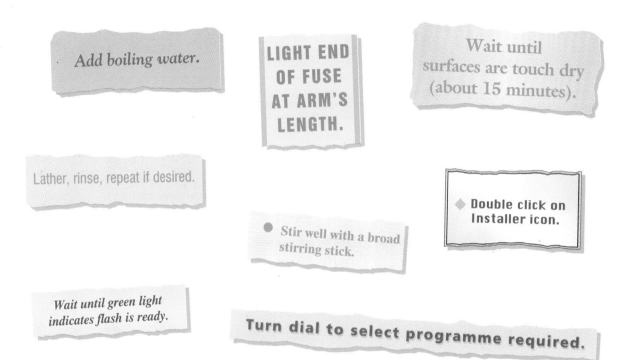

Add boiling water.

LIGHT END
OF FUSE
AT ARM'S
LENGTH.

Wait until
surfaces are touch dry
(about 15 minutes).

Lather, rinse, repeat if desired.

◆ Double click on
Installer icon.

● Stir well with a broad
stirring stick.

Wait until green light
indicates flash is ready.

Turn dial to select programme required.

The instructions below come before and after the ones in the illustrations.
Can you reconstruct the full set of instructions for each product?

a Ensure that all surfaces are free from grease
and dust ...
... Apply two coats with brush or pad.

b Place upright in bottle or tube ...
... Stand well clear.

c Place bag in cup ...
... Leave for 5 minutes to bring out the full
flavour.

d Insert Disk 1 into floppy drive ...
... Follow on-screen instructions.

e Apply sparingly to both surfaces ...
... Position together accurately and then
press hard.

f Gently massage into wet hair and scalp ...
... For best results, follow with Organics
Conditioner.

g Fill dispenser with detergent ...
... Press power switch to start washing cycle.

h Depress shutter button half way ...
... Depress shutter button fully to take
picture.

2 What differences do you notice between the language
of written instructions and normal spoken English?

Choose one set of instructions.
How would you explain to a friend what to do?
Add any details you like.

This unit is about everyday activities in the home. It focuses on the following vocabulary areas:
– language found in instructions for using common products and appliances
– verbs and adjectives describing how things go wrong and how they can be put right (e.g. *crack, leak, rusty*; *mend, replace*)
– verbs for cooking and preparing food.

The Reading and Listening activity is about two people who had commercial ideas: one invented a device for keeping socks together in the wash, and the other opened a restaurant.

1 Instructions

This exercise presents instruction labels from everyday products and appliances that are found in the home. These are used for general comprehension and recognition, and also as a way of introducing two kinds of vocabulary: common action verbs, e.g. rinse, stick, spread, light, and the names of everyday products and appliances, e.g. paint, glue, washing machine.

► Workbook: Exercise A, Listening

1 Reading & presentation

● Look at the instructions together and see if students can guess what products they belong to.

● Give time for students to read the instructions that come before and after and try to reconstruct the complete instructions. Discuss the answers together. Answers:

  a Stir well with a broad stirring stick. (a can of paint)
  b Light end of fuse at arm's length. (a firework/rocket)
  c Add boiling water. (a tea bag)
  d Double click on Installer icon. (a computer)
  e Wait until surfaces are touch dry (about 15 minutes). (a tube of glue)
  f Lather, rinse, repeat if desired. (a bottle of shampoo)
  g Turn dial to select programme required. (a washing machine or dishwasher)
  h Wait until green light indicates flash is ready. (a camera)

2 Speaking activity

● Look at the instructions again, and focus on

  – the verbs used, which are typical of this style of language; compare these with equivalent verbs in everyday English:

INSTRUCTIONS	'NORMAL'
ensure	make sure
place	put
apply	put on
insert	put in
depress	press down

  – the 'reduced' structures which are typical of instructions (e.g. *Place bag in cup*, instead of *Put the bag in the cup*).

● Divide students into pairs or small groups, and give each pair or group a different set of instructions to work on. Together, they prepare a 'spoken' version of the instructions.

● Ask one student from each group to give their explanation to the class. If any points are unclear, other students should ask questions.

Vocabulary option
Write key verbs and nouns on the board, e.g.

add	press	surface
rinse	ensure	button
light	apply	switch
stir	insert	

Optional extension
Ask students to think of another product, and write a simple set of instructions for using it. They read out their instructions, and the rest of the class guesses what the instructions are for.

Homework option: Students could write their instructions at home, and read them out in the next lesson.

2 What needs doing?

This exercise is about things that often go wrong in the home, and what can be done to put them right. The main vocabulary focus is on words and phrases used for saying what's wrong (e.g. it's leaking, it's got a puncture, there's a ... missing*), but the exercise also introduces ways of saying how to put things right (e.g.* replace, repair, stick together*) and the structure* it needs + -ing.

1 Presentation & listening

- Look at each picture in turn, and ask students to say what's wrong. As you do this, check that students know how the words in the box are used in context, and write key phrases on the board. Expected answers:

  A *There's a damp patch* on the ceiling. Probably the roof *is leaking*, and perhaps *there's a* tile *missing*.
  B The bike *has got a puncture* (a flat tyre).
  C The glass under the frame *is cracked* (*there's a crack in it*), the frame *is rotten*, and the paint *is peeling* (*off*).
  D *There's a stain* on the shirt (perhaps an ink stain), *there's a* button *missing*, *there's a tear in it* (*it's torn*).
  E The handle *has come off* (*has broken off*).

- In pairs, students decide what needs doing in each situation.

- 🔲 Taking each picture in turn, ask students what they decided. Then play that section of the recording. As you go through, build up a list of 'repairing' verbs on the board:

repair	sew (up/on)	replace	stick (on)
scrape (off)	repaint	mend	

2 Speaking activity

- In pairs, students find out how many of the jobs they and their partner could do.

- As a round-up, ask a few students whether they or their partner are more practical. Find out if there are any students who could do all of the jobs themselves.

3 Creative cooking

This exercise is based on a reading text, which gives a recipe for using up food you happen to have in your fridge. It focuses on verbs used to describe cooking and preparing food.

1 Presentation

- Introduce the idea underlying the reading text – that sometimes you want to make a meal from whatever you happen to have in your kitchen.

- Look at the verbs in the box, and present any that students don't understand. Then ask students to fill the gaps in the recipe. Expected answers:

1 peel	4 melt	7 simmer	10 sprinkle	12 pour
2 slice	5 fry	8 add	11 bake	13 serve
3 chop	6 add	9 stir		

Ask students whether they think the dish sounds good to eat or not.

2 Speaking activity

- Working in groups, students write a list of five or six ingredients. They can either write fairly easy combinations (e.g. *potatoes, cheese, onion, butter*) or more difficult ones (e.g. *yoghurt, garlic, chocolate, wine*).

- Groups exchange lists of ingredients. They try to think of a dish that would include as many of the ingredients as possible, and write a recipe for it like the one in the reading text.

- Each group reads out their recipe in turn. Ask the rest of the class whether they would eat the dish or not.

➤ Workbook: Exercise B

Presentation option
Show how these words can be used either as nouns or as verbs:

It's torn	There's a tear in it
It's cracked	There's a crack in it
It's stained	There's a stain on it
It's leaking	There's a leak in it

Grammar option
Present *needs + -ing* on the board:

The chair needs	mending
	painting

Ask students to use this structure in discussing how to solve the problems.

🔲 The tapescript is on page 106.

Role-play option
Students work in pairs. Student A chooses one of the situations, and tells B what the problem is and how it happened. Student B gives advice about how to put it right. Then they change roles.

➤ Workbook: Exercise C

Language note
To *mix* is to put two (or more) things together: *Mix the tuna with the onion. Mix the tuna and onion (together).*

To *stir* is to move things round (with a spoon): *Stir the milk (round) slowly.*

To *simmer* is to boil slowly.

To *cook* is a general word – it can include boiling, frying, baking, etc.

Optional lead-in
Write a few ingredients on the board (e.g. *potatoes, cheese, onion, wine*). Ask students to suggest possible dishes you could make with them, e.g.

Bake the potatoes, put cheese and onion in them, and drink the wine.

2 What needs doing?

1 What's wrong with the things in the pictures?
Use words from the box to help you.

crack	come off
leak	missing
peel	rotten
stain	damp
tear	puncture

What do you think needs
doing to put things right?

🔲 Now listen to the
suggestions in the recording.
Are they the same as yours?

2 Work in pairs. Find out which of you is more practical. Which of the jobs would
you be able to do yourself, and which would you get someone else to do?

3 Creative cooking

What do you do when friends turn up unexpectedly and you haven't done any shopping?
Answer: do the best you can with what you've got! This new series offers imaginative recipes that require only the
most ordinary of ingredients. This week, a delicious combination of tuna, apple and brandy!

*B*AKED TUNA *and* APPLE FLAMBÉ

What you've got

1 onion	1 apple	some stale bread
1 tin tuna	100 g butter	a bottle of brandy

First .....1..... the onion and the apple. Thinly .....2..... the onion, and .....3..... the apple into small pieces. .....4..... the butter in a pan, and .....5..... the onion gently in the butter until it begins to turn yellow. Then .....6..... half a cup of water. Bring to the boil and leave to .....7..... for a few minutes. .....8..... the tuna and the chopped apple, and .....9..... thoroughly. Put the mixture in an ovenproof dish. .....10..... breadcrumbs over the top, and .....11..... in a hot oven for 30 minutes or until it is golden brown. Warm a small glass of brandy and .....12..... it over the baked tuna. Set light to it, and .....13..... immediately.

1 Fill the gaps in the recipe with verbs from the box.

sprinkle	serve	fry	melt
simmer	slice	add	pour
bake	chop	peel	stir

Would you eat baked tuna and apple flambé?

2 Work in groups.
On a piece of paper, write a list of ingredients
suitable for the magazine series.

Give your list to another group, who will write a recipe for you.

What do you think of the result?

4 They did it themselves

READING

1 Read through the article quickly, and find answers to these questions.

a What does Andrea Gordon's invention do?
b How did she start thinking about it?
c How does it work?
d What was the main problem in producing it?
e Is she going to give up acting?

ME AND MY GIZMO
Socking it to 'em

ACTRESS Andrea Gordon has got little feet coming out of her ears. At least, she has since she turned her hand to invention. She is the proud inventor of a foot-shaped, plastic device which keeps your pairs of socks together in the washing machine.

So how did the idea occur to her for such an important breakthrough in domestic technology? Archimedes would have approved of her answer.

'It was just a string of little coincidences,' says Andrea modestly. 'A group of us were having dinner after working all day in the studio, and we got talking about universal problems like traffic congestion and lost socks.

'One of the actors said he had ended up taking his washing machine apart to retrieve a sock and had to spend all day Saturday putting it back together again.' The problem was defined.

'I just got thinking, "Why doesn't somebody invent a peg or something just to keep them together?"' Indeed. 'I was just thinking about it and a couple of hours later I was drying up the dishes and I put the tea-towel in one of those plastic grips you get.' Eureka!

'It seemed so obvious that it would work,' she confesses, 'that I was sure someone must have thought of it already.' Nobody had. 'So when I lost an expensive £20 silk sock, that was what finally persuaded me to go for it.'

BUT WAS THIS a real problem for which people really needed a solution? MIA Marketing thought so, and took on the idea.

'I don't set out to solve the world's problems,' says Andrea, 'but at least it's one annoying little thing out of the way. This invention is going to reduce stress levels, so I've done my bit.'

Once the real need for this gizmo had been established, the process of testing began. 'It wasn't easy,' remembers Andrea. 'The first plastic cracked.' They eventually settled on the more expensive thermoplastic polyurethane elastoma, a plastic that retains its shape in boiling water, and even in the rough and tumble world of sock-washing.

NOW LITTLE FEET are available from major shops at £1.95 for a pack of five. According to the advertising blurb on the packet, they are 'suitable for men's, women's and children's socks' and they come in different colours for 'all the family'.

SO WILL THIS breakthrough change Andrea's life? Will she be turning down acting work to become a full-time inventor? 'Acting is what I do,' she insists. 'But I'm glad I saw this idea through. A lot of people have ideas and they don't do anything about them, or they are put off by people not listening to them.'

So now you know – marketing people will listen to anything that might make money.

William Mayes

2 Now read the article more carefully.
What is the significance of the following?

– the studio
– a tea-towel
– a silk sock
– MIA Marketing
– stress levels
– elastoma

4 They did it themselves

This combined Reading and Listening activity is about two people who have had enterprising ideas. The reading activity is a newspaper article about an actress who has invented a device for keeping socks together in the wash. The listening activity is an interview with a French restaurant owner who has just opened a new restaurant in England.

Reading skills: *skimming for general idea; understanding irony.*
Vocabulary focus: *understanding idiomatic expressions.*
Listening skills: *listening to confirm hypotheses.*

Reading

- Tell students they are going to read about an invention, but do not say what it is. Ask them to read the article quickly, and find answers just to the five questions in 1.
- Discuss the answers together. Answers:

  a It keeps your pairs of socks together in the washing machine.
  b At a dinner party, people started talking about lost socks.
  c You put both socks through the holes in the plastic, and it grips them.
  d The plastic cracked in boiling water.
  e No.

- Give time for students to read the text again and find answers to the questions in 2.
- Go through the answers together. Answers:

  the studio: the actors at the dinner party had all been working there (probably a recording studio).

  a tea-towel: the plastic grips she used to hold her tea-towels gave her the idea (a tea-towel = a cloth used for drying dishes).

  a silk sock: losing an expensive silk sock made her think her idea was worthwhile.

  MIA Marketing: the company who produced 'Little Feet'.

  stress levels: she thinks 'Little Feet' will reduce stress levels.

  elastoma: the heat-resistant plastic that 'Little Feet' are made of.

- Discuss the answers to Questions 3 and 4 together. Expected answers:

  3 *a* she started inventing things
     b we started talking
     c in the end (after trying different solutions) he took …
     d I started thinking
     e decide to do it, take action
     f adopted, accepted
     g made my contribution (to society)
     h decided to use
     i took it to its conclusion
     j discouraged

  4 Amusing and ironical. Examples of irony (pretending to treat the invention as much more important than it really is): 'the proud inventor', 'important breakthrough in domestic technology', 'Archimedes would have approved', 'Eureka!', 'the rough and tumble world of sock washing'.

Note on title
'Sock it to 'em!' is a colloquial expression meaning 'show your strength, show what you can do (to sock = to hit). In the title of the article it is of course a play on words, as the article is about socks.

Note
The aim of this stage is to give students practice in 'skimming' quickly to understand the main points. To encourage this, you could set a time limit (e.g. two minutes). Alternatively, ask students to read quickly and raise their hands when they've finished.

Option: paired reading
Ask students to read and discuss the questions in pairs, or to read alone first and then compare their answers with their partner.

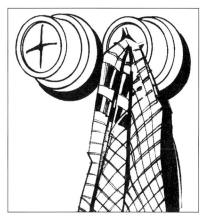

Plastic grip for hanging tea-towels

Note
This is a discussion question, with no 'correct' answer. If students interpret the article in a different way, encourage them to support their own point of view.

Listening

- Read through the eight statements, then ask students to read the publicity leaflet. Discuss which statements are explained by the leaflet, and how. Possible answers:

  a Yes. It was a way of using up spare dough when they baked bread.

  b Yes. It has a bread base, and has other things sprinkled on it (*fromage frais* = curd cheese).

  c Not really explained. The ingredients seem rather different (e.g. fromage frais, bacon).

  d Not really explained. It seems to be popular in France.

  e Yes. Prices will be reasonable (£5 with wine).

  f Yes. It's cooked quickly in a hot oven.

  g Not explained.

  h Not explained.

- [cassette icon] Play the recording. Then discuss which of the eight statements are now explained more clearly. Possible answers:

  b It was the 'ancestor' of the pizza: cheap ingredients, fast to cook, not expensive to eat.

  c Not as filling as pizza, tastier, moister, cheaper.

  g It will be more fun, with a relaxed atmosphere.

  h It will be more sociable. You have the food in the middle and you share it.

- If necessary, play the recording again. Ask students to note down what they think are the three main attractions of La Tarte Flambée. Then build up a list on the board. Possible answers:

  – fun to eat in
  – good food
  – different from other restaurants
  – not expensive
  – lively atmosphere

Discussion

- Ask students whether they think Little Feet or La Tarte Flambée will be a success. Then tell them the following information:

  – A year after the launch, Little Feet were on sale in around ten countries, and available from supermarkets, department stores and by mail order. Sales had reached two million, and were still going well.

  – A year after opening, La Tarte Flambée was doing well. It was busier during the tourist season (spring and summer), but during the winter was still very busy at weekends. The owner was considering opening other branches.

Optional lead-in

Use the picture of the *tarte flambée* as a basis for asking questions, e.g.

What do you think it's made of? What do you think it tastes like? Do you have anything like that in your country?

Note

Although the language he uses is fairly simple, the restaurant owner speaks with quite a strong French accent. If students have serious difficulty in understanding him, let them read the tapescript as you play the recording.

[cassette icon] The tapescript is on page 106.

Self-study Workbook

Exercise A: Getting the picture
Instructions for using a camera. Students add missing parts to the text and focus on key words.

Exercise B: Things need doing
Vocabulary connected with problems in the home. Students choose words to fill gaps in sentences.

Exercise C: Verbs in the kitchen
Verbs connected with preparing food. Students complete an acrostic.

Idioms: Parts of the body (1)
Common idioms with parts of the body (e.g. *pull someone's leg*).

Listening: How to do it
People demonstrating how to paint a door, play the recorder, and mend a puncture. Students predict what words they will hear, then listen for key points.

Word building: Prefixes (1)
Use of *un-*, *in-*, etc. to give opposite meaning.

3 These conversational expressions appear in the article.
What do you think they mean?

a ... she *turned her hand to* invention
b ... and we *got talking*
c ... he had *ended up* taking ...
d I just *got thinking* ...
e ... persuaded me to *go for it*
f ... and *took on* the idea
g ... so I've *done my bit*
h ... they eventually *settled on* ...
i ... I *saw* this idea *through*
j ... they are *put off* by people not listening ...

4 **Do you think the style of the article is**

– serious and analytical?
– enthusiastic and persuasive?
– negative and critical?
– amusing and ironical?

Find examples from the article to support your point of view.

LISTENING

1 Here are eight statements about a dish called *tarte flambée*, and a new restaurant which will soon be serving it.

a 200 years ago, people had a good reason for cooking tarte flambée.
b It's similar to pizza.
c It's different from pizza.
d People will like it.
e It's not expensive.
f It's quick to cook.
g Eating in La Tarte Flambée will be very different from eating in a formal gastronomic restaurant.
h It will also be more fun than other fast food restaurants.

Read the publicity material. Which of the statements does it help to explain?

2  Now listen to the restaurant's owner, Philippe Roy, talking about his new restaurant. What does he say that helps to explain the eight statements?

3 What would you say are the three main attractions of La Tarte Flambée?

DISCUSSION

Do you think either Little Feet or La Tarte Flambée will be a commercial success?
Why / Why not?

Your teacher will tell you how well they were doing a year after they were launched. Did they do as well/badly as you expected?

La Tarte Flambée

La Tarte Flambée will soon be opening, bringing you an authentic taste of Alsace and a new eating experience.

The Tarte Flambée was first made in Alsace, eastern France, over 200 years ago. Villagers gathering to bake their bread in the communal oven would roll any spare dough thinly, sprinkling this with handy ingredients such as fromage frais, onions and bacon. It was then cooked quickly in the hot oven (hence flambée). The dish soon grew to become the centrepiece of all social occasions.

I've created La Tarte Flambée so that you too can enjoy a taste of Alsace in a warm and friendly atmosphere. Prices will be very reasonable – in fact you can enjoy a traditional tarte flambée and a glass of wine for only £5!

Philippe Roy

Study pages

Grammar study: -ing forms

1 Verbs and nouns

Look at the words in italics. What's the difference between those in A and those in B?
What's the connection between them?

A	*Nicotine* is bad for your health. I enjoy *music*. Thank you for the *present*.
B	*Smoking* is bad for your health. I enjoy *walking*. Thank you for *inviting* me.

Complete these sentences with *-ing* forms instead of the nouns in italics, so they have roughly the same meaning.

a He's very good at *maths*.
b He wastes all his money on *the lottery*.
c She went out without *her coat*.
d *Factory work* can be very boring.

2 Verb + -ing

admit	consider	involve	risk
avoid	deny	miss	suggest

All the verbs in the box can be followed by *-ing* forms. Fill the gaps with suitable verbs.

a He .... being in the building at the time, but .... shooting the security guard.
b Her job .... travelling all over the world.
c I was about to cook lunch when he .... getting a take-away instead.
d It's great that the children can read now, although I really .... reading them a bedtime story.
e The Stock Market isn't for me. I don't want to .... losing all my money.
f Let's go now to .... getting stuck in the traffic.
g Now we can afford it, we're .... buying a new car.

Now complete these sentences.

a The walls are a bit thin, so could you avoid ...
b I love living in the country, but I miss ...
c Learning a language involves ...
d I'm tired of living alone. I'm considering ...

3 Preposition + -ing

-ing forms often follow verbs and phrases with prepositions. Here are some examples:

> I'm thinking *of starting* my own business.
> Are you accusing me *of cheating*?
> He's not very good *at making* polite conversation.

Fill the gaps in these sentences. Include a preposition and an *-ing* form.

a At last she succeeded .... Mount Everest.
b I absolutely insist .... the meal.
c Would you be interested .... the Folk Festival?
d He's not used .... on his own.
e They tried to prevent us .... the building.
f He never forgave her .... his Persian carpet.
g I prefer watching videos .... the cinema.
h She's really looking forward .... school.

4 Other people's actions

Look at the examples. Which use a passive form?

> I don't mind *you correcting my mistakes*.
> I don't like *people smoking in the house*.
> I can't stand *being laughed at*.
> I don't mind *you phoning me at work*.
> I hate *being called 'Miss'*.

Imagine these things happening to a young child. How do you think she feels about them?

– her parents give her sweets
– she gets bullied at school
– her parents often go out in the evening
– people pat her on the head

Now think about your own childhood. What did you like/dislike people doing?

5 Infinitive or -ing?

Look at these pairs of examples. What do they tell you about the verbs *like*, *remember*, *forget* and *try*?

1 a I like singing in the shower.
   b I like to pay my bills as soon as I receive them.

2 a I don't remember seeing you here before.
   b I must remember to post that letter.

3 a I'll never forget shaking Mick Jagger by the hand.
   b I forgot to write down their telephone number.

4 a We tried to open the door, but it was locked.
   b – I can't get the video to work.
      – Why don't you try changing the plug?

Choose the best answer.

a – He won't help me.
    – Well, have you tried *asking/to ask* him?
b I remember *riding/to ride* on a steam train when I was eight.
c Don't forget *ringing/to ring* me when you get home.
d I tried *lighting/to light* a fire, but the wood was damp.
e Cats like *keeping/to keep* themselves very clean.

Grammar study C: -ing forms

1 Verbs & nouns

> Nouns and -ing forms

- Use the examples to establish that
  - the words in Box A are nouns, the words in Box B are -ing forms of verbs (gerunds)
  - -ing forms can be used in the same way as nouns: as the subject of a sentence, as the object, or after a preposition.
- Students replace the nouns with -ing forms. Possible answers:
  - a He's very good at doing maths / solving mathematical problems.
  - b He wastes all his money on gambling / buying lottery tickets.
  - c She went out without putting her coat on.
  - d Working in a factory can be very boring.

2 Verb + -ing

> Verbs which are followed by -ing forms

- Go through the verbs in the box and check that students understand what they mean. Then do the exercise round the class. Answers:
  - a admitted, denied
  - b involves
  - c suggested
  - d miss
  - e risk
  - f avoid
  - g considering
- Ask students to do the second part of the exercise in pairs, and then go through the answers together. Possible answers:
  - a … making too much noise, … playing loud music.
  - b … being able to go to the theatre, … having shops nearby.
  - c … working hard, … listening carefully.
  - d … advertising for a partner, … sharing a flat with friends.

3 Preposition + -ing

> Prepositional phrases with -ing forms (think of doing, good at doing, etc.)

- Give time for students to do the exercise, then go through the answers together. Possible answers:
  - a in climbing, in getting to the top of
  - b on paying for, on making
  - c in coming to, in seeing
  - d to living, to being
  - e from leaving, from entering
  - f for ruining, for dropping ash on
  - g to going to
  - h to going to, to leaving.
- Build up a list of verbs and phrases on the board:

be thinking of	insist on	forgive s.o. for
accuse s.o. of	be interested in	prefer … to
be good at	be used to	look forward to
succeed in	prevent s.o. from	

Focus especially on the phrases be used to, prefer … to, and look forward to. Point out that to here is a preposition (not to + infinitive). If necessary give more examples to show how to is followed by a noun or -ing:
  - I'm looking forward to their visit.
  - I'm looking forward to seeing them.

4 Other people's actions

> Verb + -ing with change of subject

- Build up a table of verbs expressing likes and dislikes on the board:

	love	
	like	
I	don't mind	wet weather
	don't like	walking on the rain
	hate	
	can't stand	

- Add to the table, to show how we can talk about what other people do (change of subject) and what is done to us (passive):

	love	wet weather
	like	walking in the rain
I	don't mind	people smoking
	don't like	people tickling me
	hate	being tickled
	can't stand	being shouted at

If necessary, do some basic transformation practice, e.g. People shout at me – I hate it.
  - → I hate people shouting at me, I hate being shouted at.
- Make sentences round the class or in pairs. Possible answers:
  - She likes being given sweets / She loves her parents giving her sweets.
  - She hates people bullying her / She doesn't like being bullied.
  - She doesn't mind her parents going out in the evening.
  - She can't stand people patting her on the head / She hates being patted on the head.
- Students write similar sentences about their own childhood. As a round-up, ask a few students what they wrote.

5 Infinitive or -ing?

> Verbs followed by infinitive or -ing, with a difference in meaning (like, remember, forget, try)

- Use the examples to focus on these differences:
  - 1 a like doing = enjoy
    - b like to do = you think it's right, you usually do it (I don't enjoy paying bills on time, but it makes me feel good to do it.)
  - 2 a remember doing = remember something you did, or something that happened in the past
    - b remember to do = remember what you need to do
  - 3 a forget doing = forget something you did, or something that happened in the past
    - b forget to do = forget what you need to do
  - 4 a try to do = make an effort to do something difficult (We tried to open the door, but we didn't succeed.)
    - b try doing = do something to see if it helps (Try changing the plug – perhaps that will solve the problem.)
- Ask students to do the second part of the exercise in pairs, and then go through the answers together. Answers:
  - a asking
  - b riding
  - c to ring
  - d to light
  - e to keep

Language awareness C: British and US English

This activity focuses on words which have different meanings in British and US English, and also on differences in spelling and grammar.

1 Vocabulary

- Look at the box of British English words and check that students know what they mean.

- Give time for students to match the US English and British words. This can be done in groups, using a dictionary. Then go through the answers together. Answers:

sidewalk = pavement; fall = autumn; closet = cupboard; drapes = curtains; line = queue (to stand in line = to queue); freeway = motorway; garbage = rubbish; truck = lorry; yard = garden; elevator = lift; candy = sweets.

- ▣ Play the recording. Students answer the questions:
  – He offered to help the woman wash up.
  – In US English *wash up* means 'wash your face and hands' (in British English it means 'wash the dishes').

- Look at the words in Section 1*b*, and see if students know what they mean in British and US English. Answers:

  a BEng = underpants (you wear them under trousers)
     USEng = trousers
  b BEng = a tunnel for pedestrians (e.g. under a road)
     USEng = underground railway
  c BEng they give you a bill in a restaurant
     USEng = a bank note (e.g. *$100 bill*)

  d BEng = a small bag for money
     USEng = a bag for keeping personal things in (BEng: *a handbag*)
  e BEng = fried potatoes (e.g. *chicken and chips*)
     USEng = thin slices of fried potato in a packet (BEng: *crisps*)

2 Spelling

- Ask students to write the US spellings of the words. They should look up any they do not know in an English–English dictionary. Then go through the answers. Answers:

  a honor; color b center; theater c traveled; marvelous

3 Grammar

- Look at the sentences and ask students how they think they should be in British English.

- ▣ Play the recording and establish what the answers should be. Answers:

  a at the weekend   c write to me   e I haven't made.
  b on Tuesday   d loves riding   f I've got

▣ The tapescript is on page 107.

Pronunciation C: rising and falling tones

This activity focuses on the way we use a falling tone when giving new information and a rising tone when repeating given (or known) information.

1 Presentation

- ▣ Play the two conversations and focus on B's replies. Bring out these points:
  – In both conversations, B's voice *falls* where the main stress of the sentence is.
  – *Conversation 1:* B's voice falls on *meeting* and rises on *Tuesday*. This is because *our meeting* is the main new information (*on Tuesday* is 'given').
  – *Conversation 2:* B's voice falls on *Tuesday*. This is because *on Tuesday* is the main new information (*our meeting* is 'given').

2 Listening & practice

- ▣ Play the conversations and ask students to identify the rising and falling tones. Answers:

  1 / You might see Boris / in Moscow. /

  2 / I leave here / on Friday. /

  3 / I bought it / in Paris. /

  4 / The one on the left / is Don's. /

  5 / I learned German / at school. /

- ▣ Play the conversations again. Students practise saying B's replies.

3 Prediction task & listening

- Pairwork. Students decide how B's replies would be said.

- ▣ Play the conversations. Point out that in these examples, the *sense* of what A says is repeated by B, rather than the actual words. Most likely answers are:

  1 fall on *at home* (new)
     rise on *most of the time* (given, = 'over the holiday')
  2 fall on *shopping* and *walk* (new)
     rise on *Saturday* and *Sunday* (given, = 'the weekend')
  3 fall on *enjoy* and *lonely* (new)
     rise on *most of the time* and *sometimes* (given, = the time I spend on my own)
  4 fall on *time* and *often* (new)
     rise on *working* and *holiday* (given, = 'these days')

Self-study Workbook

Study Skills C: Approaching a reading text   *See notes on page 129.*

Language awareness: British and US English

1 *a* One of the most obvious differences between British and US English is in common vocabulary. Can you match these American words with their British equivalents? Use a dictionary to help you.

sidewalk	fall	closet	drapes
line	freeway	garbage	
truck	yard	elevator	candy

lift	rubbish	sweets	motorway
pavement	garden	wardrobe	
curtains	lorry	autumn	queue

b 🔲 You will hear a short anecdote about an Englishman visiting the US.

– What did the Englishman offer to do?
– Why did his hosts laugh?

Here are some other words that mean different things in British and US English. Find out what they mean in each.

a pants   *c* a bill   *e* (potato) chips
b a subway   *d* a purse

2 Some words are spelt differently. Here are some British English words. How would an American spell them? Use a dictionary if necessary.

a honour; colour   *c* travelled; marvellous
b centre; theatre

3 There are also some minor differences in grammar. Here are some sentences in American English. How would they be different in British English?

a I saw my friend Sally on the weekend.
b The President was in Moscow Tuesday.
c Don't forget to write me.
d He loves to read in bed.
e I already boiled the water, but I didn't make the coffee yet.
f I found London very strange at first, but now I've gotten used to it.

🔲 You will hear an American talking about the differences. Listen and check your answers.

Pronunciation: rising and falling tones

1 🔲 Look at these conversations and listen to B's replies. Where does her voice *rise* and where does it *fall*? What is the difference between the two replies?

1 A I've arranged to see Sue on Tuesday.
   B / But our meeting's / on Tuesday. /
2 A See you at the meeting on Friday.
   B / But our meeting's / on Tuesday. /

2 🔲 Listen to these conversations. Decide which sections of B's replies have a *rising tone* and which have a *falling tone*.

1 A I'm going to Moscow.
   B / You might see Boris / in Moscow. /
2 A When are you going to Malaysia?
   B / I leave here / on Friday. /
3 A I like your jacket. Where did you get it?
   B / I bought it / in Paris. /
4 A Is this Don's bag?
   B / The one on the left / is Don's. /
5 A How did you learn to speak German?
   B / I learnt German / at school. /

Now try saying them yourself.

3 Look at B's replies in these conversations. Which sections do you think will have a rising tone, and which will have a falling tone?

1 A Did you do much over the holiday?
   B / We just stayed at home / most of the time. /
2 A What did you do at the weekend?
   B / On Saturday / I went shopping / and on Sunday / I went for a walk. /
3 A What's it like living on your own?
   B / I really enjoy it / most of the time / but it does get a bit lonely / sometimes. /
4 A Are you still playing football these days?
   B / When I'm working / I don't get much time / but when I'm on holiday / I often play. /

🔲 Now listen and see if you were right.

Working it out

1 Mysteries of the universe

must, might, can't • infinitive forms

1 Read the texts and choose opinions that are closest to your own.
Give reasons for your opinions.

A

Many people are convinced that there is life elsewhere in the universe. Scientists are busy searching for evidence of other forms of life, in the form of radio signals, but so far have found no trace.

> There must/might/can't be life elsewhere in the universe

B

Every year, a number of people claim that they were abducted by aliens. They usually say that they were taken on board an alien spaceship for scientific experiments and released a few hours later.

> Aliens must/might/can't be abducting human beings on a regular basis.

C

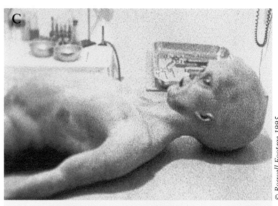

© Roswell Footage 1995

This still is from a film claiming to show an autopsy on a dead alien who crash-landed in the Nevada Desert in 1947. The owner says it was kept secret for years by the US Military. But is it a fake?

> Aliens must/might/can't have landed on Earth.

D

A number of huge shapes were drawn on the ground in Nazca, Peru, around 2000 years ago. Since they are visible only from the air, some believe they were drawn by aliens.

> The Nazca lines must/might/can't have been drawn by aliens.

2 Now read the article *Life Elsewhere?* on page 93. What opinions does the writer have? Have you changed any of your opinions after reading the article?

This unit is concerned with the language of making deductions and giving explanations. It focuses on three main areas:
– the modal verbs *must*, *might* and *can't* with present and past infinitives
– 2nd and 3rd conditionals
– talking about appearance, using *look*, *seem* and *appear*.

The fourth activity develops writing skills, and deals with ways of explaining reason and purpose.

1 Mysteries of the universe

This exercise deals with the issue of whether there is intelligent life elsewhere in the universe, and whether aliens have visited the Earth. This topic provides a natural context for the language of making deductions and giving opinions, and is used as a way of presenting the modals must, might *and* can't *followed by infinitive forms. Three infinitive forms are introduced here: the simple infinitive,* be + -ing, *and* have + -ed *(including the passive* have been + -ed).

➤ Focus on Form: Exercise 1
➤ Workbook: Listening

1 Discussion & presentation

● Read through the texts, and check that students understand them. Focus on any new vocabulary, e.g. *evidence (of)*, *found no trace (of)*, *were abducted*, *a still* (= a picture from a film), *an autopsy*, *a fake*, *aliens*.

● Divide the class into pairs. Students consider the four statements, and decide which choice represents their opinion.

● Take each statement in turn, and ask students what they think. Try to get students to discuss each statement and give reasons for their opinions, e.g.

There must be life elsewhere in the universe: – Why do you think there must be? Why haven't scientists found any trace of it? Does anyone disagree?

● Look at the way *must/might/can't* are used. Point out that
– it must be = I'm sure it is
– it might be = maybe it is
– it can't be = I'm sure it isn't.

Give examples to show how we use *must/might/can't* to talk about the present or past:

I'm sure he *lives* here (in general): he must *live* here
I'm sure he's *working* (at the moment): he must *be working*
I'm sure he *saw* me (past): he must *have seen* me.

Show these forms on the board:

He	must might can't	*live* here *be working* *have seen* me

> *Vocabulary option*
> Prepare for the discussion by giving other vocabulary connected with aliens and space, e.g. *universe*, *solar system*, *planet*, *space*, *spaceship*, *flying saucer*, *UFO* (= unidentified flying object).

> *Alternative*
> If you don't want to interrupt the flow of the discussion, you could present this language either right at the beginning or at the end of the activity.

> *Note*
> Infinitive forms are also dealt with in Study Pages A (page 16).

2 Reading and discussion

● Give time for students to read through the article.

● Establish what the writer's answers to the four statements would be. Probable answers:

There must be life elsewhere in the universe (because there are so many other stars with planets orbiting round them).

Aliens can't be abducting human beings (because they wouldn't bother to travel so far).

Aliens can't have landed on Earth (same reason; also, if they had, they would have taken over the planet).

The Nazca lines can't have been drawn by aliens (same reasons).

● Ask students if they have changed their opinion after reading the article. If they don't agree with what the article says, encourage them to say why.

> *Optional reading task*
> Write this task on the board:
>
> > **Does the writer believe that:**
> > **– there is life elsewhere in the universe?**
> > **– there is intelligent life elsewhere in the universe?**
> > **– aliens have visited Earth?**
>
> Students read and find answers to the questions.

2 Otherwise ...

This exercise links must/might/can't *with 2nd and 3rd conditional sentences, used for giving explanations. It is a straightforward sentence-making exercise, with a grammar focus.*

1 Presentation

- To introduce conditional sentences, write these sentences on the board:

> **They can't be in, because the lights aren't on.**
> **They can't be in. Otherwise ...**
>
> **They can't have recognised us, because they didn't wave.**
> **They can't have recognised us. Otherwise ...**

Ask students to continue the second sentence in each pair. (Answers: *... the lights would be on. ... they would have waved.*)

- Use this to remind students of conditional structures:
  – *would + infinitive* for talking about the present
  – *would have + -ed* for talking about the past.

- Look at the exercise, and ask students to match the other sentences. Answers:

They must be expecting guests. Otherwise the house wouldn't be so tidy.
They must have got stuck in the traffic. Otherwise they'd be here by now.
They must be on expenses. Otherwise they wouldn't be travelling first class.
They can't have gone far. Otherwise they would have taken the car.

2 Writing & speaking activity

- Working alone or in pairs, students add a sentence to each deduction, beginning with *Otherwise.*

- In turn, students read out one of their reasons. The others guess what deduction it goes with.

3 How do you picture it?

In this exercise, students listen to two interpretations of a painting, and then interpret a painting themselves. This involves language for talking about appearance and general impression, especially the verbs look, seem *and* appear.

1 Discussion, listening & presentation

- Read through the questions, then give students a few minutes to look at the picture and think about it. Go through the questions together, and see what ideas students have.

- 🎧 Play the recording. Stop after each part and establish how each speaker interprets the picture. Possible answers:

Speaker 1: The picture's saying that people in the West have too much, while in the Third World people are hungry.
Speaker 2: The figures in the picture show two sides of the woman's personality – a sophisticated, beautiful side and a darker, more primitive side.

- 🎧 Play the recording again. Ask students to listen out for examples of *look, seem* and *appear.* Answers:

look: Her face looks open, he looks like Andy Warhol, he looks hungry. She looks like a schoolgirl, the table looks like a school desk, he looks very sophisticated.
seem: She seems to be looking in front of her, there seems to be a screen. She seems to be sitting there, they seem to represent different sides of herself.
appear: An older woman who appears to be pushing her way into the picture ...

Build up tables on the board to show structures with *look, seem* and *appear*:

look	+ adjective like + noun as if + clause		seem appear	to + infinitive

[Continued on next page]

➤ Focus on Form: Exercise 2
➤ Workbook: Exercise A

Optional grammar practice
Ask students to make complete conditional sentences with *If*, e.g.

If they had recognised us they would have waved.
If they weren't expecting guests, the house wouldn't be so tidy.
If they hadn't got stuck in the traffic, they'd be here by now.

Focus on Form Exercise 2 deals with full *If* sentences.

➤ Focus on Form: Exercises 3, 4
➤ Workbook: Exercise B

Groupwork option
Students discuss the picture in pairs or groups. Then ask each group in turn for their interpretation.

Note
If necessary, explain who Andy Warhol was (a fashionable New York artist and film-maker of the '60s).

The picture in fact refers to Andy Warhol's famous 'pop' art painting of a tin of soup (shown here lying under the table). If you like, bring in a reproduction to show to the class.

🎧 The tapescript is on page 107.

Language note
Seem and *appear* can also be followed by an adjective, e.g.

They seem very excited.

2 Otherwise …

2nd & 3rd conditionals

1 Match the deductions and the reasons. What's the connection between each pair?

They can't be in.		… they would have taken the car.
They can't have recognised us.		… the lights would be on.
They must be expecting guests.		… they would have waved.
They must have got stuck in traffic.	Otherwise …	… they'd be here by now.
They must be on expenses.		… they wouldn't be travelling first class.
They can't have gone far.		… the house wouldn't be so tidy.

2 Give reasons for these deductions. Begin each reason with *Otherwise* …

– They must be hard up.   – They must have moved.   – They must be very happily married.

– They can't be hard up.   – They can't have moved.   – They can't be very happily married.

Read out some of your reasons. Can other students guess which deductions they go with?

3 How do you picture it?

look • seem • appear

1 Look at this painting, which is called *Regarding Soup*, and think about these questions.

– How old do you think the woman is?
– Who do you think the man is?
– What about the other figure?
– What's the significance of the soup?
– What is the woman doing?
– Why do you think they're wearing sunglasses?
– What do you think the picture is trying to say?

You will hear two people talking about the picture. How do they answer the questions? Do you agree with them?

Now listen again. How do the speakers use these words?

– look
– seem
– appear

2 Work in groups. Look at the painting on page 94, which is by the same artist.

How do you interpret it?

© 1994 Gabriella Roth

4 Why do they do it?

1 Why do people gamble, even though they know that they're more likely to lose money than win? Here are four different people's explanations. Read them and note down all the expressions used for talking about *reason* and *purpose*.

A I think people gamble for many reasons, but one is so as to bring some excitement into their lives. Buying a lottery ticket, for example, gives you something to look forward to, and you can have a lot of fun imagining what you would do if you won.

C People who gamble a lot probably do it for the same reason that people take drugs – it gives them some kind of a 'high'. The problem is, of course, that this sort of gambling can easily become addictive.

B The most obvious reason why people gamble is in order to make money – even if you know you may not win, there's always a chance that you will. And for many people that's the only way they could ever make a lot of money.

D Well, I play cards for money sometimes, and it's just a way of having a good time with my friends. We get together and have a nice evening – we only play for small amounts of money, so there's not much risk in it.

2 Choose one of the questions below that interests you, and make a few notes of your own opinion. Then ask two or three other people in the class what they think, and make notes of what they say.

- Why do people start smoking?
- Why do people become politicians?
- Why do people hunt wild animals?
- Why do people go sky-diving?
- Why do people fast?
- Why do people enjoy watching violent films?
- Why do people run marathons?
- Why do people become vegetarians?
- Why do people take drugs?
- Why do people keep large dogs as pets?

3 Put the opinions you have collected together in a connected series of short paragraphs, like the example below.

> There are various reasons why gambling is so popular. The most obvious reason why people gamble is in order to make money – even if you know you may not win, there's always a chance that you will. And for many people winning money from gambling is the only way they could ever make a lot of money.
>
> Another reason people gamble is to bring some excitement into their lives. Buying a lottery ticket, for example, gives you something to look forward to, and you can have a lot of fun imagining what you would do if you won.
>
> For most people, gambling is just a way of having a good time – for example, getting together with friends and playing cards for small amounts of money can be an enjoyable way of spending an evening.
>
> But people who gamble a lot probably do it for the same reason that people take drugs – it gives them some kind of a 'high'. The problem is, of course, that serious gambling can easily become addictive and there's a real danger of it ruining your life.

4 Why do they do it?

Writing skills: *giving explanations in writing; making notes and organising them into paragraphs.*
Language focus: *structures for talking about reason and purpose.*

This activity helps students to write a paragraph giving explanations. It follows these stages:
1 Reading and presentation. Students study examples and note down expressions used for talking about reason and purpose.
2 Discussion and note-making. Students find out opinions about a topic from other people in the class, and make notes.
3 Writing. Students organise their notes into a series of short paragraphs.

1 Reading & presentation

● Read through the explanations, and ask students which they think are the most convincing. Build up on the board a list of expressions used for talking about *reason* and *purpose*:

People gamble	*for many reasons* *for the same reason that …*
One **Another** **The most obvious**	*reason why people gamble is …*
People gamble	*in order to …* *so as to …* *as a way of … -ing*

2 Discussion & note-making

● Students choose one of the questions, and then sit in groups of three or four. In turn they ask other students in their group what they think about their question, and make notes.

3 Writing

● Read the connected text, and ask students what changes the writer has made to the explanations in Section 1. Bring out these points:
  1 The writer has *put the explanations in a particular order*, starting with the most obvious and finishing with the most serious/extreme.
  2 The writer has *changed the style* (especially of paragraph 3), so that the paragraphs all describe people *in general*.
  3 The writer has added a *general sentence* (sometimes called a 'topic sentence') at the beginning: *There are various reasons why gambling is so popular.* This sentence shows what the paragraphs are going to be about.
  4 The writer has added expressions to *show how the paragraphs are connected* (e.g. *Another reason people gamble is …, But …*).
● Students write a series of short paragraphs based on their notes, adding any details they like.

➤ Workbook: Exercise C

Optional lead-in
Before looking at the exercise, write the word *gambling* on the board. Ask students what forms of gambling they know (e.g. cards, roulette, lotteries, dice).
Then ask students why they think people gamble, and what they themselves think of gambling.

Language note
Instead of *reason why* we can also say *reason (that)*, with no difference in meaning, e.g.
The main reason (that) people gamble is …

Optional lead-in
To demonstrate this part of the activity, choose a question yourself, and ask a few students what they think about it. Make brief notes on the board of what they say.

Alternative
Students move freely round the class, asking four or five other students their question.

Blackboard option
Write a checklist on the board:

- **Put points in order**
- **About people in general**
- **Start with a topic sentence**
- **Show how paragraphs are connected**

Homework option
Students collect the notes in class, but write the paragraphs for homework.

Notes for Exercise 3 (cont.)

2 Speaking activity

● In groups, students look at the painting on page 94, and discuss answers to the questions.
● Ask one student from each group to report back their interpretation to the rest of the class.

Focus on Form

1 Must, might & can't

> *must, might, can't* + infinitive forms

- Do the first part of the exercise round the class. Answers:

  a They might be having lunch in the canteen.
  b She must have been driving too fast.
  c You must have been surprised.
  d You can't have enjoyed that much.
  e He might have been kidnapped.
  f There must be some explanation.
  g You can't mean that!
  h You must be joking.

- Students do the second part of the exercise alone or in pairs. Then go through the answers together. Possible answers:

  a You must be exhausted …
  b … they must be at home.
  c She can't have gone abroad …
  d … they might be sitting in the garden.
  e … he must have been wearing gloves.

2 'Unreal' conditionals

> 2nd, 3rd and 'mixed' conditionals

- Answers:

  a refers to the present (*had, would be*).
  b refers to the past (*had lived*) and the present (*would know*).
  c refers to the present (*loved*) and the past (*wouldn't have said*).
  d refers to the past (*had been driving, would have seen*).

- Read the example to show how the exercise works. Then read out 2, *If I wasn't a very polite person …*, and ask students to find a continuation: *… I would have told her what I really thought of her.*

- Students do the rest of the exercise in pairs.

- Go through the answers together. Answers:

  3 If they were on holiday, they would have sent us a postcard.
  4 If you hadn't jumped out of the way, you would have been run over.
  5 If they didn't like us, they wouldn't have invited us to their party.
  6 If she hadn't just won the lottery, he wouldn't have asked her to marry him.
  7 If he wasn't at home, he wouldn't have left the front door open.
  8 If you'd been listening to what I told you, you'd know what to do.

3 Seem & appear

> *seem/appear to* + infinitive; *seem/appear* + adjective

- Go through the text together, asking students to make sentences. Possible answers:

  She seems to be married. She appears to be living alone. She seems to have rich friends. She appears to speak fluent Spanish. She doesn't seem to go out to work. She appears to have connections with Mexico. She seems (to be) afraid of something. Something appears to have upset her. She seems to have been in Russia. She doesn't appear to understand Russian.

4 The five senses

> *look, sound, taste, smell* and *feel*

- Do the first part of the exercise round the class. Expected answers:

  a smell like   c tastes   e feels as if
  b sound as if   d looks like

- Students do the second part of the exercise alone or in pairs. Then go through the answers together. Possible answers:

  a … more like wool / nylon / synthetic material.
  b … ten years younger / more respectable.
  c … like sea water / disgusting.
  d … as if they're having a fight / like a disco.
  e … bad / as if it's gone bad.

Self-study Workbook

Exercise A: Taking sides
must, can't and conditional sentences with *If* and *Otherwise*. Students rewrite opinions using the target structures.

Exercise B: Appearance and the senses
Sense verbs: *look, sound, seem, appear*. Students rewrite sentences.

Exercise C: Reason and purpose
Reason and purpose expressions. Students write a paragraph from notes.

Idioms: Parts of the body (2)
Common idioms with parts of the body (e.g. *rack your brains*).

Listening: Life elsewhere?
Four people say whether they think there is life elsewhere in the universe. Students listen and identify the points the speakers make.

Common verbs: come
Idiomatic expressions and phrasal verbs involving the verb *come*.

Focus on Form

1 Must, might & can't

Rewrite these sentences using *must*, *might* or *can't*.

a Perhaps they're having lunch in the canteen.
b She was obviously driving too fast.
c I'm sure you were surprised.
d You didn't enjoy that much, I'm quite sure.
e It's possible that he's been kidnapped.
f Surely there's some explanation.
g Surely you don't mean that!
h I'm quite sure you're joking.

Now complete the following using *must*, *might* or *can't*.

a ... – you haven't slept for 24 hours.
b Their phone's engaged, so ...
c ... because her passport's still in the drawer.
d If they don't answer the door, try looking round the back – ...
e His fingerprints aren't on the gun, so ...

2 'Unreal' conditionals

Look at these sentences. Which refer to

– the present?
– the past?
– both present and past?

a If you had measles, you'd be covered in spots.
b If she'd lived in France, she'd know what *Ça va* means.
c If you really loved me, you wouldn't have said that.
d If he'd been driving carefully, he would have seen them coming.

Student A: **Choose an item from Box A and change it into the first half of an *If* ... sentence.**
Student B: **Choose an item from Box B to continue the sentence.**

Example:

A If they had a mobile phone ...
B ... we could have got in touch with them.

Box A

1 Unfortunately they haven't got a mobile phone.
2 I'm a very polite person.
3 I'm sure they're not on holiday.
4 It's lucky you jumped out of the way.
5 Of course they like us.
6 She's just won the lottery.
7 I'm sure he's at home.
8 You weren't listening to what I told you.

---

3 Seem & appear

Read the text, and talk about the woman, using *seem* and *appear*.

Examples:

She doesn't appear to have a job.
She seems to have had a tragedy in her life.

I don't know my next door neighbour, but I've noticed a few things about her ...

She wears a wedding ring, but hers is the only name on the door. A woman driving a Porsche often comes to visit her, and I've heard them talking together in Spanish.

I've never seen her go to work in the morning, but she's always on the phone, and she gets a lot of mail, much of it from Mexico.

Recently she put extra locks on her front door, and I've often heard her crying at night.

She has pictures of Moscow on her walls, but when I said 'Zdravstvuytye' to her the other day, she looked at me completely blankly.

---

4 The five senses

Fill the gaps using *look*, *sound*, *taste*, *smell* or *feel*, adding *like* or *as if* where necessary.

a Your socks .... rotten eggs.
b You .... you've got a cold.
c I can't eat this. It .... too salty.
d I'm not sure what it is. It .... some kind of prehistoric tool.
e My head .... someone's hitting it with a hammer.

Now complete these remarks.

a Are you sure this is cotton? It feels ...
b Now that you've shaved your beard off, you look ...
c Euurgh! Do you call this soup? It tastes ...
d What on earth is going on next door? It sounds ...
e I wouldn't eat that meat. It smells ...

Box B

a You weren't run over.
b He's left the front door open.
c We couldn't get in touch with them.
d That's why he asked her to marry him.
e That's why you don't know what to do.
f That's why they invited us to their party.
g They haven't sent us a postcard.
h I didn't tell her what I really thought of her.

---

8 In the market-place

1 The right career?

Careers guidance questionnaire

1 Which of these areas can you see yourself working in? Tick the boxes.

- ☐ business
- ✓ arts/entertainment
- ✓ education
- ✓ health and welfare
- ✓ media
- ☐ industry
- ☐ science/technology
- ☐ the environment
- ✓ politics/public life
- ☐ service industries

Other: ....

2 How true are these statements of you? Give yourself a mark out of five.

- **3** I don't mind hard physical work.
- **5** I enjoy working with my hands.
- **3** I enjoy solving problems.
- **5** I'm a good listener.
- **2** I'm good with figures.
- **4** I have a good artistic sense.
- **5** I'm a good communicator.

3 Do you have any particular skills or leisure interests?

Painting and decorating
Painting pictures
I speak Spanish and German
Sports – both watching and playing
Listening to music, socialising, walking

4 What are/were your favourite subjects at school?

Art, English, Sport
....
....

5 What do you expect from a job? Give each of these a mark out of five.

- **3** prospects for promotion
- **5** the power to take your own decisions
- **5** contact with other people
- **3** a good salary
- **4** the chance to travel
- **5** long holidays
- **3** being able to leave the job behind you when you go home

6 How true are these statements of you? Give each a mark out of 5.

- **4** I get on with other people.
- **3** I don't mind taking orders.
- **3** I need to be my own boss.
- **4** I go crazy if I do the same thing for too long.
- **3** I can cope when things get tough.
- **3** I like to look smart.
- **2** I can keep smiling – however I'm feeling.
- **4** I'm punctual.

1 Read the completed careers guidance questionnaire.
Do you see this person as

– a boss or an employee?
– working in an organisation or self-employed?
– having a safe, steady job or doing something more adventurous?

Think of a specific job for the person.

2 Now fill in the questionnaire yourself (there's a copy on page 95) and give it to the teacher.

Work with a partner. The teacher will give you two completed questionnaires. Look at them, and suggest two or three suitable jobs for the writers.

Now look at the suggestions that have been made for you. What do you think of them?

8

This unit is about careers and the world of business. It focuses on the following vocabulary areas:
– language connected with jobs and careers
– verbs and verb phrases used in talking about business (e.g. *make a profit*, *set up a business*, *be made redundant*)
– language for talking about advertising.

The Reading and Listening activity is about faxes received by companies offering them large amounts of money, and what they should do about it.

1 The right career?

This exercise takes the form of a careers guidance questionnaire, which students discuss and then complete for themselves. This introduces language for talking about various aspects of jobs: the names of general areas of work (e.g. industry, the media*), abilities and skills (e.g.* good at communicating, a sense of responsibility*), and features of jobs (e.g.* pay, working conditions, opportunities for promotion*).*

➤ Workbook: Exercise A

1 Reading, discussion & presentation

- Establish why this person has completed the questionnaire: to find out what kind of career might be suitable for her.
- Read through the first section. Focus on the areas the person has ticked, and ask students to give examples of possible jobs, e.g.
  – *arts/entertainment:* theatre director, actress, musician, painter
  – *education:* school teacher, kindergarten teacher, university lecturer, educational adviser
  – *health and welfare:* doctor, nurse, social worker, international aid worker
  – *media:* radio/TV producer, TV personality, newsreader, journalist
  – *politics/public life:* member of parliament, civil servant.
  Quickly look at the other areas and check that students know what they mean.
- Read through the other sections, focusing on any difficult items and asking students for paraphrases, e.g.
  – What's *a good communicator*? (Someone who can talk to other people easily, and can explain things to people.)
  – If you have a job with *prospects for promotion*, what does it mean? (You have a chance to be promoted.)
- Discuss what kind of job might suit this person, using the questions as a guide. Then ask students to suggest particular jobs that might be suitable, and build up a list on the board.

2 Speaking activity

- Working alone, students complete the questionnaire on page 95.
- Collect the questionnaires, and give two to each pair of students. Make sure that no one has been given their own questionnaire.
- Students look at each questionnaire in turn. They decide on suitable jobs for the writers, and write them in a list.
- Hand back the questionnaires to the students who wrote them, with the suggested jobs. As a round-up, ask students for their comments.

Language note
The arts and *the media* are both plural nouns, and are usually used with *the*. *The arts* covers all forms of art, including theatre, literature and music. *The media* covers radio, television, newspapers and magazines.

Language note
Notice how we use *good* to talk about ability:
He's *a good* listener, *a good* communicator.
She's *good at* solving problems.
I'm *good with* figures, *good with* children.

Groupwork option
Students look at the questionnaire in groups, and decide on one or two suitable jobs for the person. Then ask a student from each group to say what jobs they chose, and why.

Alternative
Make photocopies of the questionnaire and distribute them.

2 Success story

In this exercise someone tells the true story of a successful publishing company. Before they listen to the recording, students predict what order the events occurred in; this is also a chance to focus on particular expressions used in talking about companies and business.

➤ Workbook: Exercise B, Listening

1 Presentation

● Read through the sentences, explaining any new vocabulary, e.g. the *turnover* of a company (= the total amount of money it takes in); an *issue* of a magazine (= a copy); a *bank loan* (= money borrowed from the bank); a company *breaks even* (= it makes as much as it spends). Build up key expressions on the board:

take on lay off	staff	make	a profit a loss
take out pay off	a bank loan	set up a company	

● In pairs, students decide what order the events should be in. Then discuss this together, and build up a possible order on the board.

2 Listening activity

● [cassette] Play the recording, pausing from time to time to check if the order students decided is correct. The correct order is:

1 *d*   2 *h*   3 *a*   4 *l*   5 *e*   6 *k*   7 *f*   8 *g*   9 *j*   10 *c*   11 *b*   12 *i*

[cassette] The tapescript is on page 107.

3 Legal, decent, honest, truthful

This is a freer discussion activity, which looks at rules set by the Advertising Standards Authority in Britain, and at advertisements which have broken those rules. This provides the basis for a general discussion about what should and shouldn't be allowed in advertising.

➤ Workbook: Exercise C

Note on title
'Legal, decent, honest, truthful' is the slogan of the British Advertising Standards Authority.

Optional lead-in
Ask students whether there is an equivalent to the Advertising Standards Authority in their own country, and what controls there are on advertising.

1 Reading & discussion

● Look at the advertisement, and ask students to suggest why it might have been banned. Then tell them the actual reason (it used speed as the main selling point – and would therefore encourage people to drive dangerously), and ask them if they agree.

● Read through the ASA's rules, explaining any unknown words (e.g. *widespread*, *cause offence*, *race*, *inferior*, *a link*).

● In pairs or groups, students look at the advertisements on pages 96 and 97. They decide which rules the advertisements break.

● Ask students what conclusions they came to. Possible answers:

A The girls look too young to drink; encourages under-age drinking.
B Links smoking with social success.
C Suggests that children are inferior if they don't buy the product.
D Causes anxiety.
E Makes a false claim about the product.
F Might cause offence; encourages immoral behaviour.
G Unfairly attacks other products.
H Makes a false claim about the product.

Alternative
Give each group two of the advertisements to look at (so that each advertisement is being studied by more than one group).

As a round-up, take each advertisement in turn, and ask for comments from the groups that discussed it.

2 Discussion

● Ask students what other advertisements they have seen that they object to, and why. Try to broaden this out into a more general discussion of whether particular types of advertisement should be banned.

Discussion option
Discuss what some of the other guidelines might be, e.g.

Advertisers should not encourage immoral or violent behaviour.
Advertisers should not make claims about a product which are untrue, or which cannot be proved.

2 Success story

You will hear someone telling the story of a company called *Future Publishing*. Here are some of the things the person says. Put them in the order you think you will hear them.

a He set up a company called *Future Publishing*.
b Over the next eight years, their turnover rose by 90% a year.
c They kept adding new magazine titles.
d Chris Anderson was working for a company that produced a home computer magazine.
e They launched their own computer magazine.
f The next issue made a profit.
g They managed to pay off the bank loan in just three months.
h He was sacked.
i He decided to sell the company.
j They took on more staff.
k They didn't sell enough copies to break even.
l They took out a bank loan of £15,000.

 Now listen to the recording. Were you right?

3 Legal, decent, honest, truthful

1 This advertisement was banned in Britain after people complained about it to the Advertising Standards Authority (ASA). Why do you think it was banned?

The ASA provides rules for companies advertising their products in Britain. Here are some of them.

a No advertisement should cause fear or anxiety without good reason.

b Advertisements should contain nothing that is likely to cause serious or widespread offence, particularly on the grounds of race, religion or sex.

c Advertisements should not make children feel inferior or unpopular for not buying the advertised product.

d Advertisements should not imply a link between smoking and social, sexual, romantic or business success.

e Advertisers should not unfairly attack other businesses or their products.

f Advertisements should not suggest that alcohol is the main reason for the success of a party or event.

On pages 96–7 there are some ideas for advertisements. Some of them break the rules above, and some break other ASA rules. What do you think the other rules might be?

2 Are there any advertisements you've seen recently that you object to? What don't you like about them? Do you think they should be banned?

4 Dirty money

READING

1 The fax opposite was received by a small company in London in early 1995.
   Use the questions below to help you read and understand it.

   a Who is Bernard Sithole?
   b How old is he?
   c How did he get hold of the $5 million?
   d Where is the money now?

   e What does he want to do with the $5 million?
   f Why is his position 'sensitive'?
   g What does he want the recipient of the fax to do?
   h What would the recipient get from the deal?

2 Find phrases in the text that mean:

   a after working for many years
   b a business that operates successfully
   c a partner from abroad

   d helping me
   e make sure I can retire safely
   f the deal which will help us both.

DISCUSSION

Imagine that you are the Managing Director of the company that received the fax.
How would you respond? Why? What would you expect to happen if you took up
the offer?

LISTENING

You will hear part of a radio programme about companies receiving faxes like
the one you have just read. The recording is in two parts.

Part 1

1 Who is Alex Clarke?

2 What differences are there between this offer and the one you read about? Think about:
   – who sent the fax
   – how much they want to transfer
   – why they want to transfer the money
   – what they want him to do
   – how much money he could make

3 What did he decide to do? Why?

Part 2

4 Does the police inspector think Alex Clarke did the right thing? Why?

5 Here are key words from three points the inspector makes. How do they fit together?
   a bank details – headed
      notepaper – transfer –
      bank account
   b oil company – $1.5
      million – £700,000
   c charities – died – death
      duties

6 What does the presenter
   advise listeners to do if
   they receive a similar fax?
   Is that what you decided
   to do?

4 Dirty money

This combined Reading and Listening activity is about faxes sent to small businesses, tempting them into suspicious business deals with offers of huge sums of money. The reading activity is a slightly altered version of a real fax received by a company in London. The listening activity is part of a radio programme which discusses this issue.

Reading skills: *reading for main points.*
Vocabulary focus: *guessing vocabulary from context.*
Listening skills: *listening for general idea; following the main points of an argument.*

Reading

- Ask students to imagine that they work for a small company, and that one day they receive the fax on page 45. Look at the questions in 1, and ask students to read the fax and find answers to the questions.

- Discuss the answers together. Answers:

  a He has a high position in an oil corporation owned by the government of his country.
  b Probably nearly 60 (he's due for retirement).
  c From awarding contracts to companies (probably from taking bribes).
  d In the National Bank in his own country.
  e He wants to invest it abroad.
  f (Probably) because he has made the money illegally, and needs to transfer it abroad without anyone knowing.
  g To give details of his/her bank account.
  h 30% of the money.

- Look at Question 2 with the class. Answers:

  a after many years in service
  b a viable business
  c an expatriate partner
  d giving me your assistance
  e secure my period in retirement
  f this mutual benefit

Discussion

- Find out which students in the class would take up the offer and which wouldn't. Ask them to say why or why not, and what they would expect to happen (*Note:* What has actually happened in cases like this is explained in the Listening activity.)

> **Option: paired reading**
> Ask students to read and discuss the questions in pairs, or to read alone first and then compare answers with their partner.

Listening

- Tell students that in the recording they will hear about a similar case to the one they read about.

- ▢ Play Part 1 of the recording, and ask students to listen for differences between the two cases. Then discuss answers to Questions 1 to 3. Possible answers:

  1 Owner of a software company in London.
  2 Differences:
    – They wanted to transfer $32 million.
    – The money was stolen.
    – They wanted him to send headed company notepaper.
    – He could make nearly $10 million.
  3 He decided not to take up the offer, but to contact the police. He thought it seemed too suspicious.

> ▢ The tapescript is on page 108.

- Before you play Part 2 of the recording, look at Questions 4 and 5 together. Check that students know the meaning of *charities* (= organisations that help poor people) and *death duties* (= tax you have to pay when you inherit money from someone who has died).

- ▣ Play Part 2 of the recording and answer the questions. Possible answers:

4 Yes. Otherwise he would have lost a lot of money.
5 *a* Once people get your bank details and your headed notepaper, they can transfer money out of your bank account.
  b The same oil company offered $1.5 million. They collected £700,000 from people before they were caught.
  c Charities receive a fax saying that someone has died. They are asked to pay the death duties, but then they never get the money.

- As a round-up, establish what the presenter's advice is (Answer: to do nothing or to contact the police). Then find out which students decided to act correctly, in view of what they have just heard, and which would have lost all their money.

Self-study Workbook

Exercise A: The job for you?
Students write about a job they would like to have and one they wouldn't like to have, and give reasons.

Exercise B: Business verbs
Verbs and verb phrases connected with business. Students choose expressions to fill gaps in sentences.

Exercise C: Selling the product
Students design an advertisement that would not break the rules laid down by the Advertising Standards Authority.

Idioms: Describing feelings
Common idioms that describe feelings (e.g. *on top of the world*).

Listening: The new design manager
A business meeting at which four people discuss who to choose as a design manager. Students listen and distinguish the main points the speakers make.

Word building: Nouns and verbs (2)
Abstract and personal nouns that come from verbs (e.g. *invent, inventor, invention*). Nouns ending in *-er, -or, -ant, -ion, -ment, -al*.

URGENT & CONFIDENTIAL

ATTN: The President/Managing Director.   Tel/Fax ▓▓▓▓▓▓▓

Dear Sir,

INTRODUCTION & BIO-DATA

I am Prince Bernard Sithole, Minister in charge of Contracts in the ▓▓▓▓▓ Oil Corporation. My position is very sensitive. I am married with children and hold degrees in public administration and business studies. I am due for retirement any moment from now, after many years in service.

REASON(S) FOR CONTACTING YOU

I urgently need your assistance in providing me with a safe and reliable bank account with full details, viz: Name and Address of Bank, Telephone, Telex and Fax Number anywhere in the world where I can transfer the sum of **5 Million** U.S. Dollars. The purpose of the transfer is to take care of my retirement by investing in a viable business.

NATURE OF BUSINESS

The above sum (5 Million U.S.D.) arises from various contracts I have awarded since I have been in this post. For the present, I have arranged for the money to be kept in a coded bank account with the National Bank of ▓▓▓▓▓ until I am able to find a reliable overseas partner to whom it can be transferred. Once the payment has been approved, you might be required to visit our country to sign the necessary papers.

SHARING THE FUNDS

30% will go to you for making available to me a company/personal account number, giving me your assistance and keeping strictly to the rules of this transaction until the money has been transferred. 10% will be used to cover expenses: obtaining vital documents, tips, trips made by both parties, phone/fax bills, hotel bills, taxes and bank charges. 60% will be shared between me and a few colleagues of mine whose help will be needed to complete the transaction.

OTHER RELEVANT DETAILS

Everything about this transaction is real. The money is clean. After putting in so many years in service, it is only normal for me to take steps to secure my period in retirement. I have worked very hard to make this transaction possible, which means that it means a lot to me, and hopefully, with a little help from you, everything will be settled in just a matter of weeks. It will come to mean a lot to you too as we meet in your country to celebrate the closing of the deal.

If you are interested in this mutual benefit, please contact me immediately at the above fax number and also complete the attached ▓▓▓▓▓ Oil Corporation **Payment Information** form.

Thank you for your kind understanding and co-operation in anticipation.

Yours sincerely,

Prince Bernard Sithole.

PRINCE BERNARD SITHOLE

Review: Units 1–8

Find out

1 *A* Write down a short list of games that you know how to play, and/or things that you know how to cook. Show it to B.

  B Choose an item from the list that interests you, and ask A to teach you how to do it.

2 Sit in groups. What's the most interesting/ unusual painting or photo you've got at home? Describe it to the others.

  Which of the pictures you've heard about do you imagine you would like best?

3 Ask other students to tell you about

  – an advertisement they particularly like
  – an advertisement they particularly dislike.

  What is it that they like/dislike about them?

4 Find out if other students believe that

  – there's a monster in Loch Ness
  – Lord Lucan is still alive
  – the world is getting warmer.

  What reasons do they have?

Words

1 Imagine a house that has not been lived in for several years, and say what might be wrong with it. Think about

  the roof   windows   ceilings   wood

2 Add words to these lists.

  – note, notice, announcement …
  – grammar, vocabulary …
  – stir, roast, chop …

3 Imagine someone who knows nothing about *either* football *or* tennis. Think of five useful vocabulary items for them to learn, and explain what they mean.

4 In what situations might you

  – lose touch with someone?
  – make small talk?
  – make it up with someone?
  – take on staff?
  – go bankrupt?

Role-play

1 *A* You're going to be interviewed for one of these jobs. Think about what you'll say.

  > Wanted: **NANNY** to look after three young children. Some cooking and cleaning. Driver's licence essential.
  >
  > Wanted: **ENGLISH TEACHER** to teach beginners. Training given, but experience an advantage.
  >
  > Wanted: **ACTORS/ACTRESSES** for small parts in a popular daytime soap. Good acting ability essential.

  B You're about to interview A. Think of some questions you will ask him/her.

  Now conduct the interview.

2 Choose one of these situations and improvise a conversation.

  – A accuses B of something.
  – A threatens B.
  – A offers B something he/she doesn't want.

  Now report what was said to other students.

3 *A* You're just leaving school/college and you can't decide what kind of career to take up. Ask B for some advice.

  B You're a careers adviser. Try to help A decide on a career.

Writing

1 *A* B is going to look after your flat while you're away. Leave a note saying what you want him/her to do, and explaining how to use e.g. the washing machine, cooker, TV.

  B Read A's note, then imagine you've now been staying in A's flat. Write a note to leave for when he/she comes back home.

2 *A* Write five or six sentences about the history of your country. Include at least three factual mistakes.

  B Read what A has written. See if you can find the mistakes, and correct them.

3 Why do you think so many men are keen on football, but so few women are? Write a few sentences about it.

Find out

1 Revision of language from Units 4 & 6

- As a preparation, elicit verbs connected with sports/games and preparing food, and write them on the board.
- Students write lists. Then they teach their partner one of the things from their list.
- Round-up. Ask a few students what they learnt to do.

2 Revision of language from Units 3 & 7

- Tell students about a painting/photo in your own home. Use this to focus on participle phrases, and structures with *look* and *seem*.
- Groupwork. Students take it in turns to decribe their painting or photo.
- Round-up. Ask each group to tell the class about the 'favourite' painting or photo from their group, and why they would like it best.

3 Revision of language from Unit 8

- Tell students about an advertisement you particularly like or dislike (or bring in one to show to the class). Encourage them to ask you questions.
- Give time for students to think of advertisements. Then they interview each other in groups.
- Round-up. Each group reports back to the class about the advertisements they discussed.

4 Revision of language from Units 5 & 7

- Give each student a letter A, B or C, and give them one of the questions to ask. Students put their question to four or five other students.
- Ask students to report back what they found out, and what reasons were given. Use this to focus on conditionals, and structures with *must/might/can't*.

Words

1 Revision of language from Unit 6

- Students write down as many words and phrases as they can think of.
- Build up lists of words and expressions for each category on the board, e.g.
  Roof: leak, rotten wood, tiles missing.

2 Revision of language from Units 2 & 6

- Give time for students to add to the lists.
- Build up lists on the board.

3 Revision of language from Unit 4

- Students choose one of the sports, and write five words.
- Ask students to read out their words, and to explain what they mean.

4 Revision of language from Units 2 & 8

- Put the questions to the whole class. Try to get students to suggest several possible situations for each item, e.g.
  lose touch: you move to a new town, and you don't go back to visit friends; you meet someone on holiday, and then forget to write to each other; you leave school, and never see your classmates again.

Role-play

1 Revision of language from Units 1 & 8

- Preparation. Look at the jobs advertised, and establish some of the things the interviewer might want to know. Focus on the Present perfect tense and expressions for talking about ability and experience.
- Students choose a job (the same one as their partner), and prepare alone for the interview.
- Pairwork. Students conduct the interview.
- As a round-up, ask interviewers whether they would give their candidate the job, and why or why not.

2 Revision of language from Unit 5

- Preparation. Get students to suggest a few possible situations, e.g.
  A thinks B has stolen some money.
  A thinks B has been saying bad things about him/her.
  B refuses to move out of A's flat, so A threatens to call the police.
- Pairwork. Students choose one of the situations and improvise a conversation.
- Ask each pair to report what happened in their conversation, using reported speech (e.g. *She accused me of stealing her money, but I explained that …*).

3 Revision of language from Unit 8

- Preparation. Establish some of the questions B might ask, e.g.
  Do you like working with people?
  What was your best subject at school?
  Are you interested in business?
- Pairwork. Students improvise a conversation.
- As a round-up, ask a few students what careers they chose.

Writing

1 Revision of language from Unit 6

- Preparation. Build up useful expressions on the board (e.g. *turn … on; press the switch; plug … in*).
- Students write a note, then pass it to another student.
- Students write a reply, then pass it back to the student who wrote to them.
- Round-up. Students read out their notes and the replies.

2 Revision of language from Units 3 & 5

- Students write sentences, including factual mistakes.
- Students pass their sentences to another student, who tries to correct the mistakes.
- As a round-up, students read out the wrong sentences they found, and correct them. Focus at this point on cleft sentence structures (e.g. *It wasn't … It was …*).

3 Revision of language from Unit 8

- Students write sentences, expressing their opinion.
- Ask students to read out their sentences, and see if others in the class agree.

Talking points

The pictures in this activity take up themes from the following units:

A: Units 4, 7
B: Unit 8
C: Unit 4
D: Unit 7
E: Unit 6
F: Unit 4
G: Unit 3
H: Unit 8

They can either be used for revision of specific language, or as a springboard for freer activity.

The activity can be done in two ways:

1 Mini-lectures

Preparation: Students choose one of the pictures and prepare a short talk based on the topic, making brief notes if they like (but not writing the talk out).

Activity: Students give their talk in turn to the rest of the class. At the end, other students can ask questions.

2 Game

Preparation: Students prepare to talk about two or three of the pictures, looking back at the appropriate unit to recall things they might say.

Activity: One student chooses a topic and says a sentence or two about it. Another student then continues, adding another sentence, and so on.

Self-study Workbook: Review, Units 1–8

Exercise A: Multiple-choice cloze
Students choose the best words to fill gaps in a text. *10 items*

B: Cloze
Students fill gaps in a text with appropriate words. *10 items*

C: Sentence rewriting
Students rewrite sentences, using given words and any other necessary words. *12 items*

D: Correcting a text
Students identify superfluous words in a text. *10 items*

E: Word-building
Students fill gaps in a text with words derived from given words. *8 items*

Talking points

Prepare a short talk (about one minute) using one of these pictures as a starting point.

9 Possibilities

1 If we carry on like this …

will & would

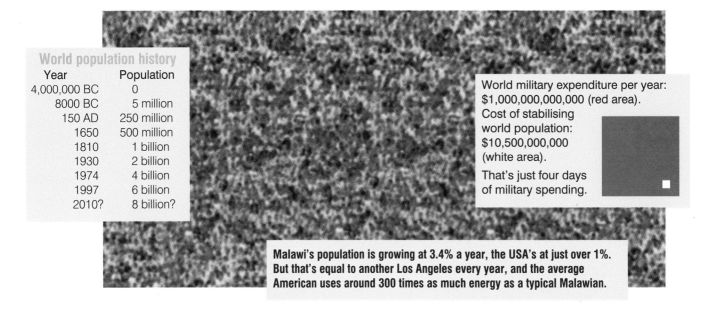

World population history

Year	Population
4,000,000 BC	0
8000 BC	5 million
150 AD	250 million
1650	500 million
1810	1 billion
1930	2 billion
1974	4 billion
1997	6 billion
2010?	8 billion?

World military expenditure per year: $1,000,000,000,000 (red area).
Cost of stabilising world population: $10,500,000,000 (white area).

That's just four days of military spending.

Malawi's population is growing at 3.4% a year, the USA's at just over 1%. But that's equal to another Los Angeles every year, and the average American uses around 300 times as much energy as a typical Malawian.

1 Here are three opinions about the problem of world population.
Read each one and summarise the main point in one sentence.
Which opinion do you agree with most?

A

If we carry on like this, the world will eventually run out of energy, clean water, food and land. Some of the poorest countries will soon have nuclear weapons, and will probably use them, as resources become scarce and wars begin to break out.

If disaster is to be avoided, we must take action now to reduce the size of the world's population.

There is much the richer nations could do to encourage people to have smaller families. For example, if they gave all women in developing countries $25 a month until the birth of their third child, this would double or triple family incomes, and most women would decide to stop at two children, so as to keep receiving the money.

B

The problem is not that there are too many people in the world, but that we have not yet developed ways of meeting their needs. The world has faced many other challenges in the past, and found ways of dealing with them – indeed, progress is made precisely because there are problems to be solved.

There have already been spectacular increases in food production to meet the demands of rising populations, and as new problems arise, so solutions will be found for them.

What is not acceptable is for rich nations to tell poor people that they're not allowed to have children. If we continue to interfere in their affairs, we will only cause suffering and resentment.

C

The main reason that poor people have a lot of children is that children represent money: they can get jobs or provide their parents with free labour.

So the answer to the population problem lies in development. If their prosperity can be increased, people will begin to have fewer children. This has already happened in most of Europe, and is happening at the moment in countries such as South Korea and Taiwan.

If the rich nations want this to happen, they must cancel the huge debts that are crippling many developing countries. This would release much-needed money for economic development, and the population problem would look after itself.

When do the writers use *will*, and when do they use *would*?

2 Write down your own suggestion for helping to solve the world population problem, and pass it to another group.

Look at the suggestion you have received. Do you think it's a good idea?
Why do you think it would or wouldn't work?

9

This unit is concerned with language for talking about possibility and probability. It focuses on three main areas:
– the contrast between *will* for making predictions and *would* for imagining possibilities
– the use of *it depends (on)*
– ways of expressing probability and certainty (e.g. *is likely to*, *is certain to*).

The fourth activity develops writing skills, and deals with language for weighing up alternatives.

1 If we carry on like this ...

This exercise is a guided discussion activity about the problem of world population, in which students read three different opinions and then make their own suggestions. The activity involves using will *for making predictions and* would *for imagining alternative possibilities.*

➤ Focus on Form: Exercise 1
➤ Workbook: Exercise A

1 Reading, discussion & presentation

- Look at the statistics at the top of the page. Establish what the point of each set of statistics is. Possible answers:

  World population history: The population of the world is not only expanding, but it's expanding at a faster and faster rate.
  Military expenditure: We could quite easily afford to stabilise the world's population – the cost would be very small compared with what we spend on weapons.
  Malawi and the USA: Population is also a problem in developed countries, because people use up more energy than they do in 'Third World' countries.

- Give time for students to read Text A, then ask them which points they agree or disagree with, and why. Then do the same with texts B and C.

- Focus on the way the writers use *will* and *would*. Ask students to find examples from the texts, and make these points:
  – The writers use *will* to talk about things they *really expect to happen*, things that they see as real possibilities (e.g. *the world will run out of energy*; *people will begin to have fewer children*).
  – The writers use *would* to talk about things they are just *imagining* as possible alternatives (e.g. *If they were offered $25 a month, women would decide to stop at two children*; *cancelling debts would release money for development*).

2 Writing & speaking activity

- Working either in pairs or small groups, students think of an idea for helping to solve the world population problem, and write it down – this could be just a single sentence, or it could be expanded into a short paragraph.

- Students pass their solution to another pair or group, who look at it and decide why they think it would or wouldn't work.

- As a round-up, ask different pairs or groups to read out the sentence they discussed and say what they thought about it.

Optional reading task

To help students focus on the texts, write these 'guiding' questions on the board before they start reading:

What does the writer think will happen? What does he/she think we should do?

Pair- and groupwork options

1 Pairwork. After reading each text, students quickly discuss with their partner which points they agree or disagree with. As a round-up, discuss the points with the whole class.

2 Groupwork. Give each group one of the texts to focus on and discuss. Then ask a student from each group to report back what the text said, and whether or not they agreed.

Vocabulary option

Use the texts to focus on useful vocabulary for talking about development and population, and write key words and phrases on the board, e.g.

**economic development
developing countries
rich/poor nations
energy
resources
prosperity
increase
reduce
expand**

2 It depends

This is a straightforward language exercise, introducing structures with It depends *followed by noun or indirect question.*

1 Presentation

- Look at the first question, and ask students to make sentences with *It depends*. Write examples on the board to show how the structure is used:

It depends	on your age.
	(on) how old you are.
	(on) whether you're under 25.

- Ask students to change the other two questions. Possible answers:

It depends (on) how you're travelling / whether you're flying or going overland.
It depends (on) when you're going; It depends on the time of year.

2 Speaking activity

- In pairs, students take it in turn to ask the questions and give responses with *It depends …* They then continue, thinking up other questions of their own.
- As a round-up, find out from different pairs how they answered the questions, and what questions they made up themselves.

3 Playing it safe

In this exercise, students listen to someone saying how dangerous New York is and what is likely to happen to you. This is used as a basis for presenting expressions of probability: likely to, unlikely to, certain to.

1 Listening & presentation

- Ask students how safe they imagine New York is, and what they think it is safe and not safe to do. Try to get a range of different ideas.
- Ask students what (if anything) they know about Harlem, Central Park and Manhattan.
- 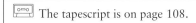 Play the recording and students answer the questions. Answers:

  a Not as dangerous as people think, no more dangerous than other big cities.
  b *Harlem:* It's not safe to walk there at night time (especially for whites).
  Central Park: It's very dangerous to go there at night.
  Manhattan: It's safe, especially if you keep to the main streets.
  What you should wear: Don't wear tourist clothes or expensive jewellery.
  How to behave: Behave like a New Yorker.

- Ask students to make four sentences from the table. Possible answers:

  You're almost certain to get mugged if you go to Central Park at night.
  You're likely to get mugged if you walk around with expensive jewellery.
  You're unlikely to get mugged if you look like a New Yorker.
  You're very unlikely to get mugged if you keep to the main streets of Manhattan.

- On the board, show these two ways of expressing probability:

| They | will certainly
will probably
probably won't
certainly won't | come on time | | They | are certain to
are likely to
are unlikely to
are certain not to | come on time |

2 Speaking activity

- Ask students to think about a city in their own area. Ask them what advice they would give a visitor about what to do and what not to do.

➤ Focus on Form: Exercise 2
➤ Workbook: Exercise B

Language note
1 *It depends (on)* is followed by a noun or an indirect question.
2 Before a question word (*how, whether*) we can leave out *on* – so we can also say *It depends how old you are*. Before a noun we must include *on* – so we cannot say ~~*It depends your age*~~.

Alternative: whole class activity
Ask the questions yourself, and get a range of different answers from the class. Then students write their own questions. They read out their questions, and other students answer them.

➤ Focus on Form: Exercise 3
➤ Workbook: Exercise C, Listening

Blackboard option
Build up a list of ideas on the board, under two headings: *Safe* and *Unsafe*.

The tapescript is on page 108.

Language note
The structure of these expressions is:
  be + adjective + to
Although they end in *-ly*, *likely* and *unlikely* are adjectives (we could also say *You might get mugged, but it isn't very likely*).
In American English, *(un)likely* can be used as an adverb (*You will likely get mugged*).

Alternative: writing activity
In groups, students write a list of *Dos* and *Don'ts* for visitors to the city where they live. Write topics on the board to help, e.g.

| driving | children | dogs |
| parking | bicycles | money |

As a round-up, students read out what they have written.

2 It depends

depend (on) • indirect questions

1 Complete the sentence beginning *It depends* …
using the questions in the green bubbles.

2 What do the answers to these questions depend
on? Have short conversations.

  a Do you think I could get a job as a taxi driver?
  b How long does it take to cook a steak?
  c What's the best place to eat around here?
  d Is Britain a good place to go on holiday?

Now ask your partner a question of your own.

How much does it cost
to get to India?

It depends …

How old
are you?

What time of year
do you want to go?

Are you flying or
going overland?

3 Playing it safe

Probability expressions

1 How safe do you think it is to walk around the
streets of New York on your own? What do you
think you should and shouldn't do?

▭ Now listen to a New Yorker talking about
the city, and answer these questions.

  a Does he think New York is a dangerous place?
  b What does he say about
  – Harlem?   – what you should wear?
  – Central Park?   – how you should behave?
  – Manhattan?
  c Write four sentences using the structures in
  the table.

You're	almost certain likely unlikely very unlikely	to get mugged if you …

Harlem

Central Park

Manhattan

2 Think about the city where you live (or near
where you live).

Is the situation similar to that in New York
or very different?
What advice would you give to a visitor?

4 Courses of action

1 Here are parts of three paragraphs, which are about three different topics. Can you reconstruct them? Write them down, adding punctuation where necessary.

> alternatively, you could try to find temporary work in a hotel or a pub

> that would be more expensive, but it would give you much more light and space

> either the government could call a general election now

> the easiest thing to do would be just to give the rooms a coat of paint

> you could quite easily find work as an au pair with an English family

> but you might find it difficult to get a work permit

> or else they could wait till next year and hope the economy improves

> in which case they would probably win with a small majority

> another possibility would be to knock down one of the walls

2 Here are some ideas in note form. Expand them into a short paragraph, beginning with the sentence given.

There are various things you could do with your money ...

keep it in a bank account

buy a flat

invest in antiques

safest

good investment
somewhere to live

rather risky?

3 Think of a topic you are familiar with, either in your own or your friends' lives or in your country, in which there are different possible courses of action. Make notes like those above. If you like, use one of these ideas:

choosing a present for someone

redecorating a room

deciding what to study

getting to know someone

improving the local environment

planning a holiday

improving sales

preventing crime

Show your notes to another student, and explain what they are about. If necessary, improve them or add to them.

Then expand them into a paragraph.

4 Courses of action

Writing skills: *writing about alternative courses of action; making notes; getting feedback and revising; expanding notes into a paragraph.*
Language focus: *linking devices used for weighing up alternatives.*

This activity helps students to write a paragraph from notes. It follows these stages:
1 *Presentation. Students reconstruct three jumbled paragraphs, and focus on linking devices.*
2 *Expanding notes. Students develop a given set of notes into a paragraph, using linking devices they have studied.*
3 *Writing. Students make their own notes about a different topic. They show their notes to other students and make improvements. They then expand their notes into a paragraph.*

1 Presentation

- Ask students to reconstruct the three paragraphs. Write them on the board, getting the class to suggest suitable punctuation. Expected answers:

  You could quite easily find work as an au pair with an English family. Alternatively, you could try to find temporary work in a hotel or a pub, but you might find it difficult to get a work permit.

  Either the government could call a general election now, in which case they would probably win with a small majority, or else they could wait till next year and hope the economy improves.

  The easiest thing to do would be just to give the rooms a coat of paint. Another possibility would be to knock down one of the walls. That would be more expensive, but it would give you much more light and space.

- Draw attention to these expressions which are used to link the ideas together, and write them on the board:

  > Alternatively, ...
  > Either ... or ...
  > ..., in which case ...
  > ..., or else ...
  > One
  > Another | possibility would be ...

> **Pairwork option**
> Students reconstruct the paragraphs in pairs. Then discuss the answers together.

2 Expanding notes

- Working alone or in pairs, students write a paragraph based on the notes. They should use the linking expressions you have written on the board to help them.
- Ask students to read out their paragraphs. A possible version:

  There are various things you could do with your money. The safest thing to do would be to keep it in a bank account. Alternatively, you could use it to buy a flat, which would be a good investment and would also give you somewhere to live. Another possibility would be to invest it in antiques, but that might be rather risky.

3 Writing

- Students choose one of the topics or a similar topic of their own, and write notes in the form of a 'flow diagram' to show the different possibilities.
- Pairwork. Students show their notes to their partner, and explain what they are about. This should reveal how well the ideas fit together, and on this basis students may want to add to or improve their notes.
- Students expand their notes into a connected paragraph.
- As a round-up, ask a few students to read out their paragraphs.

> **Optional lead-in**
> To show what to do, choose a topic yourself, and write a 'flow diagram' on the board. Explain what it is about, and invite comments and questions from the class. Use this as a basis to make changes and additions.

> **Alternative**
> Students move freely round the class, showing their notes to several other people.

> **Homework option**
> Students make and improve their notes in class, but write the paragraphs for homework.

Focus on Form

1 Will or would?

> Use of *will* and *would*

● Do the first part of the exercise round the class or in pairs. Establish why *will* or *would* is used in each case, and if necessary give other examples. Answers:

a *would, he'd* (in fact he doesn't help – we're just imagining it)

b *promised she'd* (reported speech)
  I'm sure she'll (prediction – this will really happen)

c *would* (after *I wish*: in fact they don't wipe their feet)

d *I'd* (unreal condition: in fact I'm not you!)

e *I'll* (*I'll* used here to make an offer)

f *won't get re-elected* (real conditional – that will really be the result), *what it will do* (prediction)

g *Would you, I wouldn't* (we're just imagining the situation)

h *It'll take* (you're planning to go by bus, and this will be the result)
  you'd get there (imagining an alternative)

i *we'll* (= Will we still be friends? – asking yourself about the future)

2 Dependency

> Structures with *It depends (on)*

● Look at the example and ask students to complete the sentences. Answers:

It depends on what the weather's like.
It depends on whether the pilot is good or not.
It depends on the size of the plane.

● Students make sentences for the other situations in pairs. Then go through the answers together. Possible answers:

Driving test: It depends on how well you drive; it depends on whether you crash into anything; it depends on whether the examiner is in a good mood; it depends on what kind of examiner you get; it depends on whether you keep calm.

Party: It depends on how many people come; it depends on what the music's like; it depends on whether people dance.

3 Probability expressions

> be *likely/unlikely/certain to*

● Do the first part of the exercise round the class. Answers:

a ... you're very unlikely to get a table.

b She's certain to be given the job.

c ... You're unlikely to tread on a scorpion.

d There's likely to be a big crowd ...

● Students rewrite the sentences, using *certain to, likely to,* or *(very) unlikely to,* according to what they think. Possible answers:

a The population of the world is very unlikely to decline over the next ten years.

b There is likely to be intelligent life elsewhere in the universe.

c Lord Lucan is very unlikely to be found soon.

d There are unlikely to be package tours to the Moon by the year 2100.

e The Loch Ness monster is unlikely to exist.

f If you smoke heavily, you're likely to die young.

Self-study Workbook

Exercise A: Would it work?
Use of *would* for imagining things. Students read a text about a decimal time system and answer questions.

Exercise B: I'm not sure …
Sentences beginning *It depends…*. Students write sentences from prompts.

Exercise C: Probability
Probability expressions: *certain/bound/sure to, likely/unlikely to.* Students rewrite sentences.

Idioms: Streets and roads
Common idioms with words connected with streets and roads (e.g. *it's right up your street*).

Listening: Return from Berlin
Someone describes how she was robbed at a railway station in Berlin. Students listen to check predictions, and complete summary sentences.

Common verbs: see
Common uses of the verb *see*, and idiomatic expressions.

Focus on Form

1 will or would?

Look at the remarks below, and choose between *will* and *would*.

a I don't know why you never ask your father to help. The exercise *will/would* do him good, and *he'll/he'd* probably enjoy it.

b – She promised me that *she'll/she'd* phone as soon as she got home.
– Don't worry. I'm sure *she'll/she'd* ring soon.

c I wish your friends *will/would* wipe their feet when they come in.

d If I were you, *I'll/I'd* take it back to the shop.

e *I'll/I'd* carry that for you, if you like.

f If the Government doesn't cut taxes before the next election, it certainly *won't/wouldn't* get re-elected. So I expect that's exactly what it *will/would* do.

g *Will/Would* you pick up a hitchhiker late at night? I certainly *won't/wouldn't*.

h You must be crazy going by bus. *It'll/It'd* take you hours. If you went by train, *you'll/you'd* get there much faster.

i I wonder if *we'll/we'd* still be friends in 20 years' time.

2 Dependency

Look at the example situation below, and complete the sentences.

Do you think it will be a bumpy flight?

It depends on   the weather.
what …

It depends on   how good the pilot is.
whether …

It depends on   how big the plane is.
the …

3 Probability expressions

Rewrite these sentences using … *certain to / likely to / unlikely to / very unlikely to* …

a Unless you book in advance, you've got very little chance of getting a table.

b I'm quite sure she'll be given the job.

c Don't worry – you probably won't tread on a scorpion.

d I expect there'll be a big crowd at the match tonight.

Now change these sentences so that they express your own opinion.

a The population of the world will decline over the next ten years.

b There is intelligent life elsewhere in the universe.

c Lord Lucan will be found soon.

d There will be package tours to the Moon by the year 2100.

e The Loch Ness Monster exists.

f If you smoke heavily, you'll die young.

Now use *It depends* … to talk about the other two situations. Can you think of any other things the answer depends on?

Do you think I'll pass my driving test?

Do you think it'll be a good party?

10 Life, the universe and everything

1 Branches of science

1 The words in this spidergram are all to do with astronomy.
  Can you explain the connections shown by the lines?

  Example: Galileo was a famous astronomer.
              Galileo designed his own telescope.

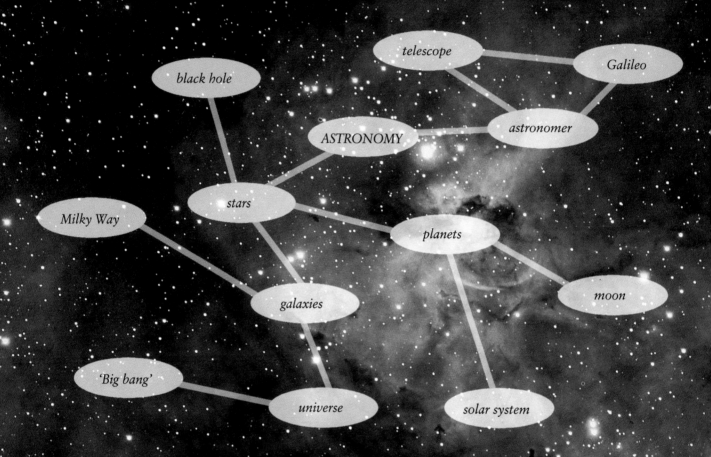

2 Look at the words below. What branch of science is each connected with?

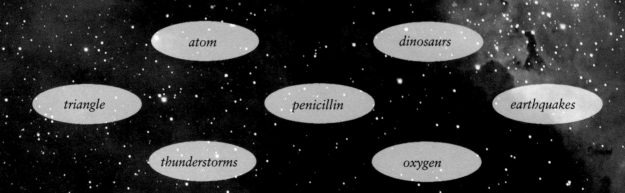

Work in groups. Choose one of the words, and use it as the starting point for your own
spidergram. Brainstorm ideas together.

Present your spidergram to the rest of the class, and explain how the ideas are connected.

10

This unit is concerned with the non-specialist language of science that people use in everyday conversation. It focuses on three main areas:
– key words and phrases used in various branches of science (e.g. *astronomy, planet, oxygen, earthquake*)
– expressions for talking about science and the environment (e.g. *pollution, chemicals, habitat*)
– language for talking about 'unscientific' beliefs (e.g. *astrology, telepathy*).
The Reading and Listening activity consists of two short science fiction stories.

1 Branches of science

This exercise is a brainstorming activity, which focuses on two types of vocabulary: the names of branches of science and the people who study them (e.g. astronomy, astronomer, biology, biologist), *and words and expressions commonly used in talking about them (e.g.* star, solar system, universe). *Students also practise explaining connections between different scientific concepts: this involves using a range of verbs, e.g.* discover, revolve, consist of.

➤ Workbook: Exercise A

1 Presentation

● To introduce the idea of the spidergram, write these items from it on the board:

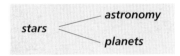

Ask what the connection between them is. Possible answer:

Astronomy is the study of the stars. Planets go round (revolve round) stars.

● Give students time to look at the rest of the spidergram and work out the connections between the items. Then discuss the answers together, and elicit any other facts that students know or are interested in. Possible answers:

Astronomers study astronomy. Galileo was an Italian astronomer. He designed his own telescope.

Many planets have moons, which revolve round them. A star and its planets together make up a solar system. There are nine planets in our own solar system.

Groups of stars are called galaxies. Our own galaxy is the Milky Way. The galaxies are all part of the universe. Some astronomers believe the universe started with a 'Big Bang' (i.e. it exploded suddenly from a single point). When stars die, they can collapse to form a black hole.

Optional extension
Ask students to suggest other items that could be added to the spidergram (e.g. *Earth, red giant, crater, infinite, rotate*), and ask them where they would be attached.

2 Writing & speaking activity

● Ask what branches of science the words are connected with. Answers:

triangle: mathematics (or geometry)
atom: physics
thunderstorms: meteorology
penicillin: medicine
dinosaurs: biology (zoology)
oxygen: chemistry
earthquakes: geology

● Divide the class into groups, and give each group one of the seven starting words. Working together, they add four or five more words to make a spidergram.

● One person from each group comes to the front of the class in turn and writes their spidergram on the board, explaining the connections between each item.

Presentation option
Build up a list of common sciences and scientists on the board:

science	scientist
astronomy	astronomer
geology	geologist
physics	physicist
biology	biologist
chemistry	chemist
mathematics	mathematician

Option for ESP classes
If students in your class have a particular interest or speciality (e.g. engineering, economics, architecture), add a starting word from their subject to those in the activity.

2 Science and the environment

This exercise is based on a survey which was carried out in 20 different countries to find out how much people know about the world we live in. There are 12 true/false questions, each relating to a different aspect of science and the environment. The answers, together with explanations, are given in the recording. Although this is primarily a reading and discussion activity, the text also introduces a range of key vocabulary connected with the environment.

1 Reading, discussion & listening

- To introduce the activity, explain that this was a quiz given to people in 20 different countries to see how much they knew about science and the environment.

- Read through the questions, but without discussing the answers at this stage. Build up new vocabulary on the board, e.g.

radioactivity	*radioactive waste*	*pesticide*
antibiotics	*nuclear power*	*species*
bacteria	*greenhouse effect*	*pollution*
virus	*atmosphere*	*cancer*

- Working alone, students write answers to the quiz.

- 🔲 Play the recording. As they listen, students check their answers. Find out who had 12 correct, 11 correct, and so on. If you like, find out an average score for the class. Answers:

1 false	4 true	7 true	10 false
2 true	5 false	8 false	11 true
3 false	6 false	9 true	12 false

2 Reading & discussion

- Turn to page 98, and give time for students to read the survey results.

- Establish where the class would have come in the survey results. Ask students if anything in the results surprises them. If you like, prompt discussion by asking questions, e.g. *Why do you think so many people got 3, 5 and 8 wrong? Why do you think East Germany did better than West Germany?*

3 Beyond science?

This is a guided discussion activity, in which students consider a range of 'unscientific' beliefs and decide to what extent they believe in them.

Discussion

- Read through the sentences, and ask students to give 'labels' to the beliefs where this is possible:

a telepathy	*d* –	*g* reincarnation
b astrology	*e* (ghosts)	*h* (psychokinesis)
c fortune telling	*f* witchcraft / the evil eye	*i* superstition

- Working alone, students record their own opinions in the table.

- Students form groups of four or five. They go through the items and compare their opinions. This should naturally lead into a discussion of the topics, with more time spent on those that students find interesting and controversial.

- As a round-up, find out what the general class opinion is about each of the items. Encourage further discussion of any points that seem to be particularly interesting, and tell the class what your own opinion is.

➤ Workbook: Exercise B

Presentation option
Write these words and expressions on the board before you begin. Check that students know what they mean by asking questions, e.g.
Can you find two things that cause disease?
What does smoke from factories cause?

Pairwork option
Students do the quiz in pairs. Then go through the answers together. See if everyone agrees, and ask students to give reasons for their answers.

Note
Students may disagree with some of these explanations, which are all from an exclusively scientific point of view. In particular, there might be discussion about item 3 (the fact that there is no evidence doesn't mean it isn't true) and item 4 (evolution is not accepted by everybody).

🔲 The tapescript is on page 108.

➤ Workbook: Exercise C, Listening

Vocabulary option
Give other words and phrases connected with these areas, e.g.
read someone's mind
tell someone's fortune
see into the future
cast a spell on someone

2 Science and the environment

1 Here are 12 true/false questions about science and the environment.
  In pairs, decide what the answers are. Can you justify your answers?

ARE THESE STATEMENTS TRUE OR FALSE?
Write T (= True) or F (= False) against each one

1 All radioactivity is made by humans. ☐

2 Antibiotics kill bacteria, but not viruses. ☐

3 Astrology, the study of star signs, has some scientific truth. ☐

4 Human beings developed from earlier species. ☐

5 All man-made chemicals cause cancer if you eat enough of them. ☐

6 If someone is exposed to any amount of radioactivity, they are certain to die as a result. ☐

7 Some radioactive waste from nuclear power stations will stay dangerous for thousands of years. ☐

8 The greenhouse effect is caused by a hole in the Earth's atmosphere. ☐

9 Every time we use coal or oil or gas, we contribute to the greenhouse effect. ☐

10 All pesticides and chemicals used on food crops cause cancer in humans. ☐

11 Human beings are the main cause of plant and animal species dying out. ☐

12 Cars are not really an important cause of air pollution. ☐

Now listen and check your answers. How well did you do?

2 The questions you have just answered were originally used in a scientific survey.
  Read about the results of the survey on page 98. How do the class results compare?

3 Beyond science?

Which of these things do you believe in? Mark your opinions in the grid.

It's not true | It's unlikely | I'm not sure | It's likely | It's definitely true

a Some people can communicate telepathically with each other.

b The star sign you were born under affects your character.

c Some people can tell the future by looking at cards.

d Dreams can warn you about events before they happen.

e People sometimes appear after death as ghosts or spirits.

f Some people have magic powers that can help or harm others.

g Some people can remember other lives they have lived in the past.

h Some people can move objects by concentrating their minds on them.

i Doing (or not doing) particular things can bring you good or bad luck.

Get together in groups, and compare your opinions.
If you disagree about any of the topics, explain why you think the way you do.

4 Science fiction

READING

The story opposite is in three parts. Read each part, and answer the questions.

PART 1

1 What is the relationship between the two men?
  Why are they at the restaurant?
  What's their connection to Miller?

2 What do these expressions tell us about the characters?
  – hideously obese
  – weasel-like
  – chortled
  – sluggishly made her way to the table
  – almost drooled

PART 2

1 What is Sloane's 'line of business'?
  Why is Wilson so fat?
  Why does Sloane fake a coughing fit?

2 What do these expressions mean?
  – what makes people tick
  – make this hit
  – Tell me another story
  – a total loony

PART 3

1 The last words of the story have been blanked out. What do you think they are?

2 Compare the words in italics with the synonyms in brackets. What extra meaning does the writer give by choosing these words?

  – *grabbed* his spoon (picked up)
  – the *monstrous* ice-cream creation (huge)
  – *slurping* the ice-cream *down* (eating)

  – it *clattered* (fell)
  – *splattered* nearby (splashed)
  – *fingering* his scar (touching)

LISTENING

You will hear a short story called *Zoo*. The story is in two parts.

1 Here are some of the elements in the first part. Try to imagine what the story is about.

the horse-spider people of Kaan	ten thousand people	six hours	Professor Hugo
a silver spaceship	barred cages	crowds of adults and children	a dollar
23rd August			the tri-city parking area outside Chicago

  ▭ Now listen to the first part of the story. How similar was it to your own ideas?

2 Here is the beginning of the second part of the story. Imagine how it might continue.

  Some two months and three planets later, the silver ship settled at last onto the familiar jagged rocks of Kaan …

  ▭ Now listen to the second part of the story.

3 Do you think the story is just for entertainment, or is the writer trying to tell us something?

4 Science fiction

This combined Reading and Listening activity consists of two short science fiction stories, both by American writers. The first story is for reading and vocabulary work, and the second is for listening.

Reading skills: *reading for implied meaning; appreciating a writer's style*
Vocabulary focus: *distinguishing precise differences of meaning between words and their synonyms*
Listening skills: *matching what you hear with your own predictions.*

Reading

Optional lead-in
Ask what the title of the story, *Dessert*, means (= last course of a meal), and discuss what the illustration shows. Ask students to imagine what the story might be about.

- Give time for students to read Part 1 of the story, and to think about the questions. To help with difficult words, they could either use dictionaries or try to guess them from the context.

- Discuss the questions together. Possible answers:

  1 The fat man has hired the thin man to kill Miller.
    They're celebrating Miller's death.
  2 *hideously obese:* He's very fat and very ugly.
    weasel-like: He's thin, mean-looking and not to be trusted.
    chortled: He's feeling very happy (*chortle* = laugh with pleasure).
    sluggishly made her way to the table: She doesn't like her job / isn't very keen
       on serving them (*sluggishly* = slowly and unwillingly).
    almost drooled: He loves eating sweet things, he's very greedy and rather
       disgusting (*drool* = let saliva run out of your mouth).

- Give time for students to read Part 2 of the story. Establish the identity of the characters: Sloane is the thin man, or 'scarface'; Wilson is the fat man. Then discuss the questions together. Possible answers:

  1 Sloane is a professional killer.
    Wilson is fat because Miller is 'eating for him' (whatever Miller eats makes
    Wilson put on weight).
    Sloane fakes a coughing fit to cover up his laughter: he thinks Wilson is crazy.
  2 *what makes people tick* = what reasons they have for the things they do
    make this hit = commit this murder (kill Miller)
    Tell me another story = I don't believe what you're saying
    a total loony = completely mad (*loony* = lunatic)

- Give time for students to read Part 3 of the story. Again let them use dictionaries to look up the words in Question 2.

- Ask students to suggest possible endings, then tell them the real ending (Answer: 'I poisoned his dinner.').

- Discuss the words in Question 2, and try to elicit these points:
  – *grabbed* = picked up greedily, in a hurry
  – *monstrous* = horribly and unnaturally large
  – *slurping ... down* = swallowing greedily, as fast as possible, and noisily
  – *clattered* = fell noisily, bouncing across the table
  – *splattered* = splashed hard, violently
  – *fingering* = touching repeatedly, as if by habit

Listening

Groupwork option
In groups, students work out a story that would include all the elements in it. Then ask each group to tell their ideas to the class.

- Look at the ten phrases, and ask students to suggest what they think the story will be about. Prompt them to consider all the elements by asking questions (e.g. *Who do you think Professor Hugo is? What about the dollar?*).

- ▭ Play the first part of the story. Establish how the elements actually fit together. Possible answer:

  On 23rd August, Professor Hugo's silver spaceship landed in the tri-city parking area outside Chicago to exhibit the horse-spider people of Kaan. Ten thousand people paid a dollar each to see them, and crowds of adults and children filed past the barred cages for six hours.

▭ The tapescript is on page 109.

- Look at the beginning of the second part of the story, and ask students to suggest how it might continue. Get a range of different ideas.

- ▭ Play the second part of the story.

- Ask students what they think the meaning of the story is. Brainstorm different ideas, and write possible 'themes' up on the board, e.g.

> *What do zoo animals really think of us?*
> *What is 'normal'?*
> *People always find some way to make money.*
> *Are cages for keeping you in or keeping*
>   *others out?*

Self-study Workbook

Exercise A: Five scientists
Science vocabulary. Students read texts about five famous scientists. They relate vocabulary to topics, and answer true/false questions.

Exercise B: Environmental issues
Vocabulary related to environmental problems. Students write short paragraphs based on prompts.

Exercise C: Believe it or not?
Students write short paragraphs about one of the issues in 10.3 (*Beyond science*).

Idioms: Things people say
Common idioms about communication (e.g. *put someone in the picture*).

Listening: Reading the tarot
Someone tells a person's fortune from tarot cards. Students predict what they will hear, and then complete summaries.

Word building: Adjectives and nouns (2)
Nouns ending in *-(i)ty, -ence/-ance, -ency/-ancy, -th, -ness*.

Dessert

by Robert E. Rogoff

I

The waitress hovered around their table like a moth near a light. Finally, the hideously obese man waved her away.

'We're not ready to order yet,' he said. 'Come back in a few minutes.'

After the waitress departed, the weasel-like man with the scar across his face addressed his dining companion seated across the table from him. 'I can assure you as we sit here tonight that Miller is quite dead or will be within minutes.'

The obese man chortled. 'That is good news.' He turned his massive body and snapped his fingers. The chair groaned in protest.

The waitress sluggishly made her way to the table. 'What'll it be, honey?'

'I'm celebrating tonight,' said the obese man. 'Let me have a super duper hot fudge sundae with the works.' He almost drooled as he said this.

'And you, dearie?' the waitress asked scarface.

'Just coffee for me, dearie.' He grinned, showing a crooked row of teeth.

The fat man looked as serious as his Buddha-like face allowed. 'You'll receive the other ten thousand as per our agreement.'

II

Scarface grinned again and rubbed his hands together. 'Mr Wilson,' he said. 'In my line of business it pays to get to know what makes people tick. If you don't think it too presumptuous of me, I'd like to inquire –' He stopped abruptly as the waitress approached to fill his coffee cup. After she slowly melted away to the recesses of the dingy restaurant, he continued, 'I was wondering … just exactly why did you have me make this hit?'

Wilson picked up his fork and rubbed a finger across its tines. 'I suppose I can tell you. I don't care whether you believe me or not.'

'Why wouldn't I believe you?'

'Mr Sloane, the sundae I ordered was the first food in years not on my very strenuous 400-calorie-a-day diet.'

Sloane suppressed a smile. Tell me another story, he thought.

Wilson continued. 'Despite eating almost nothing since 1985, my weight has ballooned to over four hundred pounds. Last month I

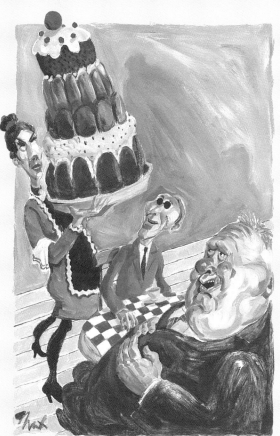

discovered – never mind how – that Miller was eating for me. He ate the food and I gained the weight.'

Sloane laughed but covered it by faking a coughing fit. This guy was loony. But a job was a job. He would take anyone's money, even a total loony like Wilson.

III

The waitress appeared and placed the sundae before Wilson. Wilson grabbed his spoon and eagerly attacked the monstrous ice-cream creation. He lifted the first spoonful. 'Here's to the demise of Miller,' he said, slurping the ice-cream down.

Suddenly he dropped the spoon. It clattered to the formica table top. A clump of fudge-covered ice-cream splattered nearby.

'Are you okay?' asked Sloane.

'I don't feel too well,' moaned Wilson. A glazed look came into his eyes. 'Oh, no. Don't tell me …'

'What?'

'How did you do it?' he demanded. He was beginning to feel dizzy. And afraid.

'Do it?' asked Sloane, fingering his scar.

'How did you kill Miller?'

Sloane smiled crookedly. 'Nothin' to it, Mr Wilson. ⬛⬛⬛⬛⬛⬛⬛⬛⬛⬛ '

Study pages

Grammar study: time

1 Time expressions

Each of these sentences contains one mistake. Can you correct them?

a I saw him on the day before yesterday.
b He made a lot of friends during he was at university.
c I've been learning English since four years.
d Would you like to come to dinner the next Friday?
e They were delayed during six hours.
f She hasn't woken up already.
g We bought this flat before six years.
h He's retiring in five year's time.
i We got to the airport until 5 o'clock.

2 Expressions with 'time'

Fill the gaps with expressions from the box.

in time	at the same time	for a time
on time	after a time	at the time
some time	from time to time	at one time

a I don't see them very often, but they drop in
....
b Her great grandfather emigrated to America
.... during the 1890s.
c The train was exactly ....
d They were very happy at first, but .... they
began to drift apart.
e It was a stupid thing to do, but I was only 15
....
f If you want to get there .... for the
fireworks, you'd better hurry up.
g The trouble was, he thought he could ride a bike
and read a comic ....
h .... , dinosaurs used to roam the Earth.
i I have to go away .... , but I promise I'll
write to you every day.

3 Time periods

Look at these sentences. In Box A, the time period begins and ends in the past. What about the others?

A	I was at university from 1987 to 1991, and then I worked as a courier for two years.
B	I've been collecting stamps for more than 20 years. I've had this album since I was ten.
C	I'm on holiday for another six weeks, but I'm only staying here until the end of August.
D	I'll be away for six days. I'll be in New York from the 3rd to the 5th, and then I'm going to visit my sister in California.

Write four things about yourself, one for each time period.

4 Two types of activity

Look at the sentences in A and B.

A	We spent two hours watching the TV. We watched the TV for two hours. *(This is how we passed the time)*
B	It took us two hours to drive to Berlin. We drove to Berlin in two hours. *(This is something we achieved, and how long it took us)*

Rewrite these sentences, using structures from the box.

a We sunbathed from two till three.
b I started cooking dinner at 5.30 and it was ready
at 7.00.
c I started reading the report on Monday, but I
didn't finish it till Friday.
d We started playing cards at 6.00 and we finished
at midnight.
e I started university in 1990, and I got my degree
five years later.

5 Two kinds of sequence

Why do the sentences in A use the Past simple tense and the sentences in B use the Past perfect tense?

A	When he *sat* down, the chair collapsed. When I *read* his note, I knew it was all over. When the dentist *gave* me the injection, I felt a stab of pain.
B	When he'*d sat* down, he began to eat his lunch. When I'*d read* his note, I threw it on the fire. When the dentist *had given* me the injection, she smiled and said 'OK? Ready for the drill?'

Make up sensible endings for these sentences.

a When the plane landed ...
b When the plane had landed ...
c When I'd finished the housework ...
d When she walked into the room ...
e When the lights went out ...
f When he'd drunk the whisky ...

Grammar study D: time

1 Time expressions

> Common mistakes involving time expressions

- Give time for students to study the sentences and correct the mistakes. Then discuss the answers together, and focus on any points that students are unclear about. Answers (with comments in brackets):

  a I saw him the day before yesterday. (*the day before yesterday* is a fixed phrase with no preposition)

  b He made a lot of friends while he was at university. (*during* + noun, *while* + clause; cf. *He made a lot of friends during the war*)

  c I've been learning English for four years. (*for* + a period, *since* + a starting point; cf. *I've been learning English since September*)

  d Would you like to come to dinner next Friday? (*next Friday* = from now, *the next Friday* = the following Friday; cf. *He came again the next Friday*)

  e They were delayed for six hours. (*for* + time period, *during* + noun; cf. *He fell asleep during the concert*)

  f She hasn't woken up yet. (= She's still asleep; cf. *She's woken up already* [= sooner than expected])

  g We bought this flat six years ago. (time period + *ago* [= 'before now'], *before* + noun or clause; cf. *We bought this flat before the war*)

  h He's retiring in five years' time. (*s'* with plural nouns, *'s* with singular nouns; cf. *He's retiring in a year's time*)

  i We got to the airport by 5 o'clock. (*by* = 'not later than', *until* says how long something continued; cf. *We stayed there until 5 o'clock*)

2 Expressions with 'time'

> The use of the word *time* in prepositional phrases

- Go through the exercise and focus on the meaning of each phrase. Give more examples if necessary. Answers:

  a from time to time (= sometimes, now and then)
  b some time
  c on time (= at the correct time)
  d after a time
  e at the time (= then, when I did it)
  f in time (= early enough)
  g at the same time
  h at one time (= once)
  i for a time

3 Time periods

> Referring to time in the past, up to now, from now on, and in the future

- Establish what the four time periods are:

  A: beginning and ending in the past
  B: beginning in the past and going on up to now
  C: from now into the future
  D: beginning and ending in the future

- Focus on the tenses and time expressions used in each time period:

  A: Past simple tense (*I was, I worked*), *from … to, for*
  B: Present perfect tenses (*I've been collecting, I've had*), *since* and *for*
  C: Present tenses to refer to the future (*I'm, I'm staying*), *for* and *until*
  D: Future tense and *going to* (*I'll be, I'm going to get*), *from … to, for*

- Students write sentences about themselves. As a round-up, ask a few students to read out their sentences.

4 Two types of activity

> *spend (time) doing* vs *take (time) to do*; *for* vs *in*

- Focus on the difference between the sentences in A and those in B:

  A: Watching TV is just an activity – you spend time doing it, but you aren't trying to achieve anything.
  B: Driving to Berlin has a particular goal – you want to get there, and it takes you a certain time to do it.

- Students rewrite the sentences. Then go through the answers. Possible answers:

  a We sunbathed for an hour.
  b I cooked the dinner in an hour and a half.
  c It took me five days to read the report.
  d We spent four hours playing cards.
  e It took me five years to get my degree (or: I spent five years at university).

5 Two kinds of sequence

> *when* + Past simple vs *when* + Past perfect

- Use the examples to make these points:
  The two boxes show two different kinds of sequence.
  1 The sentences in A are all about an immediate reaction. With all of them, we could say *at that moment* (e.g. *She gave me an injection, and at that moment I felt a stab of pain*). We join them with *when* + Past simple.
  2 The sentences in B all have the idea of 'one thing after another' or 'first … and then' (e.g. *First she gave me the injection, then she smiled*). We join them with *when* + Past perfect.

- Ask students to do the second part of the exercise in pairs, and then go through the answers together. Possible answers:

  a … I woke up, … there was a loud bang.
  b … I took my seat-belt off, … we all got out.
  c … I made a cup of coffee, … I went to the shops.
  d … everyone turned to look at her, … I knew something was wrong.
  e … everyone stopped talking, … I had to stop reading.
  f … he threw the bottle in the river, … he started on the vodka.

Language awareness D: conversational fillers

This activity focuses on words and phrases commonly used as 'fillers' in conversational English, to give the speaker time to think or to modify what he/she is saying.

well	really	basically
um	you know how it is	er
sort of	you know	
I mean	or something	

1 'Meaningless' fillers

- Write the sentence *I tripped and fell over* on the board. Then read it out adding *well*, *um* and *sort of*:
  Well, um, I sort of tripped and fell over.
  Discuss why people often add phrases like these to what they say, and make these points:
  – They don't add anything to the meaning.
  – People often use them to give themselves time to think, or if they can't express themselves clearly.
  – Students don't need to use them, but to understand spoken English it may be important to recognise them.

- Ask students if they know any other phrases like these in English, and write them on the board.

- 🔲 Play the recording, and establish what each person is trying to say. Answers:
  1 She finds it hard to stop smoking.
  2 She thinks smoking is a disgusting habit.
  3 He's tried to give up several times.

- 🔲 Play the recording again. Students listen and note down all the fillers they hear.

- Build up a list on the board:

2 Fillers that show attitude

- Explain that we often add expressions which show our attitude to what we're saying (e.g. that we feel it strongly, or we're not sure).

- 🔲 Play the recording, pausing after each item to establish what expressions the speakers use. Answers:
  A – let me see, as far as I remember
    – I think, or something like that
  B – the fact is, to be honest, and that's how it is
    – it just can't be helped
  C – I was just thinking, one possible idea might be, or something like that, it's just an idea
    – What do you think?
  D – the fact is, let's face it
    – if you ask me, that's how I see it

3 Activation

- Pairwork. Students choose a situation and improvise a conversation, using 'fillers' where they seem natural.

- As a round-up, ask a few pairs to improvise their conversation in front of the class.

> 🔲 The tapescript is on page 109.

Pronunciation D: high key

This activity focuses on the way we make a 'step up' in pitch to indicate a contrast with what is expected or with what has gone before.

1 Presentation

- 🔲 Play the two versions of the remark, and focus on the differences between them:
  – The first time the remark is 'normal' – it's just a statement of fact. The voice *stays down* on *married*.
  – The second time, the voice *goes up* on *married*. This gives an extra implied meaning: 'This is unexpected news' or 'I can't quite believe it myself'.

- If you like, get students to practise saying the remark with and without a 'step up'.

2 Listening & practice

- 🔲 Play the remarks, pausing after each pair. Ask students to match them with the implied meanings, and to identify where the speaker's voice goes up. Answers:
  1 *a*, then *b* (step up on *tennis* in *b*)
  2 *b*, then *a* (step up on *eight o'clock* in *b*)

3 *b*, then *a* (step up on *asparagus* in *b*)
4 *a*, then *b* (step up on *late* in *b*)

- Ask students to choose one remark and to say it in one of the two ways. Other students try to identify which meaning it has.

3 Prediction task & listening

- Pairwork. Students decide where they think the speaker's voice will go up.

- 🔲 Play the conversations, checking the answers as you go. Point out that the speaker's voice will go up on words which contrast with what has gone before. Answers:
  1 step up on *president* (contrast with *prime minister*)
  2 step up on *Sarah* (contrast with *Paul*)
  3 step up on *cheaper* (contrast with *more expensive*, which is what we'd expect)
  4 step up on *Saturday* (contrast with *Friday*)
  5 step up on *maths* (contrast with *French*)

- Ask students to say the remarks, focusing on the points where they should 'step up'.

Self-study Workbook

Study Skills D: Summarising information　　　*See notes on page 129.*

Language awareness: conversational fillers

1 In everyday conversation, people often use 'fillers' such as *um*, *well* and *sort of*. Can you think of any others?

[cassette] You will hear three people talking about smoking. Note down the fillers the speakers use. Why do you think they use them? How necessary do you think they are?

2 We often use other expressions in conversation, which help to explain our attitude (e.g. *as far as I'm concerned, I think*).

[cassette] You will hear people saying the things below. What else do they say? Listen for expressions which mean the same as the expressions in brackets.

A
It was quite a small room, and it had yellow wallpaper with pictures of penguins on it.
(I'm trying to remember)
(I'm not sure)

B
I've been very busy recently and I haven't had time to look at it.
(I'm telling you the truth)
(It's beyond my control)

C
Let's organise a fancy dress party.
(I don't want to force this idea on you)
(Do you agree?)

D
This government doesn't care about people's welfare at all. It's only interested in winning the next election.
(This is definitely true)
(This is my opinion)

3 Work with a partner. Choose one of the situations below, and improvise a conversation. Use any fillers you like to help you.
   a You are your partner's boss, and you're giving him/her the sack.
   b Tell your partner your earliest childhood memory.
   c What do you think is the most serious danger to mankind? Tell your partner about it.
   d Invite your partner to come and stay for the weekend.

Pronunciation: high key

1 [cassette] You will hear this remark said twice:

Sonia and I have decided to get married.

What is the difference in the way the remark is said? What difference is there in meaning?

2 [cassette] You will hear each of the remarks below said twice. Each time, decide which of the two implied meanings fits better, *a* or *b*.
   1 He's decided to take up tennis.
      a He's been thinking about it for some time, so I'm not surprised
      b That's odd – he's not normally interested in sports.
   2 She was asleep by eight o'clock.
      a It's her usual bedtime.
      b It was unusually early for her.
   3 It tastes like asparagus soup.
      a That's what I think it is.
      b That's funny – I was expecting chicken soup.
   4 He arrived late again this morning.
      a I'm not surprised – he's often late.
      b I wonder what's wrong – he's usually on time.

Now try saying the remarks yourself. See if other students can tell which meaning you are trying to express.

3 In each of these remarks the speaker is making a contrast. Underline the word where you think the speaker's voice will go *up*.
   1 Although the prime minister is head of the government, it's the president that has most of the power.
   2 I was expecting Paul to call, but when I answered the phone, it was Sarah.
   3 Surprisingly, the tickets are cheaper than a year ago.
   4 We went there on Saturday, not Friday.
   5 Oh, I thought the French exam was easy. It was the maths exam I didn't like.

[cassette] Now listen and see if you were right. Then practise saying the remarks yourself.

Evaluating

1 For better, for worse

1 Do you think things have got better or worse in your country over the last 20 years or so? Which of these statements do you think are true?

a Children have | more / less | fun than they used to.

b Cities have become | dirtier. / cleaner.

c There's a | greater / smaller | variety of fruit and vegetables than there used to be.

d Young people used to behave | more / less | responsibly than they do now.

e Holidays have become | cheaper. / more expensive.

f There are | more / fewer | opportunities for women than there used to be.

g People are | more / less | prejudiced against foreigners than they used to be.

h More / Fewer | people wear perfume these days.

[cassette icon] You will hear some people talking about how life in Britain has changed. Do they say the same things as you? What other changes do they mention?

2 Now write two sentences of your own. Think of one change for the better in your lifetime and one change for the worse.

This unit is concerned with language for evaluating. It covers three main areas:
– making comparisons between the past and the present
– saying whether or not things are worth doing
– describing advantages, using causative verbs (e.g. *enable*, *prevent*).
The fourth activity develops writing skills, and deals with language for weighing
up advantages and disadvantages.

1 For better, for worse

*This exercise is about the way life has changed, and whether things are better or
worse now than they used to be. It introduces time comparison structures, and
revises comparative forms (-er than, not as … as …) and used to.*

➤ Focus on Form: Exercise 1
➤ Workbook: Exercise A

1 *Discussion & presentation*

- Working alone or in pairs, students look at each statement and choose the
  version they think is true.

- Go through the statements with the whole class, and see if they agree about
  them. Ask further questions to encourage discussion (e.g. *In what way do
  children have more fun? What can they do now that they couldn't do before? Is
  there anything they could do before that they can't do now?*).

- Show these three ways of comparing the past and the present:

  1 by saying how things have changed:
    Cities *have become* cleaner
  2 by comparing 'now' with the past:
    Cities *are* cleaner *than they used to be*
  3 by comparing the past with 'now':
    Cities *used to be* dirtier *than they are now.*

  Show how comparisons between different times use the same structures as other
  comparisons:

Tokyo	is cleaner than isn't as polluted as	Los Angeles.
Tokyo	is cleaner than isn't as polluted as	it used to be.

- 🔲 Play the recording. Pause after each section and check which statements
  represent what the speakers say. Answers:

  a Children have less fun than they used to.
  b Cities have become dirtier.
  c There's a greater variety of fruit and vegetables than there used to be.
  d Young people used to behave more responsibly than they do now.
  e Holidays have become cheaper.
  f There are more opportunities for women than there used to be.
  g People are less prejudiced against foreigners than they used to be.
  h More people wear perfume these days.

2 *Writing & speaking activity*

- Working alone or in pairs, students write two or more sentences of their own,
  using the structures you have presented.

- In turn, students read out their sentences. Ask the rest of the class if they agree,
  and why or why not. Where students have written something controversial, try
  to get a variety of opinions from the class and encourage discussion.

Blackboard option
Build up a list of statements on the
board representing the majority
class opinion. Students can then
look at this as they listen to the
recording.

Language note
In comparisons with *used to*, the
verb *be* is repeated, e.g.
He *is* kinder than he used to *be*.
Other verbs are not repeated, e.g.
He *works* harder than he used to.
(not … ~~used to work~~)

Optional comprehension check
Ask questions to check that
students understand the details of
what each speaker says, e.g.
Speaker 1: Why is life difficult for
young people? What's wrong with
schools?

🔲 The tapescript is on page 109.

2 What's the point?

This exercise introduces structures used for saying whether things are worthwhile or not. Students use these structures to talk about a range of issues.

➤ Focus on Form: Exercise 2
➤ Workbook: Exercise B, Listening

1 Presentation

● Look at the table, and establish how the expressions are used and what they mean. Build up this presentation on the board:

It's a good idea It's not a good idea	to give ...		It's worth(while) It's not worth There's no point in	giving ...

It's a waste of time	to give ... giving ...

● Ask students what they actually think about giving money to beggars. Get them to use the structures you have presented in their replies.

2 Writing & speaking activity

● Working alone, students write sentences about the topics in the list.
● Students sit in groups. They read out their sentences, and discuss their opinions with others in the group.
● As a round-up, ask each group which topic led to most discussion, and ask them to summarise what they said.

> *Language note*
> *It's not worth doing* and *There's no point in doing* mean roughly the same; they both mean 'you can do it, but it will achieve nothing'. *It's a waste of time* (+ *-ing* or *to*) has a similar meaning, but is stronger.

> *Practice option*
> Elicit other examples using these expressions, to check that students can use them, e.g.
> You can take a bus, but it's only five minutes' walk away.
> → There's no point in taking a bus.

> *Alternative*
> Students move freely round the class, reading their sentences to other students and finding out what they think.

3 Gadgets

This exercise focuses on a range of causative verbs, which are often used for talking about advantages and benefits. Students use these verbs to talk about gadgets and what they might be used for.

➤ Focus on Form: Exercise 3
➤ Workbook: Exercise C, Listening

1 Presentation

● Students look at the gadgets and match them with the descriptions.
● Look at the gadgets together, and discuss the answers. Ask students to say whether they think the gadgets would be useful. Answers:

A saves you from having to look a fish in the eye ...
B enables you to transfer chopped vegetables ...
C makes it easier for you to put in your eyedrops.
D prevents you from feeling dizzy ...
E allows you to take off your shoes ...
F discourages people from treading on your toes ...

● Show what structures are used with the verbs in the box, and check that students know what they mean:

It	enables allows encourages makes it easier for	you to + inf.	It	stops prevents discourages saves	you from+ ing

2 Speaking activity

● In pairs, students discuss what the gadgets on page 99 might be used for.
● Discuss the gadgets with the whole class. Possible answers:

A allows you to cut a cake fairly (so everyone gets the same size slice).
B enables you to switch the light on/off when you're carrying things.
C prevents the ice from coming out of the glass when you drink.
D makes it easier to kill cockroaches with your slipper.
E enables you to sit down in a crowded underground train.
F prevents you from missing the station if you fall asleep in the metro (the sign says 'I am having a short sleep. Could you please wake me up when I reach the stop printed below. Many thanks.').
G enables you to smoke up to 14 cigarettes at once.
H helps you to keep fit while using the phone.

> *Language note*
> It enables/allows you to do sg. = you *can* do it
> It stops/prevents you from doing sg. = you *can't* do it
> It encourages you to do sg. = you *want to* do it
> It discourages you from doing sg. = you *don't want to* do it
> It saves you from doing sg. = you *don't have to* do it

> *Optional extension*
> Students think up a similar invention of their own, and draw a rough sketch of it. They then explain to other students what it is for and how it works.
> They could also write a description of it for homework.

2 What's the point?

1 Which of the expressions in the table are followed by *to* and which by *-ing*? Which of the expressions mean roughly the same?

2 What do you think about these things? Write three sentences like those in the table, and add a reason.

– going on a diet to lose weight
– taking part in political demonstrations
– keeping people alive who are in a terminal coma
– keeping old photos and letters
– giving money to help famine victims

Now find out if other people in the class agree with you. If they disagree, find out why.

It's a good idea It's worth(while) It's not worth There's no point in It's a waste of time It's not a good idea	giving money to beggars to give money to beggars

3 Gadgets

Causative verbs

1 Here are some pictures of gadgets taken from a book called *101 Unuseless Japanese Inventions*.

Which gadget

– allows you to take off your shoes without bending down?
– prevents you from feeling dizzy if your office is on the 40th floor?
– saves you from having to look a fish in the eye when you chop its head off?
– discourages people from treading on your toes when you're in the underground?
– makes it easier for you to put in your eyedrops?
– enables you to transfer chopped vegetables directly into the pan?

A

B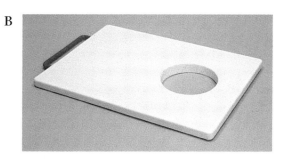

C

D

E

F

make it (easier) allow enable prevent stop save encourage discourage

2 Look at the gadgets on page 99. What do you think they are used for, and how do they work? Talk about them using the verbs in the box.

4 Pros and cons

1 Look at the text, which describes some of the advantages and disadvantages
of living in a foreign country.

How could you fit the sentences on the left into the text? How do you think they improve it?
Where would you divide the text into paragraphs?

One of the most exciting things about
being abroad is that …

Another interesting thing is that …

But being in a foreign country can also
be difficult. One problem is that …

As a result …

> Everything you do is a challenge. You feel you've really
> achieved something if you manage to go across town by bus or
> buy a loaf of bread. Everything's slightly different from your
> own country – the food, the buildings, the way people dress.
> It's rather like being a child again and seeing everything for
> the first time. Even when you're having a good time, you
> remain an outsider. Even if people are really friendly, you can
> never completely become part of their world. You can easily
> feel lonely, and start missing your family or friends. That's
> when you want to go back home again.

2 Match the topics on the left below with the comments on the right.
Expand them into sentences using the expressions in the box.

advantage of	disadvantage of	trouble with
(good) thing about	drawback of	problem with

being an only child
having older brothers and sisters
having younger brothers and sisters
living with your parents
living on your own
growing up in a city
growing up in the country

you don't have to do your own washing
you have more chance to play outside
you don't have to tidy up for anyone else
you often have to look after them
you meet people with all kinds of different backgrounds
you don't get new clothes very often
you often have no one to play with

3 Look at the topics again. Which of them have you experienced yourself?
Choose one, and find someone else who has had the same experience.

Together make brief notes under two headings: *Good points* and *Bad points*.

Expand your notes into two paragraphs, one describing the good points and
the other the bad points.

4 Pros and cons

Writing skills: *writing about advantages and disadvantages; organising information into paragraphs; 'signposting' paragraphs (indicating to the reader what they are about).*
Language focus: *expressions for talking about advantages and disadvantages.*

This activity helps students to organise information into paragraphs. It follows these stages:
1 *Presentation. Students study a text and decide how to organise it into paragraphs including topic sentences and linking devices.*
2 *Language focus. Students expand ideas into sentences using particular expressions.*
3 *Writing. Students make notes about a topic, and then expand them into two paragraphs.*

1 Presentation

- Quickly read through the text, and establish that as it stands it doesn't make much sense. Ask students to suggest how to fit the extra sentences into it, and how to divide it into paragraphs. Expected answer:

  One of the most exciting things about being abroad is that everything you do is a challenge. You feel you've really achieved something if you manage to go across town by bus or buy a loaf of bread. *Another interesting thing is that* everything's slightly different from your own country – the food, the buildings, the way people dress. It's rather like being a child again and seeing everything for the first time.

  But being in a foreign country can also be difficult. One problem is that even when you're having a good time, you remain an outsider. Even if people are really friendly, you can never completely become part of their world. *As a result,* you can easily feel lonely, and start missing your family or friends. That's when you want to go back home again.

- Discuss how the extra sentences improve the text. Establish these points:
  – They help to show how the different parts of the text belong together.
  – They let the reader know what you're talking about (e.g. *I'm saying that this is exciting; now I'm going on to a different point*).

2 Language focus

- Look at the expressions in the box. Emphasise that we always say
  – the advantage/disadvantage/drawback *of*
  – the good/bad/interesting thing *about*
  – the trouble/problem *with*.
- Ask students to make sentences from the notes. Possible answers:

  One problem with being an only child is that you often have no one to play with.
  The main disadvantage of having older brothers and sisters is that you don't get new clothes very often.
  The trouble with having younger brothers and sisters is that you often have to look after them.
  One advantage of living with your parents is that you don't have to do your own washing.
  One of the best things about living on your own is that you don't have to tidy up for anyone else.
  The main advantage of growing up in a city is that you meet people with all kinds of different backgrounds.
  The good thing about growing up in the country is that you have more chance to play outside.

3 Writing

- Students choose one of the topics and form pairs or small groups with others who have chosen the same topic. Working together, they discuss the topic and make brief notes.
- Working together or alone, students expand their notes into two connected paragraphs, using the text in Stage 1 as a rough model.

Presentation idea
Prepare a 'model' version on an OHP slide to show to the class.

Language note
A *drawback* is a disadvantage of something that otherwise has many advantages.
Trouble is normally only used with *the* (*The trouble with being an only child …*). All the other expressions can be used with *the, a, one, another, one of the,* etc.

Optional lead-in
To show what to do, choose a topic yourself, and write brief notes under two headings: *Advantages* and *Disadvantages*.

Homework option
Students make notes in class, but write the paragraphs for homework.

Focus on Form

1 Time comparison

> Time comparison with *-er than* and *not as … as*

- Read the sentences with the class, and discuss the question. Answer:

  She's talking about ten years ago. Since then she has got married, had children and given up her job.

- Look at the topics in the box and establish what they might include (e.g. *appearance* might include clothes, make-up, hairstyle, how old you look).

- Students write sentences about themselves.

- Pairwork. Students show each other their sentences.

- As a round-up, ask a few students what they found out about their partner.

2 There's no point …

> *There's no point in / It's not worth* + *-ing*; *It's not a good idea to*

- Look at the examples and establish these points:
  - *There's no point in/It's not worth* taking a camera = You can do it, but there's no advantage.
  - *It's not a good idea to* take a camera = Something bad could happen as a result (e.g. it might get stolen).

- Pairwork. One student reads out the sentences in Box A in two ways, and the other student finds a suitable continuation each time.

- Go through the answers together. Answers:

  a It's not worth taking the lift: he only lives on the first floor.
     It's not a good idea to take the lift: someone got stuck in it the other day.

  b There's no point in offering him a bribe: he's far too honest.
     It's not a good idea to offer him a bribe: he'll probably report you to the police.

  c It's not worth inviting him: he's always busy on Friday nights.
     It's not a good idea to invite him: he's terribly boring.

  d There's no point in taking that cough mixture: it won't do you any good.
     It's not a good idea to take that cough mixture: it'll make your hair fall out.

3 Causative verbs

> *force/enable/encourage s.o. to* + inf.; *prevent/save/ discourage s.o. (from)* + *-ing*

- Students make sentences from the table. Possible answers:

  One good thing about having a credit card is that it saves people carrying cash around all the time.
  The trouble with having a credit card is that it encourages you to spend more than you can afford.

  One good thing about being drunk is that it enables you to forget all about your troubles.
  The trouble with being drunk is that it prevents people from thinking clearly.

  One good thing about having a large dog is that it forces you to go for a long walk every day.
  The trouble with having a large dog is that it discourages people from visiting you.

- Students write a sentence about one of the topics in the box.

- Students read out their sentences in turn. The rest of the class guess what the sentence is about.

Self-study Workbook

Exercise A: Then and now
Time comparison structures. Students paraphrase given sentences.

Exercise B: Giving advice
It's (not) a good idea to …, *It's (not) worth …*, *There's no point in …* Students write a paragraph giving advice to a foreign visitor to their country.

Exercise C: Good and bad effects
Causative verbs. Students write sentences about a town planning scheme, then write part of a letter.

Idioms: Other people
Common idioms describing people and how you react to them (e.g. *she leaves me cold*).

Listening: Panel discussion
A radio panel discussion about third world charities. Students listen and identify points made by the speakers.

Common verbs: take
Common uses of the verb *take*, including phrasal verbs and other idiomatic expressions.

Focus on Form

1 Time comparison

Here are some sentences written by a 28-year-old woman in which she says how she has changed over a period of time.

> I was much more fashion-conscious then, more ambitious, more interested in making money.
>
> I'm not nearly as well off financially as I was then.
>
> I go out in the evenings far less than I used to.
>
> I'm not as selfish as I was then. Nowadays I haven't got time to think about myself.
>
> I'm not as physically active as I used to be — I used to do lots of dangerous sports, but nowadays I'm quite happy just going for a walk.
>
> I'm a lot happier than I was, much more relaxed, and much more confident, too.

How long ago do you think she is talking about, and what do you think has happened in between?

Now think of a time when you were different from the way you are now, and write a similar set of sentences. Use this list of topics to help you.

appearance	interests	attitudes
personality	social life	food
money	fitness	knowledge
work	skills	happiness

When you've finished, show your sentences to another student. Can they guess how long ago you're talking about, and what has happened in between?

2 There's no point ...

Student A: Read out each remark in Box A twice, once using *There's no point in ...* or *It's not worth ...*, and once using *It's not a good idea to ...*

Student B: Read out a suitable continuation from Box B.

Examples:

A There's no point in
   It's not worth   taking a camera.
B You aren't allowed to take photos anyway.

A It's not a good idea to take a camera.
B There are a lot of thieves about.

Box A

a Let's not take the lift ...
b Don't offer him a bribe ...
c Let's not invite him ...
d Don't take that cough mixture ...

Box B

... it'll make your hair fall out.
... he's terribly boring.
... he'll probably report you to the police.
... it won't do you any good.
... he only lives on the first floor.
... he's far too honest.
... someone got stuck in it the other day.
... he's always busy on Friday nights.

---

3 Causative verbs

Make six sensible sentences from the table.

One good thing about The trouble with	having a credit card being drunk having a large dog	is that ...

... it	forces you	from thinking clearly.
	enables you	to go for a long walk every day.
	prevents people	carrying cash around all the time.
	saves people	to forget all about your troubles.
	encourages you	from visiting you.
	discourages people	to spend more than you can afford.

Now choose an item from the box below, and make a sentence about one of its advantages or disadvantages. Can other students guess what item you're talking about?

Example: It prevents you from getting to sleep.
Answer: Drinking coffee.

doing military service	drinking coffee
having a mobile phone	not having a TV
having a burglar alarm	reading in bed
having an alarm clock	being very tall

12 Yourself and others

1 The egg test

Many countries have a tradition of painting patterns on eggs at Easter time.

Before you start the activity, choose two of the eggs below: the one you like most, and the one you like second best.

1 *a* The eggs in the picture were used as part of a personality test in a magazine.
Here are two of the interpretations. Which of the eggs do you think they go with?

Everything in its place
You're a naturally cautious person, and sometimes you tend to be a bit too precise and fussy. You always make sure you do everything thoroughly. In fact sometimes you're so afraid of making mistakes that you're not satisfied until you've cleared up every single point.

Admired by everyone
You're an active and sociable person who likes to take part in things and enjoys being the centre of attention. Although you have a tendency to be rather vain and self-centred, other people don't seem to mind, probably because you give people at least as much as you take from them.

b These sets of character adjectives go with the other eight eggs.
Which do you think go with which?

- superstitious, optimistic
- calm, reflective
- placid, easy-going
- cheerful, sociable, talkative
- sensitive, insecure
- inquisitive, nosy
- light-hearted, carefree, optimistic
- passionate, aggressive, determined

Now check your answers against the magazine's interpretations on page 100.

2 Look again at what the magazine says about the two eggs you chose.
Does it describe what you're really like?

This unit is about your own personality and your relationship with other people. It focuses on the following areas:
– describing personal characteristics (including 'character' adjectives, e.g. *optimistic, talkative, inquisitive*)
– things that people look for in relationships with a partner (e.g. *honesty, sense of humour*)
– talking about other relationships (e.g. between colleagues, neighbours, family members).

The Reading and Listening activity is about tattoos.

1 The egg test

This exercise is based on a personality test from a magazine, in which people's character is supposedly revealed by the design that appeals to them most on painted eggs. This is used as a way of introducing a range of adjectives which describe personality.

1 Reading & presentation

- Introduce the activity by telling students that this is a personality test. Ask them to cover the page below the pictures, and choose the two eggs they like best and second best. They should note down which eggs they have chosen.

- Read through the two interpretations. As you do so, build up a list of these 'character' adjectives on the board:

cautious	sociable
precise	vain
fussy	self-centred
active	

Discuss which eggs the two interpretations might go with, and ask students to give reasons for their choice. Answers:

Everything in its place: D
Admired by everyone: H

- Look at the list of character adjectives. Focus on their meaning by asking questions and giving simple examples (e.g. If I'm *superstitious*, what do I believe? If I'm *cheerful*, I'm always smiling).

- In pairs, students try to match the sets of adjectives with the eight remaining eggs (not D and H). Then discuss the answers together. Answers:

A sensitive, insecure
B calm, reflective
C light-hearted, carefree, optimistic
E passionate, aggressive, determined

F cheerful, sociable, talkative
G inquisitive, nosy
I superstitious, optimistic
J placid, easy-going

2 Discussion

- Give time for students to read through the interpretations on page 100.
- Pairwork. Students tell each other which eggs they chose, and whether they think the interpretations really say something about them.
- As a round-up, ask a few students what conclusions they came to.

➤ Workbook: Exercise A

Option
Choose two eggs yourself at this stage. Then introduce the round-up discussion in Stage 2 by telling the class which eggs you chose.

Note
The texts contain the expressions *tend to* and *have a tendency to*. This is a good opportunity to present them.

Language notes
Sensitive can have a positive or a negative meaning in English. Compare:
She's a wonderfully sensitive person. (= she has fine feelings)
Be careful what you say to him: he's terribly sensitive. (= easily hurt)

Inquisitive and *nosy* both mean 'wanting to find out about things'. *Nosy* is more negative (= sticking your nose into other people's business).

Optional extension
Develop this into a more general discussion of personality tests, horoscopes, etc. and whether they really tell you anything about your personality.

2 Relationships

In this exercise seven different people say what they look for in a relationship with a partner. This leads to a discussion of what is most important in a relationship. Although this is mainly a listening and fluency activity, it introduces a number of key words and expressions for describing personal qualities (e.g. honesty, respect, sense of humour).

➤ Workbook: Exercise B

1 *Listening & presentation*

- 🔲 Play the recording, pausing after each speaker. Students listen and note down a key word or expression each time, representing the main point the speaker makes.

🔲 The tapescript is on page 110.

- Discuss the answers together, and build up a list of points on the board:

> **honesty**
> **mutual interests**
> **a beautiful partner**
> **friendship**
>
> **leading your own life**
> **admitting mistakes**
> **not being too serious**
> **love**

  🔲 As you do this, play the recording again, pausing after each speaker and checking in more detail that students have understood.

- Brainstorm other things that might be important in a relationship, getting students to suggest as many ideas as possible. Add them to the list on the board.

2 *Writing and speaking activity*

- Working alone, students write down the three most important things they themselves would look for in a relationship, choosing from the list on the board.
- Pairwork. Students read out their list to their partner, and say why they think those things are important.
- As a round-up, ask students to read out their lists, and see how many students agree with each other.

> *Alternative*
> Students move freely round the class, telling each other what they wrote, until they find someone who has the same list as theirs.
> As a round-up, find out how many students managed to find a 'partner'.

3 Social comment

This is a freer activity, in which students interpret and discuss cartoons, all of which are about relationships.

➤ Workbook: Listening

1 *Speaking activity*

- Divide the class into pairs or groups. Give time for students to look at the cartoons and interpret them, and to decide which ones need captions.
- Discuss the cartoons together. Ask students to say what they think they are about, and to suggest possible captions. Then tell them the original captions. Answers:
  A (envy between neighbours) Caption: They'll be unbearable when they get the swimming pool.
  B (wife and husband) No caption.
  C (loneliness) Caption: Look, we'll be back tomorrow, I promise, but we've got to go now, it's late, now you go to bed. It won't be long …
  D (unwelcome visitors) No caption.
  E (bringing up children) Caption: Well, you did say they should go outside and get some fresh air.
  F (father and son) Caption: You may not remember me. I was always in bed by the time you got home.

2 *Discussion*

- In groups, students consider each cartoon and decide whether it would be suitable for publication in their own country. Ask them to consider these points:
  – Would people understand it? Would they find it funny? Why?/Why not?
  – Is the problem it deals with universal or 'British'? What about the people and places shown?
  – Would it need changing in any way?
- As a round-up, ask each group what they decided.

> *Homework option*
> Students find other cartoons (in their own language) which are about relationships.
> In the next class, they show them and talk about them in English.

2 Relationships

1 🔲 You will hear seven people saying what they look for in a relationship. Listen, and note down the main point each speaker makes.

What other things might be important in a relationship? Add other ideas to the list.

2 Choose three things you yourself would look for in a relationship, and write them down in order of importance.

Does anyone else have exactly the same list as you?

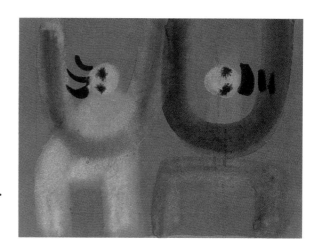

3 Social comment

1 Look at these cartoons, four of which have their captions missing. Which of them do you think is about

– the relationship between wife and husband?
– the relationship between father and son?
– the problems of bringing up children?
– envy between neighbours?
– unwelcome visitors?
– loneliness?

Which four cartoons do you think need captions? Choose one of them, and make up a caption for it.

The teacher will read out the original captions. Were they as good as yours?

A

B

C

D

2 These cartoons were all originally published in Britain.

Imagine you were making a collection of cartoons entitled *Social Comment*, for publication in your own country. Which of these cartoons would you include? Which wouldn't you include? Why?

E

F

4 Skin deep

READING

1 *Before you read*

Without looking at the article, try to guess the answers to these questions.

a Why are tattoos associated with sailors?

b How is tattooing done?

c How far back does tattooing go?

d Where on the body do people have tattoos?

e Does it hurt?

f Is it dangerous?

g How long do tattoos last?

h Can tattoos be removed?

Now read the article. What were the answers?

2 **Look at these tattoos. Which of the styles described in the article do you think they are?**

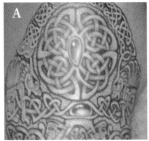 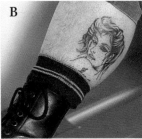  

3 **What problems might you have if you**

a went to a 'scratcher'?

b took aspirin before being tattooed?

c had a tattoo on your cheek?

d tattooed the name of someone you're in love with?

e had a tattoo removed?

LISTENING

You will hear an interview with a tattoo artist.

1 Imagine you were conducting the interview. What would you ask him about?

Write down two or three questions.

Now listen to the interview. Does he answer any of your questions?

2 *a* **What does he say about**

– Holland?   – portrait and reproduction work?   – department stores?

– scars?   – tattoos on the face and hands?   – the Royal Family?

b **Who is Winnie and what does he look like?**

3 **Imagine someone gave you a voucher for a free tattoo.**
Would you use it? If so, what would you have done?

4 Skin deep

This combined Reading and Listening activity consists of a magazine article about tattooing and an interview with a tattoo artist.

Reading skills: *matching information with your own predictions.*
Listening skills: *matching what you hear with what you want to find out.*

Reading

- Look at the questions in 1 and ask students to suggest answers. Get as many different ideas as you can.

- Give time for students to read the article and find answers to the questions. Then discuss the answers together. Answers:

  a Because they were introduced into Europe by Captain Cook and his crew, and so became popular with sailors.

  b With a cluster of needles (a tattoo gun).

  c At least 4,000 years.

  d Anywhere where you have skin. The most popular places are arms and shoulders.

  e Yes, but it hurts less after the first two minutes.

  f No, as long as it is done properly by a qualified tattoo artist.

  g All your life.

  h Yes, but it leaves a scar.

- Discuss Questions 2 and 3. Answers:

  2 A Celtic B Portrait C Tribal D Oriental

  3 (Expected answers)

  a You might be infected.

  b You would bleed more.

  c It would change shape as you got older; you'd never be able to cover it up.

  d You might fall in love with someone else.

  e It would be expensive and painful; you'd have a scar for the rest of your life.

Listening

- Before you play the recording, ask students to think of two or three questions they would ask a tattoo artist and write them down. If you like, build up a list of 'class questions' on the board.

- 🔲 Play the recording, pausing from time to time to check if any of the questions have been answered.

- Discuss Question 2. If necessary, play the interview again, and pause at relevant points. Answers:

  a – People come to his studio from *Holland* and other countries.
    – The only thing you can swap (= exchange) a tattoo for is a *scar*.
    – He does more *portrait and reproduction work* (i.e. art) than he used to.
    – He refuses to do *tattoos on the face and hands*.
    – You'll never be able to get a tattoo done in a *department store*.
    – In the early 19th century, the British *Royal Family* were heavily tattooed.

  b Winnie is one of his clients. He's got a castle tattooed over 80% of his body.

- Ask students, in view of what they have read and heard, whether they would have a tattoo done if they had a free voucher. Ask them what kind of tattoo they would choose.

Optional lead-in
Ask if anyone in the class has ever been tattooed, or knows anyone with a tattoo.
Discuss what they think of tattoos (e.g. whether they find them attractive, pointless, unpleasant, etc.).

Optional vocabulary work
Write words from the text on the board, and ask students to try to find out what they mean from the context, e.g.

on display	**palette**
onomatopoeic	**blur**
knotwork	**sag**
jab	

🔲 The tapescript is on page 110.

Optional discussion
Focus on any of the students' questions that were not answered by the tattoo artist. See if anyone in the class can suggest an answer. If you like, ask students to find out the answers for homework.

Self-study Workbook

Exercise A: Personality adjectives
A wordsearch puzzle containing character adjectives.

Exercise B: Laura's dream
An account of a dream from a book about interpreting dreams. Students predict how the dream links with the person's real life, then read the interpretation.

Idioms: Reactions
Common idioms for describing reactions (e.g. *turn a blind eye to something*).

Listening: Two jokes
Two jokes about relationships, with pauses. Students listen and at each pause predict the next line.

Word building: Prefixes (2)
Use of prefixes *mis-*, *dis-*, *over-*, *under-* and *re-*.

Skin Deep

Not so long ago, tattoos were definitely NOT the thing to do. Fashions change, however, and tattoos are fast becoming a common sight. But before you rush to join the likes of Edward VII, Janis Joplin and Sean Connery, pause for a moment – getting a tattoo is a lot easier (and cheaper) than getting rid of one.

The art of tattooing goes back a long way. The Egyptians used to tattoo each other 3,000 years ago, and the oldest known example is on the body of a 4,000 year old 'ice-man' who was found frozen in mountain snow on the Italian–Austrian border in 1993. The picture shows a tattoo on the upper arm of another ice-man, who died 2,500 years ago in Siberia, and who is now on display in a Moscow museum.

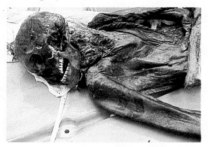

In more modern times, tattoos were reintroduced to Europe by Captain Cook and his crew on their return from Tahiti in 1771 – hence the traditional association of tattoos with sailors. The word 'tattoo' itself comes from the Tahitian word 'tatau' – onomatopoeic for the sound made by their tattooing instrument.

There are a number of major styles of tattoo, including *Tribal* (bold, simple patterns in black ink), *Celtic* (intricate knotwork, again usually black), *Oriental* (fish, clouds, dragons, etc.) and *Portrait* (images taken from photos, usually in black and grey ink). But nowadays almost any kind of image can be turned into a tattoo, in a full range of colours, and on almost any part of the body.

Technically, the only places you *can't* get tattooed are your hair, teeth and nails, but parts of the body which may change shape with ageing (such as the stomach, which tends to get bigger and sag) are best avoided. Arms and shoulders are the most popular, and one reason for this is that while these areas can be displayed in public, it is equally easy to conceal them under a shirt. For the same reason, many people choose the left wrist (which can be covered by a watch) or the feet and ankles. Some even use a shaved area of the head – and can then grow their hair to cover it up again if they want to.

Tattoos are put in place by means of a tattoo gun, which has a cluster of needles which jab in and out rapidly. The artist changes colours by dipping the tip of the gun into various colour inks as a paint artist does into a palette. Being on the receiving end of a tattoo gun is a painful process, especially for the first couple of minutes; after that, the body's natural pain-killers – endorphins – start to come into play, and the pain apparently subsides into a kind of vibrating, buzzing sensation. The use of aspirins is not recommended, as they thin the blood and can lead to bleeding.

Though not pleasant, the process is not dangerous, provided the tattoo is applied by a qualified artist in a clean and properly supervised environment. Infections can, however, result from using a 'scratcher' – someone who's bought a tattoo gun by mail order and has no idea how to use it safely. For this reason, many US states have strict safety regulations concerning tattooing, and four have banned it altogether.

The main disadvantage of tattoos is that they're permanent. It is true that they tend to blur (and possibly sag) with age – but they don't go away. So it is not a decision to be taken lightly. If you might want a job as a bank clerk in a few years' time, think twice before tattooing that fire-breathing dragon on your hand. And by all means tattoo a heart with your partner's name on your arm – provided you're sure you'll feel the same way for ever.

Tattoos can be removed, but it can be a painful process and it can leave scars. Only laser treatment can remove them completely, and this is *very* expensive. In other words, it is much easier to get a tattoo than to remove one. In a recent survey, one third of men and women questioned regretted getting tattooed. So the undecided would be well advised to stick to those temporary tattoos that you put on for the evening and remove with baby oil the next day.

E Study pages

Grammar study: pronouns and determiners

1 How many?

What's the difference between the sentences in A and those in B?

A	*All* new cars are fitted with seat-belts. *Most* flats have central heating these days. *Many* deaf people are good at lip-reading. *Very few* people live to a hundred. *Almost no* pandas survive in the wild.
B	*All (of)* these clothes need washing. *Most of* the rooms have got a private bath. *Many of* his novels are set in India. *Very few of* the audience understood Italian. *None of* his children went to university.

Here are some other quantity expressions. How could you use them to replace the phrases in italics?

hardly any   not many   quite a few   nearly all

Add a suitable quantity expression to these sentences.

a Police officers carry guns.
b Men wear earrings nowadays.
c My friends are communists.
d The shops around here open on Sunday.
e Children are vaccinated against polio.
f The students in this class are female.

2 Yourself and each other

Look at these sentences. What's the difference between *blame yourself* and *blame each other*?

a You mustn't blame yourself – it wasn't your fault.
b The two drivers blamed each other for the accident.

Fill the gaps with a verb from the box plus either *myself/yourself* etc. or *each other / one another*.

be ashamed of	help	talk to
enjoy	introduce	recognise
express		

a I believe neighbours should .... when times are bad.
b We'd like to .... I'm Bob, and this is Hilary.
c They haven't .... since they split up last year.
d Take your hands off me! You should ....
e He can understand French, but he can't .... very easily.
f Just .... to anything from the fridge.
g Now everybody, just relax and .... !
h When they met again ten years later, they hardly ....

3 I did it myself

What extra meaning is given to each of these sentences by the words in italics?

a	My sister likes detective stories, but I prefer science fiction *myself*.
b	– I'm starving. – Yes, I'm pretty hungry *myself*.
c	– Isn't that a Picasso over there? – No. I painted it *myself*.
d	Mummy didn't help me tie my shoelaces. I did them *by myself*.

Complete these sentences, using *yourself*, *himself*, etc.

a All their friends recommended the play, so they …
b Did someone give her that car, or did she …?
c Do you like our house? We …
d Some people are crazy about Volvos, but I …
e – Who helped him with his homework?
– No one! He …

4 One and ones

A	I'd like a Coke. A large one, please. The green sweets are horrible, but I rather like the red ones.
B	I usually drink instant coffee, but I occasionally drink Turkish (coffee). I don't like white bread. I prefer brown (bread).
C	Do you want a can opener or a bottle opener? I haven't got any tennis balls, but I've got some table tennis balls.

When do we use *one* and *ones*? When can't we use *one* and *ones*?

Complete these remarks, using *one/ones* where possible.

a This screwdriver's too big. Have you got … ?
b Are those plastic flowers or … ?
c Italian ice-cream is much better than …
d Would you like a vanilla ice-cream or … ?
e I hate hot weather; I much prefer …
f The older children are allowed to go home for lunch, but … at school.
g That's not a carving knife – it's a …
h This exercise is boring. Can we … ?

Grammar study E: pronouns and determiners

1 How many?

All, most, many, etc., and all of, most of, many of, etc.

- Look at the sentences in Box A and Box B, and establish these points:
  – If we are talking in general (cars, flats, deaf people) we use *all*, *most*, *many*, *few* and *no*.
  – If we are talking about particular things (*these* clothes, *the* rooms, *his* novels) we use *all (of)*, *most of*, *many of*, *few of*, *none of*.
- Discuss how we could use the other expressions to replace those in the boxes. Possible answers:

  Hardly any pandas survive in the wild. Hardly any of the audience understood Italian.

  Not many people live to be a hundred. Not many of the audience understood Italian.

  Quite a few deaf people are good at lip-reading. Quite a few of his novels are set in India.

  Nearly all flats have central heating these days. Nearly all (of) the rooms have got a private bath.

- Students add quantity expressions to the sentences. Possible answers:

  a Most police officers carry guns.
  b Quite a few men wear earrings nowadays.
  c Hardly any of my friends are communists.
  d None of the shops around here open on Sunday.
  e Nearly all children are vaccinated against polio.
  f Most of the students in this class are female.

2 Yourself & each other

Reflexive and reciprocal verbs

- Look at the examples and establish the difference:
  – *blame yourself* = you say it's your (own) fault.
  – *blame each other* = you say it's the other person's fault and the other person says it's your fault.
- Before you do the exercise, write these forms on the board:

myself	*ourselves*
yourself	*yourselves*
himself	*themselves*
herself	

- Students fill the gaps with suitable verbs. Answers:
  a help each other
  b introduce ourselves
  c talked to each other
  d be ashamed of yourself
  e express himself
  f help yourself
  g enjoy yourselves
  h recognised each other

3 I did it myself

Emphatic pronouns: myself, yourself, themselves, etc.

- Point out that we can use *myself*, *himself*, etc. just to give emphasis. Look at the examples and establish what extra meaning the words in italics give to the sentences:
  1 *myself* = in contrast to my sister
  2 *myself* = also (not only you)
  3 *myself* = I did it, not anyone else
  4 *by myself* = without help (from anyone else)
- Students complete the sentences. Possible answers:

  a ... decided to see it themselves.
  b ... buy it herself? / pay for it herself?
  c ... built it ourselves.
  d ... don't think much of them myself /... prefer BMWs myself.
  e ... did it by himself.

4 One & ones

Use of one and ones to replace a noun

- Use the examples to make these points:
  – With count nouns (*a Coke, sweets*), we can use *one* or *ones* instead of repeating the noun.
  – We can't use *one* or *ones* with non-count nouns (*coffee, bread*), so we either repeat the noun or just leave it out.
  – With double-noun phrases (*can opener, tennis balls*), we have to repeat the noun (we can't contrast *a can opener* with 'a bottle one' or *tennis balls* with 'football ones').
- Ask students to do the exercise in pairs, and then go through the answers together. Possible answers:

  a ... a smaller one?
  b ... real ones?
  c ... American (ice cream).
  d ... a chocolate one?
  e ... cold weather.
  f ... the younger ones have to stay ...
  g ... bread knife.
  h ... do a different one?

Language awareness E: regional accents

This activity is concerned with different major accents of English: United States, Australian, Scottish, Welsh, Irish, London and Northern English. The aim of the activity is to help students develop a 'feel' for different English accents.

1 Identifying accents

- ▭ Look at the maps, and identify where the places are. Then play the recording. Pause after each speaker, and quickly check that students understand what he/she is talking about. Then ask them where they think the speaker comes from. Answers:

  1 D Wales
  2 C London
  3 A Scotland (west coast)
  4 F United States (west coast)
  5 G Australia
  6 E Southern Ireland
  7 B North-west England

2 Features of accents

- ▭ Play the recording of each speaker reading the sentence. Pause after each speaker and ask students what they noticed about the way the person spoke. Bring out some of these typical features:

Welsh: Intonation: even pitch throughout sentences. Pure vowels instead of diphthongs: *eight, phone, hello.* /æ/ in *answer, last.* Aspirated /t/ in *almost, hesitated, it.* Clear /l/ in *almost, hall.*

London: Glottal stop instead of /t/ in *eight, it, Peter.* /h/ dropped in *hesitated, hello.* /aʊ/ in *phone, hello.* /aɪ/ in *eight, hesitated.*

Scottish: /r/ pronounced at front of mouth, rolled slightly. Pure vowels, not diphthongs: *eight, phone, hesitated.* /ɑ/ sound in *rang, happened.* /uː/ in *you.*

United States: /r/ rolled. /ɑː/ in *o'clock.* /d/ rather than /t/ in *eight o'clock, hesitated, Peter.* /æː/ in *answer, last.*

Australian: Close /æ/ (almost /e/) in *rang, answer, happened.* /d/ rather than /t/ in *eight o'clock, hesitated, Peter.* /aɪ/ in *eight, hesitated.* /aʊ/ in *phone, moment, hello.* /ə/ sound at end of *hesitated* and *answer it.*

Southern Irish: Rolled /r/. Lilting ('sing-song') intonation. /ɑː/ in *o'clock.* /ɔɪ/ in *I, decided.* Stress on third syllable of *hesitated.* /æ/ in *answer, last.*

Northern English: Long pure vowels instead of diphthongs: *eight, phone, moment.* /h/ dropped in *hesitated.* Short /æ/ in *answer, last.*

3 Extension

- Ask students to tell you occasions where they've heard these or other accents, and whether they had difficulty in understanding them.

> ▭ The tapescript is on page 111.

Pronunciation E: low key

This activity deals with two common occasions when we make a step down in pitch: to mark the end of a section of speech, and to indicate a piece of extra information.

1 Presentation

- ▭ Play the recording, and use it to establish that
  - the speaker's voice *goes down* on the word *Two*. This indicates that this is the *end of a section* of speech: now she will go on to something different.
  - the speaker's voice *goes up* on the word *third*. This is to announce *a new section*, and *contrast* it with the last one (the same use as in Pronunciation D).
- If you like, get students to practise saying the remark with a 'step down' and a 'step up'.

2 Listening & practice

- ▭ Play the recording, which consists of four separate stretches of speech. Ask students to identify where the speaker's voice goes down and where it goes up. Answers:

  1 down on *Moscow*; up on *Delhi*
  2 down on *talk*; up on *next*
  3 down on *Freud* (and staying down on *thought about it*); up on *Jung*
  4 down on *thirty* (and staying down on *people*); up on *food*

- Students practise saying the remarks.

3 Presentation

- ▭ Play the recording and discuss how the extra information is marked out. Establish that it is partly by pausing, but mainly by a *change in level*: the voice drops and gives the extra information at a *lower pitch* than the rest. (This enables the speaker to mark out extra information without making significant pauses.)

4 Prediction task & listening

- Pairwork. Students decide which parts are extra information, and mark them with brackets.
- ▭ Play the conversations, checking answers as you go. Ask students to try saying the remarks, stepping down on the extra information. Answers:

  1 (who's a doctor)
  2 (a friend of mine)
  3 (entitled 'Falling Leaves')

Self-study Workbook

Study Skills E: Developing a piece of writing *See notes on page 129.*

Language awareness: regional accents

1 ▣ You will hear seven people talking about their childhood. Where do you think they come from? Match them with the places shown below.

2 ▣ You will hear the same speakers reading this extract from a novel. What features of the accent do you notice?

It was almost eight o'clock when the phone rang in the hall. I hesitated for a moment, then decided to answer it. 'Hello' said a voice. 'It's Peter. What happened to you last night?'

3 Can you think of other examples of these regional accents that you've heard before (e.g. elsewhere in this book, on television, people you've met)?

Pronunciation: low key

1 ▣ Listen to the recording, and notice how the speaker says the underlined words. Where does her voice *go down*, and where does it *go up*?

... Right, so that's the answer to Question Two. Now the third question you'll probably find a bit easier ...

2 ▣ Listen to these stretches of speech. Underline the words where the speaker's voice goes down, and where it goes up.

1 ... and that's how we eventually got to Moscow. Getting to Delhi wasn't nearly so exciting ...

2 ... I'd like to thank Dr James for coming to talk to us. Our next speaker is from the University of Oxford ...

3 ... So that was really what Freud thought about it. Now Jung's ideas about dreams were quite different ...

4 ... so we're expecting about thirty people. As for the food, that's being taken care of by my brother-in-law ...

Now try saying the remarks yourself, making 'steps up' and 'steps down' on the underlined words.

3 In writing, we can mark out extra information by using commas or brackets.

Examples:

Mr Brown, the managing director, has asked me to contact you.
I've got an elder brother (who lives in Canada) and two younger sisters.

▣ Listen to the recording. How do we mark out extra information when we speak?

4 Which parts of these remarks do you think are 'extra information'? Put brackets round them, and then try saying each remark.

1 ... my sister who's a doctor is a neighbour of yours ...

2 ... and so I went to see Marco a friend of mine about the problem ...

3 ... her fourth book entitled 'Falling Leaves' was probably her most popular...

▣ Now listen and see if you were right. Then practise saying the remarks again.

1 Was justice done?

> should(n't) have done /been + -ing

82-year-old man who shot burglar must pay him £4000

AN 82-YEAR-OLD MAN who shot a burglar who was trying to break into his allotment shed was ordered to pay him £4000 damages yesterday. Ted Newbery had been sleeping in the shed to try to stop vandals destroying his allotment. He fired through a hole in the door when he heard voices outside. Mark Revill, 28, was hit in the chest and arm by 50 shotgun pellets as he and another man tried to smash their way into the shed. They had gone there to steal, knowing that the pensioner had a television set and a washing machine in the shed.

Mr Newbery had slept in the shed every night for four years because of vandalism,

the court was told by the defence. That night, he heard a loud banging on the door, and a voice saying 'If the old man's in there, we'll do him.' He was absolutely terrified, and fired the gun in self-defence. As a result of the incident, Mr Revill lost two fingers, and has partially lost the use of one arm.

Mr Justice Rougier ruled that Mr Newbery had acted out of all proportion to the threat. He had not acted in panic, but had planned his response in advance, and it had been reckless to shoot the shotgun through a hole in the door, while not being able to see what he was shooting at.

Mr Justice Rougier award-

ed Revill £4000 for his injuries and loss of earnings.

The judgment caused an immediate public outcry. Tim Molloney, the Mayor of Erewash, launched an appeal to raise money to pay Mr Newbery's bill, and started the fund with a contribution of £100. Since then, money has been pouring in from all

over the country. A London restaurateur was one of the dozens to call *The Times* to express his anger over the affair. Husseyin Ozer, 42, said he would sell his Rolex watch to pay the award. 'I am outraged. The old saying that an Englishman's home is his castle does not seem to be true any more,' he said.

---

1 **Read the newspaper story. Which of the opinions below do you agree with? Give each a score from 0 (= strongly disagree) to 5 (= strongly agree).**

 A Mr Newbery was right to try to defend himself, but he should have fired a warning shot, or shouted a warning first.

 B Mr Newbery had no right to shoot Mr Revill, even in self-defence. He should have been sent to prison for what he did.

 C As the police weren't protecting Mr Newbery, he had no choice but to try to protect himself.

 D It was Mr Revill's own fault if he was injured – he shouldn't have been trying to break in.

 E The Mayor of Erewash was quite right to start a fund to help Mr Newbery.

 F The whole thing's crazy. Mr Revill should have been ordered to pay Mr Newbery £4000, not the other way around.

2 **Read the article** *Yes, justice was done* **on page 101, and answer the questions.**

 Now look at the six opinions again. Have you changed you mind about any of them since reading the article?

This unit is concerned with language for commenting on past actions and saying whether or not they were right. It focuses on three modal verb areas:
– *should/shouldn't have done* and *should/shouldn't have been doing*
– *needn't have done* and *could have done*
– *might have done*.

The fourth activity develops writing skills, and deals with language for contrasting ideas and balancing an argument.

1 Was justice done?

This exercise is based on a real newspaper story about a man who took the law into his own hands to defend his property against thieves, and leads to a discussion of whether he was right or wrong. It introduces the structures should/shouldn't have -ed *and* should/shouldn't have been -ing, *and also other expressions for talking about right and wrong (e.g.* have a right to, be to blame for, his own fault).

➤ Focus on Form: Exercise 1
➤ Workbook: Exercise A

Language note
An *allotment* is a small piece of land which you can rent in a town for growing vegetables. Usually each allotment has a *shed* for keeping tools, chairs, etc.

1 Reading, discussion & presentation

● Before students read the text, write these key words on the board and establish what they mean:

allotment	*shotgun*
shed	*reckless*
vandals	*a public outcry*
pensioner	*launch an appeal*

Optional pre-reading task
Using the words on the board and the headline of the article, ask students to guess what the story will be about.

● Give time for students to read the text. Then establish the main points by asking questions, e.g. *What did Ted Newbery do in his shed? Why? Why did he have a shotgun? What did he do with it? Why did the judge say he'd been 'reckless'? What did the public think about it? What did they do?*

● Use examples from the text to show how we use *should(n't) have -ed* and *should(n't) have been -ing*:

> He <u>fired</u> at them
> He <u>shouldn't have fired</u> at them
>
> They <u>were trying</u> to break in
> They <u>shouldn't have been trying</u> to break in

Practice option
Give simple examples using the past simple and continuous, and ask students to make sentences using *should/shouldn't*, e.g.

You didn't tell me.
→ You should have told me.

They were playing in the road.
→ They shouldn't have been playing in the road.

● In pairs or groups, students read through the opinions and give each one a score from 0 to 5.

● Discuss the opinions together, and build up a 'class score' on the board.

2 Reading & discussion

● Give time for students to read the text on page 101. Then discuss the questions under the text. Possible answers:

1 People can't be allowed to shoot anyone who steals from their property. It isn't a fair comparison: Mr Revill intended to damage Mr Newbery's property, and also to attack him.
2 He took the law into his own hands.
3 *Similar:* The owner shot without warning.
   Different: The Scotsman was completely innocent; he was killed; the owner wasn't put on trial.
4 They increase violent crime.

Presentation option
Write these expressions on the board:

> He was right/wrong to...
> He had no right to...
> It was his own fault that...
> He was to blame for...

If necessary, give other examples to show what they mean.

● Look again at the statements in 1, and ask students if their opinion has changed. Discuss whether they think the article on page 101 is right or not.

Pair- or groupwork option
Divide students into pairs or groups again to discuss this. Then have a round-up with the whole class.

2 Mistakes

This exercise introduces the structures could have *and* needn't have, *and gives further practice of* should(n't) have. *Students look at situations in which people made mistakes, and then talk about a similar incident from their own experience.*

➤ Focus on Form: Exercise 2
➤ Workbook: Exercise B, Listening

1 Presentation

- Look at the first situation. Establish that:
  – *needn't have … could have* fits the meaning better, because it means 'it was unnecessary to dress up' (he spent a long time dressing up, and no one else did)
  – *shouldn't have … should have* would mean ' I was wrong to dress up' (i.e. something bad resulted from it, e.g. he missed his train).
- Ask students to suggest endings for the other two stories. Possible answers:

  We shouldn't have parked at a bus stop. We should have used the car park.
  I needn't have climbed all those stairs. I could have used the lift.

Practice option
Elicit other examples of these structures, e.g.
I changed $100 at the border, but then I didn't spend any of it.
→ I needn't have changed the money. I could have kept it in dollars.

2 Writing & speaking activity

- Working alone, students think of a time they (or someone they know) made a mistake. They write a sentence using one of the structures in the box.
- Students sit in groups. In turn, they tell the other students their story, including the sentence they have written.
- As a round-up, ask each group to tell their most interesting story to the rest of the class.

3 Speaking your mind

This exercise introduces common expressions with might have done, could have done *and* needn't have done *in conversational English. Students look at remarks in isolation, and then hear them in context.*

➤ Focus on Form: Exercise 3
➤ Workbook: Exercise B

1 Presentation & listening

- Look at the remarks and ask students to suggest situations in which they might hear them.
- 🔲 Play the recording, in which students hear the remarks in context. Pause after each section and establish what happened and what the remark meant. Possible answers:

  1 A and B were expecting guests. A forgot to tell B that the guests had cancelled the visit. (*You could have told me* = Why didn't you tell me?)
  2 Parent to a child who has just run out into a road. (*You could have been knocked over* = You were lucky not to be run over)
  3 A and B were invited to dinner, but the hosts served frozen pizza. (*We might as well have stayed at home* = it wasn't worth going out)
  4 A and B are tidying their flat, clearing up, etc. before going out or expecting visitors. A left B to do all the work. (*You might have offered …* = Why didn't you offer…?)
  5 Someone watching/listening to football results. (*I might have known* = I expected it)
  6 A and B have been talking to some boring people. B was rude to them, and A was embarrassed. (*You needn't have been …* = It wasn't necessary)
  7 Someone is being given a present (probably flowers). (*You needn't have bothered* = It wasn't necessary)

Note on title
Speaking your mind is an idiom that means 'saying what you really think'.

🔲 The tapescript is on page 111.

Language note
Might/could have done is used here in three different senses:
1 as a less direct way of saying *should have done* (*You could have told me, You might have offered …*)
2 to say that it wasn't worth doing something (*We might just as well have stayed at home*)
3 to imagine something that didn't in fact happen (*You could have been run over*).

2 Speaking activity

- Ask students to suggest suitable remarks for the situations. Possible answers:
  – You could have been mugged. You might have been attacked.
  – You could have told me you'd be late. You might have phoned me.
  – You needn't have slapped him. You could have just told him not to do it.
  – You might have remembered to send me a card.
  – You could have told me you didn't like fish. I might just as well not have bothered to cook anything. I might as well have given you a sandwich.

2 Mistakes

could/needn't/should(n't) have done

1 Here is the end of a story. Choose the structures
that you think fit the meaning best.

> … Of course, as soon as I went in the room, I realised that I
> *needn't/shouldn't* have spent all that time dressing up in a dinner
> jacket. I *could/should* have just worn jeans, like everyone else.

Now look at these other two stories.
How do you think they end?

> … and there was a police truck
> towing away our car. It was our
> own fault, of course. We …

> … It was only when I
> finally staggered up to
> the ninth floor that I
> realised that 'Aufzug'
> means 'lift'. So it
> turned out that I …

2 Think of a time when something similar happened to you, and
write a sentence about it using one of the structures in the box.

Tell another student what happened.
Include your sentence in what you say.

could have	should have
needn't have	shouldn't have

3 Speaking your mind

couldn't /needn't /might have done

1 Look at each of these remarks. What can you tell about the speaker and the situation?

1 You could have told
me earlier.

2 You could have been
knocked over.

3 We might just as well
have stayed at home.

4 You might have offered
to lend a hand.

5 Huh! I might have
known!

6 You needn't have
been quite so rude.

7 You needn't have
bothered.

Now listen to the remarks in context. Were you right?

2 Think of things you might say to
– someone who's been walking around the streets alone late at night
– someone who's just arrived at your house three hours late
– someone who's just slapped a child
– someone who's forgotten your birthday
– someone who hasn't eaten a meal you've cooked.

4 Points of view

1 Look at paragraphs A–D. What do they have in common, and how are they different? What expressions do they use to contrast the two different points of view?

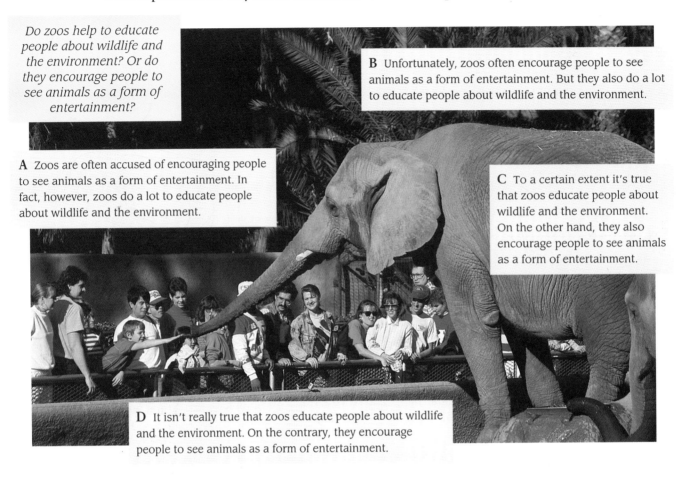

Do zoos help to educate people about wildlife and the environment? Or do they encourage people to see animals as a form of entertainment?

B Unfortunately, zoos often encourage people to see animals as a form of entertainment. But they also do a lot to educate people about wildlife and the environment.

A Zoos are often accused of encouraging people to see animals as a form of entertainment. In fact, however, zoos do a lot to educate people about wildlife and the environment.

C To a certain extent it's true that zoos educate people about wildlife and the environment. On the other hand, they also encourage people to see animals as a form of entertainment.

D It isn't really true that zoos educate people about wildlife and the environment. On the contrary, they encourage people to see animals as a form of entertainment.

2 Choose one of these opinions. What arguments are there for and against it? Make some notes.

> Sending criminals to prison is a complete waste of time.

> Women and men now have equal opportunities in society.

> Doing military service makes young people into better citizens.

Develop your notes into a short paragraph (two or three sentences) that represents your own point of view. Use the expressions in Part 1 to help you.

3 Here is a longer version of paragraph C in Part 1. Notice how examples and further comments have been added to it.

> To a certain extent it's true that zoos educate people about wildlife and the environment – or at least they try to. It's common in zoos nowadays to find information about where the animals live in the wild and how they behave, or about how different animals depend on each other for survival.
>
> On the other hand, they also encourage people to see animals as a form of entertainment. You can see this in any monkey house: usually, people go there not to learn about how monkeys behave, but because they find their behaviour amusing. In fact, many species of monkey are in serious danger because of what human beings are doing to them, and this is really a reason to be angry, not to laugh.

Expand your own paragraph in a similar way.

4 Points of view

Writing skills: *balancing different points of view; developing an argument.*
Language focus: *expressions used for contrasting ideas.*

This activity helps students to develop an argument in writing. It follows these stages:
1 *Presentation. Students compare different paragraphs about the same topic.*
2 *Paragraph writing. Students make notes and develop them into a short paragraph.*
3 *Extended writing. Students expand their paragraph into a longer piece of writing.*

➤ Workbook: Exercise C

1 Presentation

● Look at the paragraphs and discuss what they have in common. Answer:

They contrast two opposing ideas: the idea that zoos educate people, and the idea that zoos encourage people to see animals as entertainment.

● Discuss how the paragraphs are different. Answer:

A strongly emphasises the idea that zoos educate people.
D strongly emphasises the idea that zoos encourage people to see animals as entertainment.
B and C both balance the two ideas, saying they are both true.

● Focus on the range of expressions used to contrast the two ideas, and build them up on the board:

Mild:	Unfortunately, ... But also ...
↑	To a certain extent it's true that ... On the other hand ...
↓	Zoos are often accused of ... In fact, however, ...
Strong:	It isn't really true that ... On the contrary, ...

Optional lead-in
Brainstorm arguments for and against keeping animals in zoos, and write ideas on the board.

Note
Other expressions for contrasting ideas are given in the Reference Section, page 123.

2 Paragraph writing

● Students choose the topic that interests them most, and make brief notes of arguments for and against. They can do this working alone, or they can form groups with other students who have chosen the same topic.
● Students develop their notes into short paragraphs.

Whole class option
Choose one of the topics with the class. Then brainstorm arguments for and against, and build them up on the board. Students use this as the basis for writing their paragraphs.

3 Extended writing

● Look at the text and discuss how paragraph C has been expanded. Bring out these points:
  – The writer has added *particular examples* to illustrate the points (e.g. information in zoos, monkey houses).
  – The writer has *modified* the first argument by adding 'or at least they try to'.
  – The writer has developed the second argument, to lead to a *conclusion* (that animals are in danger, so we should be angry).
● Students expand what they have written into at least two paragraphs, presenting two opposing points of view and developing them.
● As a round-up, ask a few students to read out what they have written.

Groupwork option
Students sit with other people who chose the same topic. In turn, they read out what they have written.

Homework option
Students make notes in class, but write the paragraphs for homework.

Focus on Form

1 Forms of 'should'

should/shouldn't + infinitive forms

- If necessary, look again at Grammar Study A, Exercise 5 (page 16), and review the various infinitive forms that can come after *should/shouldn't*.
- Look at the example, then ask students to do the exercise in pairs.
- Go through the answers together. Answers:

  a She shouldn't have taken the car without asking.
  b There should be a name-plate on the door.
  c You should have been wearing a crash helmet.
  d They shouldn't have pulled down that lovely old house.
  e Those children shouldn't be playing in the road.
  f This mistake should have been noticed before.
  g They should have been wearing gloves.

2 Needn't, couldn't & should(n't)

needn't have done, could have done, should(n't) have done

- Do the exercise round the class or in pairs. Possible answers:

  B He needn't have got to the airport so early. He could have arrived later. He should have arrived an hour before his flight.
  C He should have sat in his own seat. He should have looked at his boarding pass to see which was his seat.
  D He shouldn't have used his mobile phone during take-off. He should have made his phone call before he got on the plane.
  E He needn't have brought his own food.
  F He shouldn't have smoked in the toilet.
  G He should have kept his table up. He should have written his postcards earlier.
  H He needn't have taken a taxi. He could have taken the airport bus.

3 Could have & might have

could have , might have, might as well have

- Look at the first sentence in Box A, and ask students to find a suitable continuation in Box B. Answer:

  g We might as well have stayed at home and watched TV.

- Students do the rest of the exercise, either writing their answers or working in pairs.
- Go through the answers together. Answers:

  2 e You could/might have told me you'd be late.
  3 a You could/might have drowned.
  4 f We might as well have walked.
  5 b You could/might have been struck by lightning.
  6 c I might have known he'd turn up late.
  7 d You could/might have sent me a postcard.

Self-study Workbook

Exercise A: They were all to blame
Forms of *should/shouldn't*. Students read short news stories and write sentences saying what was wrong.

Exercise B: Could, should, needn't and might
Could have, should have, needn't have, might have.
Students rewrite sentences.

Exercise C: Contrasting ideas
Students expand contrasting pairs of opinions into paragraphs.

Idioms: All in the mind
Common idioms connected with understanding and misunderstanding (e.g. *bark up the wrong tree*).

Listening: Mistakes
Two people talk about embarrassing mistakes. Students predict answers to questions, then listen to check.

Common verbs: put
Common uses of the verb *put*, including phrasal verbs.

Focus on Form

1 Forms of 'should'

Rewrite these remarks using an appropriate form of *should*.

Example:

What's he doing sitting in my chair?
Answer: *He shouldn't be sitting in my chair.*

a She had no right to take the car without asking.
b Why isn't there a name-plate on the door?
c I can't understand why you weren't wearing a crash helmet.
d It was a mistake to pull down that lovely old house.
e It seems wrong for those children to be playing in the road.
f Why wasn't this mistake noticed before?
g It's their own fault: they weren't wearing gloves, were they?

2 Needn't, couldn't & should(n't)

Look at the comic strip below. Talk about the mistakes the man made, using *needn't*, *couldn't*, *should* and *shouldn't*.

Example:

He needn't have bought his whisky and cigarettes at a supermarket. He could have got them in the duty free shop.

3 Could have & might have

Match the remarks in Box A with the most suitable continuations in Box B. Fill the gaps in the continuations with *could have*, *might have* or *might as well have*.

Box A

1 I don't know why we bothered to see that film.
2 I thought you'd lost your way.
3 Didn't you see the red flag flying?
4 It wasn't really worth taking a taxi.
5 You shouldn't have sheltered under a tree.
6 That's just typical of him.
7 I didn't know you'd been on holiday.

Box B

a You .... drowned.
b You .... been struck by lightning.
c I .... known he'd turn up late.
d You .... sent me a postcard.
e You .... told me you'd be late.
f We .... walked.
g We .... stayed at home and watched TV.

When my uncle flew to Spain last year, he'd never been on a plane before, and he got quite a few things wrong …

A He went to the supermarket and bought whisky and cigarettes.

B He got to the airport five hours before his flight took off.

C When he got on board, he sat in the first empty seat he saw.

D As they were taking off, he made a call on his mobile phone.

E Then he ate the sandwiches he'd brought for the journey.

F After lunch, he went to the toilet and had a cigarette.

G As they were landing, he pulled down his table and started to write postcards.

H At the airport, he paid a fortune for a taxi to the city centre.

14 Body and mind

1 Small but deadly

DANGER OF CHOLERA IN REFUGEE CAMPS, WARNS UN

Teenagers say Aids is their biggest fear

Britain to keep rabies law

Tourists warned after malaria death

1 Look at these newspaper headlines. Imagine what the articles that go with them might say. Which pictures go with which headlines? What's the connection?

2 Work in groups. Choose one of the diseases. Discuss what you know about it and what you think you know. Try to answer these questions.

   a How widespread is the disease?
   b What causes it and how is it transmitted?
   c What are the symptoms?
   d How can you avoid catching it?
   e Is it curable?

Now check your answers in the back of the book. Use a dictionary to help you.

Did you find out anything that you didn't know before? Tell the rest of the class about it.

This unit is about health, illness and medicine. It focuses on the following areas:
– language for talking about diseases and symptoms (e.g. *infectious*, *cure*, *temperature*)
– language for talking about medical treatment (e.g. *operation*, *vaccinate*, *x-ray*)
– alternative forms of medicine (e.g. *traditional medicine*, *homeopathy*).

The Reading and Listening activity is based on the sleepwalking scene from Shakespeare's *Macbeth*.

1 Small but deadly

This exercise is about four of the world's most serious diseases: malaria, cholera, Aids and rabies. Students brainstorm how much they know, and then read information about the diseases.

➤ Workbook: Exercise A

1 Introduction

- Ask students to match the headlines with the pictures, and say what the connection between them is. Possible answers:

    A Rabies. You can catch rabies from being bitten by a dog or a wild animal.
    B Malaria. You can catch malaria from being bitten by a mosquito.
    C Aids. You can catch Aids from having casual sex.
    D Cholera. You can catch cholera from drinking dirty water.

- Discuss briefly what the articles might be about, e.g.
    – People in refugee camps are living in unhygienic conditions (over-crowded, dirty water, no proper toilets, etc.), so there is danger of cholera.
    – A survey of teenagers' attitudes (perhaps about sex, or perhaps about risks in their lives).
    – You are not allowed to bring live animals into Britain, because of the danger of rabies.
    – Someone has died of malaria in a tropical country where tourists go (e.g. Kenya, Thailand).

2 Discussion, reading & presentation

- Groupwork. Each group chooses one of the diseases (whichever they find most interesting). They discuss what they know about it and make notes in answer to the questions (even if they are not sure of the answers).

- Each group turns to the back of the book and reads about the disease they discussed (Aids p. 98, malaria p. 101, cholera and rabies p. 102).

- If groups chose different diseases, ask each group to report back what they found out. If groups chose the same disease, simply ask each group what they found out that was different from what they thought before.

- Focus on the language contained in the texts that is important for talking about diseases, and write key expressions on the board:

catch (malaria)	an outbreak (of cholera)
infectious	a (cholera) epidemic
to cure a disease	symptoms
curable	treatment
incurable	

> **Whole class option**
> Choose one of the diseases, and elicit information from the whole class, building up notes on the board. Then divide the class into groups to talk about the other three diseases.

2 Medical treatment

This exercise introduces words and expressions for talking about medical treatment. Students listen to seven short scenes and identify what is happening, using the presented language to talk about them.

➤ Workbook: Exercise B

1 Listening & presentation

- 🔲 Play the recording, pausing after each scene. Ask students to explain what is happening. Get them to use words from the box to do this, and focus on the way the words are used. Possible answers:
  1 A doctor or nurse is *giving* someone a *vaccination* (e.g. against cholera).
  2 Someone is *having an X-ray*.
  3 A dentist is *examining* someone's teeth. She finds that one of the teeth needs *a filling*.
  4 A child has cut his knee, hand, etc. A parent is *putting a plaster on it*.
  5 A *surgeon* is *performing an operation* on someone's heart.
  6 A doctor is *prescribing medicine* for a patient.
  7 Someone is *taking* a child's *temperature*, by putting a *thermometer* in his/her mouth.

🔲 The tapescript is on page 111.

Presentation option
Show these pairs of verbs and nouns on the board:

examine	examination
operate	operation
prescribe	prescription
vaccinate	vaccination
inoculate	inoculation

2 Speaking activity

- To introduce this part of the activity, tell the class about an experience you have had (or which you know about) which you were reminded of by one of the scenes in the recording (e.g. a visit to a dentist, an occasion when a doctor prescribed the wrong medicine, a time when you injured yourself, a film you saw showing an operation).
- Give students a few moments to think of an experience, making brief notes if they wish.
- Groupwork. In turn, students tell their experience to the others in the group.
- As a round-up, ask each group to tell their most interesting experience to the rest of the class.

3 Alternative medicine

This is a freer listening and discussion activity, in which students consider the relative advantages of conventional and alternative medicine.

➤ Workbook: Exercise C, Listening

1 Listening & discussion

- 🔲 Play the recording, pausing from time to time if necessary. Then discuss the first three questions. Possible answers:
  – *'Western' method of treatment:* an injection at the hospital to relieve the pain. Result: the patient could walk after two or three days.
  – *Traditional method of treatment:* give the patient a special drink, then chant and 'move' the poison out of the patient's body with the fingers. Result: the patient was cured immediately.

- Discuss what the speaker seems to think about what he saw (he seems very impressed, though he can't explain it). Then ask students what they think about it and whether they think there is any explanation for it.

Optional lead-in
Find out how much students know about scorpions (e.g. where you find them, how you get stung by them, why they are dangerous). Ask them what they would do if they were stung by a scorpion.

🔲 The tapescript is on page 111.

2 Speaking activity

- Look at the forms of alternative medicine in the list, and check that students know what they are and roughly what they involve:
  – *folk medicine:* treatment with traditional herbs, etc.
  – *acupuncture:* treatment by sticking needles in certain parts of the body
  – *homeopathy:* treatment with very small quantities of a drug that would produce similar symptoms (see Workbook Exercise C)
  – *hypnotherapy:* treatment by hypnotising the patient
  – *faith healing:* treatment by faith (often the healer touches the patient).

- Ask students if they know anyone who has used them, and/or whether they themselves would use them. Encourage students to tell stories that they know, and also to discuss what they think of these forms of medicine.

Groupwork option
Students work in groups. Each group chooses one of the forms of treatment to discuss. They then report back to the rest of the class, and see if other people agree with their conclusions.

2 Medical treatment

1 🔲 You will hear seven short scenes. Listen and say what is happening in each one. Use the words in the box.

examine	surgeon
filling	temperature
operation	thermometer
plaster	vaccination
prescribe	x-ray

2 Do any of the scenes you heard remind you of a similar experience of your own? Tell other students about it.

3 Alternative medicine

1 🔲 You will hear a story about two different methods of treating a scorpion sting. Listen and answer the questions.

a What was the 'Western' method of treatment?
b What was the traditional method of treatment?
c What was the result of each form of treatment?

What does the speaker seem to think about what he saw?

What do you think about it?
Can you think of an explanation for what happened?

2 Do you know anyone who has used any of the treatments below? What were they treated for?

– traditional folk medicine   – hypnotherapy
– acupuncture   – faith healing
– homeopathy

Would you consider using any of these treatments as an alternative to going to the doctor? Why / Why not?

4 All the perfumes of Arabia

READING

Have you ever seen or read Shakespeare's *Macbeth*?

yes   *no*

What do you know about the characters in the box? How do they fit into the story?	Read the synopsis of the play on page 103.
Now check your answers on page 103.	What have you learned about the characters in the box?

Macbeth	the three witches	King Duncan	Macduff
Banquo	Lady Macbeth	Duncan's sons	

READING AND LISTENING

You will read and hear the sleepwalking scene from *Macbeth*.

PART 1: LINES 1–31

Read lines 1–31. How many of these questions can you answer?

a Where is Macbeth?
b According to the gentlewoman, what does Lady Macbeth do at night?
c Why won't the gentlewoman reveal what Lady Macbeth says?
d What is she doing with her hands?

🔊 Now listen to a modern English version of these lines. Are your answers still the same?

PART 2: LINES 32–68

Read lines 32–68. Use the notes under the text to help you understand it, but do not try to understand every word.

🔊 Now listen to the same lines being performed by Shakespearean actors, and answer the questions.

a How would you describe what's wrong with Lady Macbeth?
b During this part of the scene, Lady Macbeth relives some of the things that happened earlier in the play. Can you identify some of them? Use the synopsis to help you.

PART 3: LINES 69–80

🔊 Listen to the last lines of the scene, and follow them on the page.
What does the doctor seem to be saying, and how does he seem to feel?

4 All the perfumes of Arabia

This combined Reading and Listening activity consists of the sleepwalking scene from Shakespeare's Macbeth. *Students read the scene with notes to help them, and listen both to a modern English 'translation' and to an authentic performance of the scene. The aim of this activity is to help students understand and appreciate Shakespeare in English.*

Reading skills: *reading for general idea; understanding Shakespearean English.*
Listening skills: *listening to dramatic dialogue.*

Note on title
The title is taken from lines 50–51 of the scene from *Macbeth*: 'All the perfumes of Arabia will not sweeten this little hand'.

Reading

- Before you start the activity, find out how familiar students are with Shakespeare's *Macbeth*. Do this by a show of hands (e.g. *How many of you have seen* Macbeth *in translation? Who knows roughly what the story is about?*).

  If most students know something about the story of *Macbeth*, follow the choice shown by the 'Yes' arrow: elicit information about each of the characters, then ask students to read the synopsis.

  If most students are unfamiliar with *Macbeth*, follow the choice shown by the 'No' arrow: give time for students to read the synopsis, then check comprehension by eliciting information about the characters.

- Establish these basic facts:

  Macbeth: He murders Duncan (King of Scotland) and becomes King in his place.
  Banquo: A Scottish general. Macbeth has him killed, and he then appears as a ghost at Macbeth's banquet.
  The three witches: They tell Macbeth he will become King of Scotland.
  Lady Macbeth: She persuades Macbeth to murder King Duncan, and helps him do it. Later, she is tormented by guilt and kills herself.
  King Duncan: King of Scotland. He is murdered by Macbeth while he is a guest at his castle.
  Duncan's sons: When Duncan is murdered, they escape. The elder son (Malcolm) returns to fight Macbeth, and at the end of the play he becomes King of Scotland.
  Macduff: Macbeth kills his family. Macduff joins Malcolm in raising an army against Macbeth, and kills him.

Homework preparation option
Ask students to read the synopsis at home before the lesson. Then begin the lesson by checking basic facts about the characters.

Reading & listening

Part 1: lines 1–31

- Either let students read lines 1–31, or read this part aloud and ask students to follow. They should not try to understand every word, but just try to get a general idea of what the two characters are talking about.

- See how many of the questions students can answer. If they can't answer a question, move on to the next one – do not give the answers at this point.

- ▭ Play Part 1 of the recording, which is a modern English 'translation' of the same lines. Then check the answers to the questions. Answers:

  a He's away fighting a war ('gone into the field').
  b She gets out of bed and writes letters in her sleep.
  c Because she hasn't got a witness to confirm that what she says is true.
  d She's rubbing them together, as if she's washing them.

▭ The tapescript is on page 112.

Part 2: lines 32–68

- Students read lines 32–68, using the notes to help them. Again they should read to get the general idea, rather than try to understand every word.

- ▭ Play Part 2 of the recording, which is from a performance of the play by the BBC. Then discuss the questions. Establish these points:

  a – She's tormented by guilt and imagines that she still has blood on her hands.
  b – Murdering Duncan (*'tis time to do it*; *who would have thought the old man to have had so much blood in him? Here's the smell of the blood still*)
     – Encouraging Macbeth to murder Duncan (*Fie, my lord, fie! A soldier and afeard?*)
     – Macduff arriving to collect Duncan (*There's knocking at the gate*)
     – Murdering Macduff's family (*The Thane of Fife had a wife; where is she now?*)
     – Murdering Banquo, and his ghost appearing at the banquet (*Banquo's buried, he cannot come out on's grave*)

- ⌷ Play the last part of the scene, while students follow. Establish these points from what the doctor says:

  - He has heard rumours of evil deeds and of trouble to come (*Foul whisperings are abroad, unnatural deeds do breed unnatural troubles*).
  - He thinks Lady Macbeth needs a priest, not a doctor (*More needs she the divine than the physician*).
  - He asks the gentlewoman to keep an eye on her (*Look after her, … still keep eyes upon her*).
  - He is astonished by what he has seen (*My mind she has mated and amazed my sight*).

Self-study Workbook

Exercise A: Talking about diseases
Students complete an acrostic puzzle from gapped sentences.

Exercise B: The man who was dead
A joke with gaps. Students fill the gaps with words from a box.

Exercise C: Homeopathy
A text about homeopathy. Students read and answer questions.

Idioms: Money
Common idioms connected with money (e.g. *sell something under the counter*).

Listening: The limits of medicine
A psychotherapist talks about the connection between mind and body. Students listen and match what she says with their own opinion.

Word building: Nouns and verbs (3)
Nouns ending in *-y, -ment, -ance, -ence, -al*.

Act V Scene 1

Enter a Doctor of Physic and a
Waiting-Gentlewoman

DOCTOR I have two nights watched with you, but can perceive no truth in your report. When was it she last walked?

GENTLEWOMAN Since his majesty went into the field I 5 have seen her rise from her bed, throw her nightgown upon her, unlock her closet, take forth paper, fold it, write upon't, read it, afterwards seal it, and again return to bed; yet all this while in a most fast sleep.

DOCTOR A great perturbation in nature, to receive at 10 once the benefit of sleep and do the effects of watching. In this slumbery agitation, besides her walking and other actual performances, what, at any time, have you heard her say?

GENTLEWOMAN That, sir, which I will not report after 15 her.

DOCTOR You may to me; and 'tis most meet you should.

GENTLEWOMAN Neither to you nor anyone, having no witness to confirm my speech.

Enter Lady Macbeth with a taper

20 Lo you! Here she comes. This is her very guise; and, upon my life, fast asleep. Observe her; stand close.

DOCTOR How came she by that light?

GENTLEWOMAN Why, it stood by her. She has light by her continually; 'tis her command.

25 **DOCTOR** You see her eyes are open.

GENTLEWOMAN Ay, but their sense are shut.

DOCTOR What is it she does now? Look how she rubs her hands.

GENTLEWOMAN It is an accustomed action with her to 30 seem thus washing her hands. I have known her continue in this a quarter of an hour.

LADY Yet here's a spot.

DOCTOR Hark! She speaks. I will set down what comes from her to satisfy my remembrance the more strongly.

35 **LADY** Out, damned spot! Out, I say! – One: two: why then, 'tis time to do't. – Hell is murky! – Fie, my lord, fie! A soldier and afeard? – What need we fear who knows it, when none can call our power to accompt? – Yet who would have thought the old man 40 to have had so much blood in him?

DOCTOR Do you mark that?

LADY The Thane of Fife had a wife; where is she now? – What, will these hands ne'er be clean? – No more o'that, my lord, no more o'that. You mar all with this starting. 45

DOCTOR Go to, go to: you have known what you should not.

GENTLEWOMAN She has spoke what she should not, I am sure of that. Heaven knows what she has known.

LADY Here's the smell of the blood still. All the 50 perfumes of Arabia will not sweeten this little hand. Oh! Oh! Oh!

DOCTOR What a sigh is there! The heart is sorely charged.

GENTLEWOMAN I would not have such a heart in my 55 bosom for the dignity of the whole body.

DOCTOR Well, well, well.

GENTLEWOMAN Pray God it be, sir.

DOCTOR This disease is beyond my practice; yet I have known those which have walked in their sleep who 60 have died holily in their beds.

LADY Wash your hands; put on your nightgown; look not so pale. I tell you yet again, Banquo's buried; he cannot come out on's grave.

DOCTOR Even so? 65

LADY To bed, to bed! There's knocking at the gate. Come, come, come, come, give me your hand. What's done cannot be undone. To bed, to bed, to bed.

Exit

DOCTOR Will she go now to bed?

GENTLEWOMAN Directly. 70

DOCTOR Foul whisperings are abroad, unnatural deeds Do breed unnatural troubles; infected minds To their deaf pillows will discharge their secrets. More needs she the divine than the physician. God, God forgive us all! Look after her, 75 Remove from her the means of all annoyance And still keep eyes upon her. So, good night. My mind she has mated, and amazed my sight. I think, but dare not speak.

GENTLEWOMAN Good night, good doctor. 80

Notes on lines 32–68

33 *set down* write down
34 *satisfy my remembrance* support my memory
36 *murky* dark
36 *Fie!* Shame on you!
37 *afeard* afraid

38 *call our power to accompt* challenge our power
44 *mar all* spoil everything
45 *starting* jumping with fright
53 *sorely charged* badly troubled
59 *beyond my practice* outside my experience

Notes on lines 69–80

73 *discharge* tell
74 *divine* priest
76 *means of all annoyance* anything that might be dangerous
78 *mated* confused

F Study pages

Grammar study: degree and comparison

1 Too and enough

too	too much	too many	enough

Add an item from the box to each of these sentences, so that they make sense.

a There weren't chairs for everyone to sit down.
b Are you old to vote?
c I'm tired to go out tonight.
d I think I've had to eat.
e She didn't run fast to catch the bus.
f Don't eat sweets or you'll be ill.
g There's just coffee for three cups.
h He took the bend quickly and skidded off the road.
i You smoke.

2 So and such

Look at these examples. When do we use *so* and when do we use *such*?

A	This coffee's so strong that I can't drink it. She drove so fast that I was terrified.
B	It was such a boring speech that I fell asleep. It was such lovely weather that we ate outside.
C	I've got so much luggage that I can't carry it all. So few people came that we cancelled the meeting.

Add *so* or *such* or *such a(n)* to the following:

cold	much food	good time
cold weather	bad food	many times
noisy	little food	intelligent
noisy party	slowly	bad temper

Choose three of the items and include them in sentences of your own.

3 Two kinds of adjective

What is the difference between the adjectives in Box A and those in Box B? What else could we say instead of *very* and *absolutely*?

A		B	
(very)	tired clever hungry upset nasty hot	(absolutely)	exhausted brilliant ravenous heart-broken revolting boiling

Which group do these adjectives belong to, A or B? Can you think of their equivalent in the other group?

angry	enormous	pleased
cold	filthy	spotless
deafening	hilarious	surprised

Student A: Ask a question using a type A adjective.
Student B: Respond using a type B adjective.

Example: A Was he upset when she left?
　　　　　　B Yes. He was absolutely heart-broken.

4 Comparison

Each of these sentences contains a mistake. Can you correct them?

a She's much more taller than her brother.
b Goats aren't as stupid than sheep.
c He writes far tidier than I do.
d I'm heavier than him ten kilos.
e He's most boring person I've ever met.
f Everest is the most high mountain in the world.
g The United States isn't nearly bigger than Canada.
h It wasn't as interesting as I expected it.

5 Numerical comparison

T-shirts $15	sweatshirts $30	jumpers $45

Sweatshirts are twice as expensive as the price of T-shirts.

Jumpers are three times as expensive as the price of T-shirts.

How would these comparisons change

a if T-shirts only cost $14?
b if T-shirts cost $16?
c if you couldn't remember the exact prices?

Complete the table, then complete the comparison beside each item. If you don't know the answer, make a guess.

Adjective	Noun		
long	length	a	The Suez Canal .... the Panama Canal.
high		b	Mount Everest .... Mount Fuji.
heavy		c	A fully grown elephant .... a baby elephant.
old		d	The Great Pyramid .... the Great Wall of China.
big		e	The Pacific Ocean .... the Indian Ocean.

Grammar study F: degree and comparison

1 Too & enough

> Too, too much/many, (not) enough

- Write these examples on the board:

too difficult	(not) enough time
too slowly	(not) good enough
too much work	(not) quickly enough
too many people	

  Use them to present the basic rules for *too* and *enough*:
  – We use *too* before adjectives and adverbs, *too much/many* before nouns.
  – *enough* comes *before* nouns, but *after* adjectives and adverbs.

- Students do the exercise. Then go through the answers:
  a There weren't enough chairs for everyone to sit down.
  b Are you old enough to vote?
  c I'm too tired to go out tonight.
  d I think I've had too much to eat (*or:* enough to eat).
  e She didn't run fast enough to catch the bus.
  f Don't eat too many sweets or you'll be ill.
  g There's just enough coffee for three cups.
  h He took the bend too quickly and skidded off the road.
  i You smoke too much.

2 So & such

> So, such and such a(n)

- Look at the examples. Establish these points:
  – We use *so* before adjectives and adverbs (*so strong, so fast*).
  – We use *such* before adjective + noun (*such a boring speech, such lovely weather*).
  – We use *so* before *much, many, little, few* (*so much luggage, so few people*).

- Students add *so, such* or *such a(n)* to the phrases. Answers:

so cold	so much food	such a good time
such cold weather	such bad food	so many times
so noisy	so little food	so intelligent
such a noisy party	so slowly	such a bad temper

- Students write sentences including three of the items.
- As a round-up, ask a few students what they wrote.

3 Two kinds of adjective

> Normal and 'extreme' adjectives

- Look at the words in the two boxes and show the connection between them: *exhausted* means 'extremely tired', *brilliant* means 'extremely clever', etc.
- Make these points:
  – The words in Box A are normal adjectives. We can make them stronger or weaker by adding *very, quite, fairly, a bit, not very*, etc.
  – The adjectives in Box B already have an 'extreme' meaning. We cannot change them by adding *very, a bit, fairly*, etc. Instead, we use words like *absolutely, totally, completely* with them.

- Look at the adjectives in the list. Establish what type they are and what their equivalents in the other group would be. Build up two lists on the board:

A	B
angry	furious
cold	freezing
loud, noisy	deafening
big, large	enormous
dirty	filthy
funny, amusing	hilarious
pleased	delighted
clean	spotless
surprised	astonished, amazed

- Ask a few questions like those in the example, and get responses from the class, e.g. *Are you feeling hungry? Is it hot in here? Is your flat clean? Was your mother angry when you came home at midnight?*
- Students continue asking and answering in pairs.

4 Comparison

> Comparative and superlative structures

- Students rewrite the sentences, correcting the mistakes.
- Go through the answers together. Answers:
  a She's much taller than her brother.
  b Goats aren't as stupid as sheep.
  c He writes far more tidily than I do.
  d I'm ten kilos heavier than him (*or* ... than he is).
  e He's the most boring person I've ever met.
  f Everest is the highest mountain in the world.
  g The United States isn't nearly as big as Canada.
  h It wasn't as interesting as I expected (*or* ... expected it to be).

5 Numerical comparison

> Comparisons with dimensions, prices, etc.

- Look at the examples, and ask students to make sentences to fit the other prices. Possible answers:
  a Sweatshirts are *more than* twice the price of T-shirts. Jumpers are *over* three times as expensive as T-shirts.
  b Sweatshirts are *nearly* twice the price of T-shirts. Jumpers are *almost* three times as expensive as T-shirts.
  c Sweatshirts are *about* twice the price of T-shirts. Jumpers are *approximately* three times as expensive as T-shirts.

- Ask students to complete the table. Answers:
  width, height, weight, age, size

  If you like, elicit other similar pairs, e.g. *deep/depth, wide/width, strong/strength*.

- Students guess how the sentences should be completed. Then tell them the answers:
  a The Suez Canal is twice as long as / twice the length of the Panama Canal (165 km, 82 km).
  b Mount Fuji is about three times as high as / three times the height of Mount Vesuvius (3780 m, 1280 m).
  c A fully grown African elephant is about 50 times as heavy / 50 times the weight of a baby elephant (5000 kg, 110 kg).
  d The Great Pyramid is nearly six times as old as / six times the age of the Kremlin (4600 years, 800 years).
  e The Pacific Ocean is twice as big as / twice the size of the Atlantic Ocean (166 million km^2, 82 million km^2).

Language awareness F: formal and informal styles

This activity is concerned with the differences between formal and informal styles of English. It focuses particularly on the use of phrasal verbs in informal English and abstract nouns in more formal English.

1 Formal & informal styles

- Look at the examples and ask students where they might expect to see or hear them. Possible answers:

  a A business letter, refusing help.
  b A policeman's report on a crime.
  c A notice or an announcement on a train.
  d A notice in a hostel, private hotel, etc.
  e Part of a speech, perhaps at the opening of a meeting.

- Ask students to 'translate' the sentences into everyday English. If you like, build up a version on the board.

- 🔲 Play the recording.

  (Answers: see tapescript.)

- Point out some of the features of formal English:
  – use of words of Latin/French origin (e.g. *assistance* instead of *help*, *proceed* instead of *go*)
  – use of phrases including nouns, instead of simple verbs (e.g. *offer you assistance* instead of *help you*, *force an entry into* instead of *break into*)
  – use of impersonal, passive structures (e.g. *is forbidden* instead of *you can't*).

2 Phrasal verbs

- Point out that in English there is often a choice of verbs with the same (or similar) meaning:
  – a verb of Latin/French origin, which is usually more formal (e.g. *I shall have to consider the matter*)
  – a phrasal verb, which is more often used in informal spoken English (e.g. *I'll have to think it over*).

- Ask students to match the phrasal verbs with the more formal verbs in the box. As you go through, present any new items and give other examples. Answers:

  a consider   *d* recover (from)   *f* ascertain
  b postponed   *e* investigate   *g* respected
  c tolerate

3 Abstract nouns

- Ask students to suggest how to make the sentences less formal, by replacing the abstract nouns with other phrases. If you like, let them look up the nouns in dictionaries. Possible answers:

  a There aren't enough qualified teachers in this area.
  b There are plenty of good restaurants near Times Square.
  c You don't have to buy it.
  d Do you mind if I smoke?
  e He often uses (*or* tends to use) formal English.

> 🔲 The tapescript is on page 112.

Pronunciation F: disagreeing politely

This activity shows how we often use rising tones when expressing polite disagreement, to give an impression of being tentative rather than contradicting strongly.

1 Presentation

- 🔲 Play the recording, and establish these points:
  – The first time, B's voice *goes down* on the word *No*. This sounds as if he's contradicting A (= 'You're completely wrong' or 'Don't be so stupid'), and might seem impolite.
  – The second time, B's voice *goes up* (or *down, then up*) on the word *No*. This is a way to correct A more politely (= 'Well, actually that's not what happened').

- If you like, make a few other remarks, and get students to practise saying *No* with a rising tone.

2 Listening & practice

- 🔲 Play the recording, pausing after each set of replies. Ask students to identify the polite reply each time, and discuss what the other reply sounds like. Answers:

  1 B is polite (A suggests 'How dare you say that?').
  2 A is polite (B suggests 'I don't want to talk about it').
  3 A is polite (B suggests 'You're quite wrong about that').

- Students practise saying the replies.

3 Presentation

- 🔲 Play the recording and establish the difference between B's two replies:

  Well yes, it can be difficult.

  (agreeing with A, a straightforward statement of fact)

  Well, it can be difficult, but I really enjoy it.

  (saying 'Yes, but ...' – partly agreeing with A, but continuing with a disagreement)

4 Prediction task & listening

- Pairs decide where B's voice will rise and fall.

- 🔲 Play the conversations, checking the answers as you go. Expected answers:

  1 He's sometimes late, but he often works at the weekend, too.

  2 I enjoyed the first half, but not the second.

  3 I used to live there, but now I've moved to London.

  4 It looks good, but it doesn't go very well.

- Ask students to practise the conversations, focusing on the intonation of B's replies.

Self-study Workbook

Study Skills F: Reading between the lines   *See notes on page 129.*

Language awareness: formal and informal

1 Here are some examples of formal English. Where would you expect to see or hear them?

   a We regret that we are unable to offer you any further assistance in this matter.

   b I was proceeding along the High Street when I observed two men attempting to force an entry into a parked car.

   c The dining car is situated towards the rear of the train.

   d The consumption of alcoholic beverages on the premises is strictly forbidden.

   e I would like to express my sincere appreciation of the fact that such a large number people have attended this meeting.

Imagine you're passing on these pieces of information to someone else. How would you express them in a more informal style?

🔲 Now listen to the recording. How similar were your answers to the ones you heard?

2 Notice that we tend to use phrasal verbs in informal English. Here are some sentences with phrasal verbs. Match them with the more formal verbs in the box.

recover	ascertain	respect	tolerate
consider	investigate	postpone	

   a I'll have to *think* it *over*.

   b They *put off* the meeting till the next day.

   c I can't *put up with* it any longer.

   d It took her a long time to *get over* it.

   e I'll *look into* it next week.

   f We need to *find out* exactly what happened.

   g I've always *looked up to* him.

3 Abstract nouns are often used in formal English. Can you identify the abstract nouns in these sentences? Rewrite them to make them less formal.

   a There's a severe shortage of qualified teachers in this area.

   b There are plenty of good restaurants in the vicinity of Times Square.

   c You are under no obligation to buy it.

   d Do you have any objection to my smoking?

   e He has a tendency to use formal English.

Pronunciation: disagreeing politely

1 🔲 You will hear this conversation twice. What is the difference between the two replies? Which reply sounds more polite? Why?

   A I hear you lost again on Saturday.
   B No, we won.

2 🔲 You will hear the questions below, with the replies said in two different ways. Which replies sound polite? How do the others sound?

   1 A I don't suppose she'll pass, will she?
      B Yes. I think she's got a good chance.

   2 A You'll be going to Italy again, won't you?
      B No, we're going to Spain this year.

   3 A You don't eat meat, then?
      B I do. I'm just not hungry.

Now listen to the conversations again, and try replying yourself in the same way.

3 🔲 Listen to these two conversations. Where does B's voice rise, and where does it fall?

   1 A Teaching must be really hard work.
      B Well yes, it can be difficult.

   2 A Teaching must be really hard work.
      B Well, it can be difficult, but I really enjoy it.

4 How do you think B's replies will sound in these conversations? Mark places where you think the voice will rise, and where it will fall.

   1 A John never seems to be here on time.
      B He's sometimes late, but he often works at the weekend, too.

   2 A Didn't you like the play?
      B I enjoyed the first half, but not the second.

   3 A You've got a house in Manchester, haven't you?
      B I used to live there, but now I've moved to London.

   4 A I like your new car.
      B It looks good, but it doesn't go very well.

🔲 Now listen and see if you were right. Then practise saying the conversations.

1 Memories

1 You will hear three people talking about their family memories.

   a 🔲 Listen to the first two and follow what they say on the page.

… Then the American Civil War. I had great-uncles who fought in that. One was killed at the Battle of Antietam, and one was wounded at the Battle of Gettysburg and another was killed at another battle somewhere. And they're all buried in the Roberts cemetery …

… I was the youngest of all these children in the family. And I was very well looked after, very spoiled by them. I could play in all their games. I was never left out. All the rest of them used to get into trouble. I never got into trouble. They used to get spanked. I never used to get spanked. So I used to, not enjoy it, but I used to get away with a lot of things …

Find examples of the passive in each extract.
Why do the speakers choose to use the passive?

   b Here is what the third speaker says, but all the verbs have been put into the active.
Where do you think the speaker might use the passive?

When I was 13, they sent my parents abroad.

My parents didn't want to disrupt my education.

They sent me to a boarding school.

I really hated it.

We had to go to bed at 9.30.

They didn't allow us to go out in the evenings.

And of course we did all use to sneak out in the evenings.

One night they caught me.

I thought they were going to expel me.

The headmistress just wrote a letter to my parents.

🔲 Now listen to the recording.

2 Think of a family memory of your own, and write one sentence using the passive.

   Tell another student about what happened. Include your sentence in what you say.

This unit is concerned with the way we use the passive in English. It focuses on three main areas:
– passives with *be* and *get* (e.g. *be punished, get caught*)
– passive reporting verbs (e.g. *is said to, is believed to*)
– passives with *have* (e.g. *have your bag stolen*).
The fourth activity develops writing skills, and deals with the language of cause and result.

1 Memories

This exercise is about people's childhood memories. This is a natural context for using the passive to talk about things that happened to you. The main focus of the exercise is on when we choose to use the passive rather than the active.

➤ Focus on Form: Exercises 1 & 2
➤ Workbook: Exercise A, Listening

1 Listening, reading & presentation

- 🔲 Play the recording of the first speaker, and let students follow the text as they listen. Identify the passive forms:

  one was killed
  one was wounded
  another was killed
  they're all buried

- Discuss why the passive is used here:
  – The speaker is interested in what *happened* to his family, not in who did these things (we don't know who killed them, buried them, etc. and it doesn't matter).

- 🔲 Play the recording of the second speaker. Identify the passive forms:

  I was very well looked after
  I was very spoiled by them
  I was never left out
  I never used to get spanked

- Discuss why the passive is used:
  – The speaker is talking about *herself* and her experiences, so she's interested in what *she did* (she played games, she got away with things) and what *happened to her* (she was spoiled, she never got spanked).
  – By using the passive, she can keep the same subject (*I*) all the time; this sounds better than if she keeps switching from *I* to *My brothers and sisters* to *My parents*.
- Look at the third speaker's sentences, and discuss where the speaker might use passive forms. (*Note:* Only sentences 1, 3, 6, 8, 9 and 10 could possibly have a passive form.)
- 🔲 Play the recording, and establish where the speaker actually uses the passive. Answers:

  my parents were sent abroad
  we were never allowed to go out
  I was caught
  I thought I was going to be expelled

2 Writing & speaking activity

- To show what to do, write a passive sentence of your own on the board. Use it as a basis to tell the class something about your childhood or your family, and encourage them to ask you questions.
- Students write a passive sentence about their childhood or their family.
- In pairs, students expand on their sentence to tell each other their family memory.
- As a round-up, ask a few students what they found out from their partner.

Language note
The second speaker uses the passive with *get*: *They used to get spanked* instead of *They used to be spanked*. This is common in conversational English, especially with certain verbs, e.g. *get killed, get stolen, get caught, get hurt*.
See *Focus on Form* Exercise 2.

Option
To show this, try reading the text using only active forms:
They used to look after me very well, they used to spoil me, they never left me out, my parents used to spank them, etc.

🔲 The tapescript is on page 112.

Homework option
Students write what they said as a paragraph (or series of paragraphs), including the sentence they wrote in class.

2 Facts and theories

This exercise introduces the passive structures is said to, is thought to, is known to, is believed to. *These structures are typical of a fairly formal style (e.g. news reports) and are introduced here mainly for recognition.*

➤ Focus on Form: Exercise 3
➤ Workbook: Exercise B

1 Presentation

- Look at the newspaper extracts, and ask students to express them in less formal English. Possible answers:

    We know that (*or* Everyone knows that) aspirins help prevent heart disease.
    People believe that the attack was carried out by a separatist group.
    They say that (*or* People say that) Queen Elizabeth I had a bath every month …
    People think that the royal couple are spending their honeymoon …

- Show the structure used with these verbs, passive verb + *to* + infinitive:

She is	**known** **said** **believed**	**to**	**be a millionaire** **be living in Singapore** **have gone abroad**

> **Language note**
> Other verbs are used in the same way, e.g. *suppose, assume, report, consider, claim.*

2 Writing & speaking activity

- Discuss whether the sentences are known to be true or whether they are just what people believe or say. Ask students to decide which verb is most appropriate. Expected answers:

    Cigarettes are known to cause cancer.
    Lord Lucan is believed/said to have taken a ferry to France.
    Dinosaurs are believed/said to have been wiped out by an asteroid.

- Students work in groups. They discuss two or three of the topics, and write a sentence about each of them.

- As a round-up, ask each group to read out their sentences. Ask other students if they agree, and let discussion develop where there is disagreement.

> **Practice option**
> Give other examples, and ask students to change them to passive structures, e.g.
> We know that the prisoner escaped.
> → The prisoner is known to have escaped.

3 Experiences

This exercise focuses on two uses of the passive with have *(have something done): to talk about things that you arrange (e.g.* I had my car serviced*), and to talk about things that happen to you accidentally or against your will (e.g.* I had my wallet stolen*). This is used as a basis for students to talk about their own experiences.*

➤ Focus on Form: Exercise 4
➤ Workbook: Exercise B

1 Presentation

- Look at the remarks and make these points:
    – All the sentences include the structure 'have something done'.
    – You can use this structure in two ways:
        1 to talk about things you arrange (someone redecorated her flat)
        2 to talk about things that happen to you accidentally or against your will (the police took away her driving licence).

- Show how this structure is formed with *have* + noun + past participle:

> *Her car is being repaired*
> *She is having her car repaired*
>
> *My bike was stolen*
> *I had my bike stolen*

> **Practice option**
> Give sentences beginning *Someone* … or *They* …, and ask students to change them to 'have something done', e.g.
> Someone took my photo.
> → I had my photo taken.
> They renewed my passport.
> → I had my passport renewed.

2 Speaking activity

- Read through the table, explaining any unknown words, e.g. *fortune, snatch* (= steal), *slap*. Then give time for students to complete it.

- Students sit in groups. They compare their answers and tell the others in the group about their experiences.

- As a round-up, ask each group to choose the most interesting experience they heard about, and tell it to the rest of the class.

> **Optional lead-in**
> To introduce the groupwork stage, complete the table yourself and tell the class about any experiences where you answered *Yes*.

2 Facts and theories

1 These sentences from newspapers and magazines are all in rather formal English.
How could you say the same things in conversational English?

> Aspirins are known to help prevent heart disease.

> The attack is believed to have been carried out by a separatist group.

> Queen Elizabeth I is said to have had a bath every month 'whether she needed it or not'.

> The royal couple are thought to be spending their honeymoon somewhere in the Caribbean.

2 Look at the sentences in the table. Are they facts or just theories?
Choose the most appropriate reporting verb.

Cigarettes are	said	to cause cancer.
Lord Lucan is	believed	to have taken a ferry to France.
Dinosaurs are	known	to have been wiped out by an asteroid.

Work in groups. Choose two or three of these topics, and try to reach agreement
about what is known or believed about them. Write sentences like those in the
table which summarise your conclusions.

– the Yeti   – Atlantis
– the death of Adolf Hitler   – Is the sea level rising or falling?
– the origins of the Aids virus   – How did the universe begin?

Now read out your conclusions. Do other students agree with them?

3 Experiences

> She had her flat redecorated last week.

> I've never had my eyes tested.

> She had her driving licence taken away last week.

> I've never had my car vandalised.

> Have you ever had anything published?

> Have you ever had your fingerprints taken?

1 What do the six remarks have in common?
What's the difference between the ones on the left and the ones on the right?

2 Complete the table.

		Yes	No
Have you ever	had your fortune told?		
	had your car or bike stolen?		
	had your bag snatched?		
	had your picture printed in the paper?		
	had your face slapped?		

Work in groups. If you answered 'Yes' to any of the questions,
tell the others what happened.

Now choose the most interesting experience in your group and
tell the rest of the class about it.

4 One thing leads to another

1 These paragraphs all contain expressions for talking about causes and results. Write them down in two lists: expressions used for describing *causes* or *origins* (e.g. *was caused by*) and expressions used for describing *results* (e.g. *led to*).

The Black Death, which swept through Europe in the 14th century, resulted in more than 3 million deaths. The plague is believed to have been caused by a virus which originated in Central Asia and may have been brought to Europe by Genghis Khan's invading armies.

The economic recession in the late 1980s caused a sharp drop in house prices. As a result, many people who would otherwise have sold their houses decided not to move. This led to a period of stagnation in the housing market, which kept house prices low for several years.

Fax and email have made it possible to communicate much faster and more effectively over long distances. One result of this has been that more people are now able to work from home instead of travelling to work.

The exact cause of the strike is still unclear, but it is thought to have been due to dissatisfaction about pay offered to part-time workers.

2 Here are three paragraphs about global warming, which all express the same idea. What is the difference between them? What other expressions could you use instead of the phrases in italics?

a Global warming has already *led to* noticeable changes in the world's climate.

b Over the past two decades, the temperature of the Earth's atmosphere has gradually increased. *As a result*, the world's climate has become less stable: some areas have experienced unusually high temperatures and droughts, while other areas have suffered from heavy rainfall and violent storms.

c Over the last two decades, the world's climate has become less stable: some areas have experienced unusually high temperatures and droughts, while other areas have suffered from heavy rainfall and violent storms. Scientists believe that these changes *are* at least partly *caused by* global warming.

3 Choose one of these headlines, and expand the ideas into a paragraph, using the expressions you have noted down. Put the ideas together in any order you like, and add any ideas of your own. Then compare paragraphs with other students.

A
EXPLOSION KILLS 20 PEOPLE

(leaking gas pipe – damaged when road was repaired – explosion – 20 people killed)

D
More illiterate children, warns report

(cuts in education – fewer teachers – more children unable to read or write)

B
INNER CITY VIOLENCE:
'We're moving out,' say residents

(increase in crime in inner city areas – people moving to suburbs – cities will become even more dangerous)

C
Arctic weather brings chaos to roads

(heavy snow and high winds – chaos on roads – cars abandoned – electricity cut off)

4 One thing leads to another

Writing skills: *Linking ideas; making logical connections.*
Language focus: *expressions for describing causes and results.*

➤ Workbook: Exercise C

This activity helps students to show logical connections between events. It follows these stages:
1 Presentation. Students study paragraphs and note down expressions for describing causes and results.
2 Discussion. Students look at similar paragraphs and discuss differences between them.
3 Writing. Students expand notes into a paragraph.

1 Presentation

- Look at the paragraphs, and ask students to identify 'cause' and 'result' expressions. Build them up on the board in two lists, writing all the verbs in the Past tense for clarity:

Cause/origin	**Result**
was caused by	resulted in
originated in	One result of this was
the cause of... was	caused
was due to	As a result, ...
	led to

> **Language note**
> The words *cause* and *result* can be used as verbs or nouns. Compare:
> – Lung cancer *is caused by* smoking.
> – *A major cause of* lung cancer *is* smoking.
> – Smoking *causes* lung cancer.
> – Air pollution *results in* global warming.
> – Global warming occurs *as a result of* air pollution.

2 Discussion

- Look at the three paragraphs and discuss the differences between them. Bring out these points:
  - In *a*, the idea is expressed in a single sentence with the structure: noun 1 – *has led to* – noun 2.
  - In *b*, the idea is expanded: the nouns in *a* become complete sentences in *b*. So the structure changes to: sentence 1 – *As a result* – sentence 2.
  - In *c*, the idea is expressed the other way round: identifying the cause instead of the result. So the structure is: sentence 2 – *are caused by* – noun 1.

- Ask students to suggest other expressions to replace those in italics. Possible answers:

  a caused, resulted in
  b As a result of this, One result of this has been that, As a consequence,
  c are due to, are the result of

3 Writing

- Read through the headlines, and make sure students understand what the notes are about.

- Students choose one topic, and expand the notes into a paragraph, linking the sentences to show causes and results.

- Students form groups with other students who have chosen the same topic. They read out what they have written, and decide which paragraph expresses the ideas most clearly.

- As a round-up, ask each group to read out the version they chose as the best.

> **Group writing option**
> Using what different students have written, each group works together to produce a collective version which incorporates the best ideas. They then read this out to the rest of the class.

> **Homework option**
> Students write the paragraphs for homework.

Focus on Form

1 Forms of the passive

> Passive form of verb tenses, infinitives and *-ing* forms

- Students do the exercise alone or in pairs. If necessary students could look at the table in the Reference Section, page 124, for help with the passive.
- Go through the answers:

    a Elections are held every four years.
    b 10 kilos of cocaine were seized by customs officials.
    c Your application is being considered.
    d I discovered that my phone was being bugged.
    e That idea has already been thought of.
    f He was given a gold watch as a retirement present (*or* A gold watch was given (to) him as a retirement present).
    g Let's wait – we might be offered a lift.
    h Do the seats have to be paid for in advance?
    i The plan should never have been allowed to go ahead.
    j She doesn't mind being asked awkward questions.
    k I'm not used to being stared at.

2 The passive with 'get'

> *get* + past participle, with particular verbs

- Point out that in informal English, we can often use *get* instead of *be* in the passive, especially with verbs used to talk about accidents or things we cannot control:

I hope I won't	be get	stuck in the lift

- Students do the exercise in pairs. Then go through the answers together. Possible answers:

    a get stolen.
    b you might get stung.
    c got expelled / got sent to prison.
    d to get mugged / to get attacked / to get killed.
    e get punished a lot / get sent to bed without any food.
    f got lost.

3 Passive reporting verbs

> *is said/known/believed* etc. *to* + infinitive

- Look at the newspaper extract and the statements. Ask students to change the statements, using passive reporting verbs, and build up sentences on the board. Answers:

    At least 80 people are known to have been killed, and many more are said to have lost their homes.
    The drinking water is believed to be contaminated by leaking oil.
    Thousands of families are reported to be camping in makeshift tents.
    The Prime Minister is understood to be visiting the area today.
    Terrorist groups are known to have been threatening to blow up the oil depot, but the explosion is thought to have been caused accidentally.

4 The 'have' passive

> *have something done*

- Look at the pictures, and ask students to say what is happening in them, using the verbs in the box. Possible answers:

    Sunday: Someone is slashing the tyres of the car.
    Monday: Someone is snatching a handbag.
    Tuesday: Someone is breaking into the house.
    Wednesday: Someone is picking the man's pocket.
    Thursday: Someone is dumping rubbish in the garden.
    Friday: Someone is breaking the window.
    Saturday: Someone is cutting the telephone wires.

- Students complete the story. Possible answer:

    Then on Monday, Sylvia had her handbag snatched. On Tuesday, they had their house broken into. On Wednesday, Jack had his pocket picked. On Thursday, they had rubbish dumped in their garden. On Friday, they had their window broken. And on Saturday, they had their telephone wires cut.

Self-study Workbook

Exercise A: Active or passive?
Active and passive forms. Students read texts and fill gaps with active or passive forms of verbs.

Exercise B: Passive forms
Students rewrite active sentences in the passive.

Exercise C: Causes and results
Expressions describing cause and result. Students complete a gapped text with expressions from a box.

Idioms: Sports and games
Common idioms that come originally from sports and games but now have other meanings (e.g. *be quick off the mark*).

Listening: Oriental spices
Someone describes spices used in oriental cookery. Students listen and match with pictures, then listen for details.

Common verbs: set
Common uses of the verb *set*, including idiomatic expressions.

Focus on Form

1 Forms of the passive

Rewrite these sentences using the passive.

a They hold elections every four years.
b Customs officials seized ten kilos of cocaine.
c We are considering your application.
d I discovered that someone was bugging my phone.
e Someone has already thought of that idea.
f They gave him a gold watch as a retirement present.
g Let's wait – someone might offer us a lift.
h Do we have to pay for the seats in advance?
i They should never have allowed the plan to go ahead.
j She doesn't mind people asking her awkward questions.
k I'm not used to people staring at me.

2 The passive with 'get'

Complete the remarks below with a 'get' passive, using an appropriate verb.

Example:

Some people are terrified of lifts. They think they're going to *get stuck*.

a You'd better lock your bike up. It might …
b Keep away from that wasps' nest, or …
c The last person they caught taking drugs on the school premises …
d If you walk around alone late at night, you're very likely …
e He had a very tough childhood. He used to …
f I never received your letter. It must have …

3 Passive reporting verbs

80 killed in oil explosion

An oil depot in the remote mountain town of Tigrit exploded late last night, starting a fire which spread through a southern suburb of the city. At least 80 people are known to have been killed.

Here are some statements people made about the explosion. Change them into sentences that the reporter might include in the newspaper article, using the structures in the box.

is are	known said believed thought reported understood	to …

> We know that at least 80 people were killed, and they say that many more have lost their homes.

> We believe the drinking water is contaminated by leaking oil.

> According to reports, thousands of families are camping in makeshift tents.

> The Prime Minister is visiting the area today, or so we understand.

> We know that terrorist groups have been threatening to blow up the oil depot, but we think the explosion was caused accidentally.

4 The 'have' passive

Use the verbs in the box to talk about what's happening in the pictures.

Now complete the story, using the 'have' passive.

break	pick
break into	slash
cut	snatch
dump	

My neighbours Jack and Sylvia are starting to believe that someone doesn't like them very much. Last Sunday, they had their car tyres slashed. Then on Monday, …

Sunday

Monday

Tuesday

Wednesday

Thursday

Friday

Saturday

16 World affairs

1 War and peace

Vietnam, 1968

towns • air bases • Vietcong • damage •
forces • launch • inflict • attack

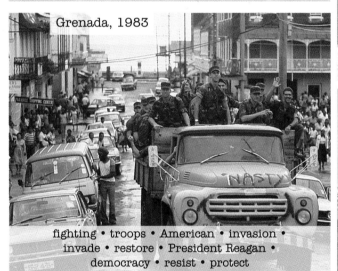

Grenada, 1983

fighting • troops • American • invasion •
invade • restore • President Reagan •
democracy • resist • protect

Rwanda, 1995

Tanzania • border • massacre •
refugees • camps • close • flee

Bosnia, 1995

presidents • peace treaty • agreement • war •
negotiations • reach • sign • end

Chechnya, 1996

Chechen fighters • town • hostages • hospital •
tanks • spokesman • surround • warn • harm

1 The photos show scenes from five different conflicts. They were all used to accompany news reports at the time.

Look at the words under each photo. Can you work out roughly what each story was?

▭ Now listen to the news broadcasts. How similar were they to what you imagined?

2 Look at these quotations, which are all about war and peace.
What point does each of them make?

> *"Peace (n.) In international affairs, a period of cheating between two periods of fighting"*
>
> AMBROSE BIERCE, 1906

> *"There never was a good war or a bad peace"*
>
> BENJAMIN FRANKLIN, 1783

> *"Patriots always talk of dying for their country, and never of killing for their country"*
>
> BERTRAND RUSSELL, 1938

> *"War can only be abolished through war"*
>
> MAO ZEDONG, 1938

> *"They make a desert and they call it peace"*
>
> TACITUS, 100 AD

Make up a 'quotation' of your own about war and peace.

This unit is about the kind of events that get into the news: relations between countries, wars, politics and social issues. It focuses on the following areas:
– language for talking about war and peace
– language for talking about political systems
– language for talking about political and social issues (e.g. unemployment, education).

The Reading and Listening activity is about working as a war correspondent.

1 War and peace

This exercise is based on news stories about five world conflicts over the last 30 years or so. It focuses on key words and expressions for talking about war and peace (e.g. invade, take someone hostage, refugee, sign a peace treaty). Students try to work out from the key words what the stories are about, and then hear a series of news broadcasts.

➤ Workbook: Exercise A

1 Presentation & listening

- Look at the pictures, and ask students if they know (or can guess) what they show, and what happened on each occasion. Use this to introduce some of the key words, e.g.
  Rwanda: the picture shows *refugees*.
  Grenada: the Americans *invaded* Grenada.

- Look at the key words you haven't covered so far, and check that students know what they mean. As you do this, get students to suggest how they might fit into a news story.

- 🔲 Play the recording, pausing after each news story to compare it with what students predicted. Build up key vocabulary on the board, focusing especially on these pairs of verbs and nouns:

VERB	NOUN
attack	attack
fight	fighting
invade	invasion
resist	resistance
damage	damage
negotiate	negotiations
agree	agreement

Groupwork option

After discussing each picture briefly, divide students into groups to work out the news stories. Give each group a dictionary to look up key words they are not sure of. Ask different groups to give their idea for each of the news stories.

🔲 The tapescript is on page 112.

Presentation option

Elicit these common phrases and write them on the board:

> *launch an attack*
> *fighting broke out*
> *put up resistance to*
> *cause damage to*
> *start/break off negotiations*
> *reach agreement*
> *take someone hostage*
> *sign a peace treaty*

---

2 Writing & speaking activity

- Look at each quotation in turn, and discuss what point it makes. Ask students whether they agree with what each quotation says, and which they agree with most.

- Either working alone or in pairs or groups, students think up a 'quotation' about war or peace and write it down.

- As a round-up, collect the 'quotations' and read them out to the class.

2 Talking politics

This exercise takes the form of a quiz, in which students find out how aware they are of politics. It introduces vocabulary for talking about political systems (e.g. government, Prime Minister, election).

1 Presentation & speaking activity

- Read through Questions 1 and 2 of the quiz, explaining any new vocabulary (e.g. *Prime Minister* = leader of the government, *the Cabinet* = the most important ministers; *general election* = election for the whole country).
- Students do the whole quiz in pairs, noting down their answers.
- Go through the answers, getting suggestions from the class and saying what answers are acceptable. Students give themselves marks. Scoring:

  1 *a* 6 points (1 for each person mentioned)
    b 2 points (1 for each answer)
  2 6 points (2 for each answer)
  3 12 points (1 for each correct pair, 1 for explaining the link)
  4 9 points (1 for each fact)
  Total: 35 points.

- Possible answers to Questions 3 and 4:

  3 Elizabeth II, Juan Carlos: both monarchs (Queen of Britain, King of Spain).
    Mozambique, Angola: both African countries, both used to be Portuguese colonies, both had long civil wars.
    Abraham Lincoln, Anwar Sadat: both presidents, both were assassinated.
    Che Guevara, Emil Zapata: both Latin American revolutionary leaders.
    Slovenia, Estonia: both European countries, both recently became independent from larger countries (Yugoslavia and Soviet Union).
    Benito Mussolini, Joseph Stalin: both dictators, both leaders of their country during World War II.

  4 Gorbachev: Leader of Soviet Union; introduced change ('perestroika') and open government ('glasnost'); gave up power to Boris Yeltsin.
    Mandela: black South African leader; fought against apartheid; was put in prison; became leader of new South Africa.
    Nixon: President of USA; ended the war in Vietnam; had to resign because of Watergate scandal.

2 Speaking activity

- Give time for students to write questions of their own. These could be about their own country or about world affairs.
- In turn, students read out their questions. Other students try to answer them.

3 Election issues

This is a freer discussion activity in which students talk about political issues in their own country. It introduces language for talking about general political and social issues (e.g. unemployment, the environment, transport).

1 Presentation & discussion

- Look at the expressions in the box, and check that students understand them. Then ask students to match the election promises with the issues. Answers:

  A Housing B Law and order C Employment D Environment E The economy

- Discuss which party in the students' own country would make each promise.

2 Writing & speaking activity

- Brainstorm other possible election issues, and write them on the board.
- Students choose three issues, and write sentences expressing their opinion about them.
- Pairwork. Students show their sentences to their partner, who guesses what party they would vote for.
- As a round-up, find out how successful students' guesses were.

➤ Workbook: Exercise B

Groupwork option
Students do the quiz in groups, all of them contributing answers. One person acts as secretary, asking the questions and noting down the answers. (*Note:* This makes it easier for students who know almost nothing about politics.)

Whole class option
Read out the questions yourself, and give time for students to write their answers, working alone. Then go through the answers and let students give themselves a score. (*Note:* This is a more serious way of doing the activity, which may suit some classes.)

Presentation option
Build up new vocabulary on the board as you go through the answers, e.g.

monarch	revolutionary
colony	independent
civil war	dictator
assassinate	resign

Alternative
If you like, replace some or all of these politicians with others.

➤ Workbook: Exercise C, Listening

Note
There may be particular issues that are important in certain countries (e.g. treatment of minorities, wars, women's rights, corruption).

Optional lead-in
Write a few sentences about one of the issues on the board. Ask students to guess which party you would vote for.

2 Talking politics

1 How politically aware are you? Answer the questions.

The teacher will tell you how to mark your answers. How well did you do?

① About your country
a Can you name
– the Minister of Foreign Affairs?
– two other members of the Cabinet?
– the last three Prime Ministers or
Presidents?
b Do you know
– how often general elections are held?
– the year of the last general election?

② Recent events
Give an example of
– a recent foreign visit by a head of state
– a recent political scandal
– a recent change of government

③ Something in common
Find pairs in the box. What connects them?

Elizabeth II	Slovenia	Josef Stalin
Mozambique	Emil Zapata	Angola
Abraham Lincoln	Anwar Sadat	Estonia
Che Guevara	Benito Mussolini	Juan Carlos

④ Famous politicians
Give three facts about each of these people.

2 Write one or two questions of your own, and find someone who can answer them.

3 Election issues

1 Look at these election promises. Which issue is each one about?

A We will use public money
to finance a much-needed
building programme in
our inner cities.

B We will find sensible
alternatives to sending
offenders to prison.

C We will not allow
foreigners to take
jobs that citizens of
this country could
do just as well.

D We will tax pollution –
the more pollution a
company causes, the
more it will pay.

D We believe that reducing income
tax will encourage people to work
hard and take more responsibility
for running their own lives.

Health
Education
Defence
The economy
Law and order
Employment
Housing
Transport
The environment
....
....
....

Think of the political parties in your country. Which of them do you think
might make each promise?

2 Imagine a general election in your own country. What other election issues
would there be? Add to the list.

Choose the three issues that you think are most important. Write two sentences
about each, saying what the problem is and what should be done about it.

Now show your sentences to another student.
Can he/she guess what party you would vote for?

4 On the front line

READING

1 Before you read the article *Images of War*, check that you understand these words, which are all connected with war. Then read the article.

devastation	guerrillas	conflict	amputate
come under fire	ambush	mine (n.)	siege

2 How do you think David Pratt would answer these questions?

  a What do you like most about being a war photographer?
  b Do you think what you do changes people's attitudes?
  c Do you get emotionally involved in what you see?
  d Does your job interfere with your personal life?
  e What do you see as the main purpose of your job?
  f Do you think you're a 'war junkie'?

3 According to the article, what did David Pratt do in these places?

  Afghanistan   Nicaragua   Cambodia   the West Bank   Yugoslavia

4 The article contains these idiomatic expressions. Can you guess what they mean?

  a Pratt admits to '*getting a buzz*' out of taking risks.
  b 'I just lay on my bed and *cried my heart out*.'
  c 'It may seem *corny*, but I just try to show it the way it is.'
  d 'War photography has become my life. It's what *makes me tick*.'

LISTENING

You will hear an interview with Gaby Rado, a television war correspondent.

1 Before you listen, look at these statements about his job. Which do you think are true and which are false?

  a Being a war correspondent is not as dangerous as people imagine.
  b The most dangerous incidents usually happen accidentally.
  c He gets so involved with what he sees that it interferes with his work.
  d What he sees often makes him feel angry.
  e It's difficult to come back from a war zone to the 'normal' world.
  f It's more difficult to be a war correspondent if you have a family.

  🔲 Now listen and check your answers.

2 He tells two stories about his experiences. Here are elements from the two stories. Which belong to which story, and how do they fit together?

the front line	dead bodies	no man's land	a baby
refugees	a young woman	a village	

DISCUSSION

Both the article and the recording focus on these aspects of reporting a war:

– the risks involved in the job   – how emotionally involved the reporters get
– coming back to the 'real' world   – the effect of the job on personal relationships

How similar are the two men's experiences? What are the differences?

4 On the front line

This combined Reading and Listening activity is about two war correspondents, one a photographer, the other a reporter. Students read an article describing the life of one of them, and then listen to a recorded interview with the other. Both the reading and the listening are concerned with the dangers of being a war correspondent, and how the job affects the people who do it.

Reading skills: *reading to find answers to specific questions.*
Vocabulary focus: *words connected with war; idiomatic expressions.*
Listening skills: *matching what you hear with your own predictions.*

Reading

- Check that students understand the words in the box, and if necessary present them using examples of your own.

- Read through the questions in 2, then give time for students to read the article and find the answers.

- Discuss the answers together. Possible answers:

  a The 'immediacy' of photography; the excitement of it.
  b Yes, photographs can change public opinion.
  c Yes.
  d Yes (he lost his girlfriend because of it).
  e To show things as they really are; to let the world know what's happening.
  f Probably, yes.

- Discuss the answers to Questions 3 and 4. Possible answers:

  3 *Afghanistan:* photographed the fighting in the capital
    Nicaragua: travelled with Sandanista guerrillas and drove into an ambush
    Cambodia: travelled across the 'killing fields' by bus, photographed victims of land mines
    The West Bank: reported on the Intifada (= Palestinian uprising)
    Former Yugoslavia: crossed from the Serbian to the Croatian side, saw the siege of Vukovar

  4 a getting excited
    b cried for a long time, and very emotionally
    c a cliché, what everyone says
    d keeps me going, gives me a reason for my life

Listening

- Look at the statements in 1 with the class, and ask them to guess whether they are true or false.

- ⊡ Play the recording, pausing from time to time to check the answers to Question 1. Answers:

  a True
  b True
  c False (he gets involved with his work and it helps him keep a distance from what's happening)
  d True
  e True
  f False (having a family helps you to adjust to the 'normal' world)

  ⊡ Establish how the elements of the two stories fit together. Then play that part of the recording again. Answers:

  Story 1: They crossed *the front line* by mistake, then went into *no man's land.* There were *dead bodies* everywhere, and they went through a *village* that was still burning.

  Story 2: They saw a group of *refugees.* One was *a young woman* who was walking across *the front line* carrying *a baby* who had died.

Optional lead-in
Write *War correspondent* on the board. Ask students whether they would like to be one, and what they imagine the job would be like. If you like, build up a list of 'plus' and 'minus' points on the board.

⊡ The tapescript is on page 112.

Language note
No man's land is the area of land between the *front lines* of two armies that are fighting each other.

Discussion

- Discuss how similar or different the two men's experiences are. Bring out these
  points:
  – Both of them clearly regard what they do as important, and get involved in
    (and upset by) what they see. They both feel sympathy with the victims of war.
  – David Pratt takes far more risks, gets far closer to the fighting, and also seems
    to enjoy danger more.
  – David Pratt seems to be more of a 'war junkie': his life is his job, and he's
    prepared to sacrifice relationships for it.
  – Gaby Rado seems to be cooler and more objective; he can stand aside from his
    job and be involved in family life.

Self-study Workbook

Exercise A: From our war correspondent
Expressions for talking about war and peace. Students
choose phrases from boxes to fill gapped sentences.

Exercise B: Points of view
Two letters to newspapers expressing controversial
opinions about world politics. Students write a letter
disagreeing with one of them.

Exercise C: Areas of government
Words for talking about political and social issues.
Students complete an acrostic.

Idioms: All at sea
Common idioms which were originally connected with
the sea and water, but which now have other meanings
(e.g. *to be out of your depth*).

Listening: A minimum wage?
A radio discussion about introducing a minimum wage for
employees. Students listen and identify points the
speakers make.

Word building: Adjectives and nouns (3)
'Families' of abstract nouns, personal nouns and
adjectives (e.g. *science, scientist, scientific*).

Images of war

What does Glaswegian David Pratt get out of being a war photographer? **Ron Farn** *explains.*

The road leading to the Pul-e-Mahmoud Khan bridge over the Kabul river was now a scene of devastation, with every building smashed beyond repair. Once at the heart of the Afghan capital, the road was almost deserted as we made our way toward the bridge which marked the front line. Suddenly a tank shell came in, followed by the rattle of automatic fire, bullets hissing past a little too close for comfort. This was far enough for me. I had all the information I needed, but David Pratt continued over the bridge to get as close as possible to the fighting, because that's what war photographers do. Why should somebody like Pratt, who studied painting and sculpture at Glasgow School of Art and later taught there, choose to go to war for a living?

"I liked the immediacy of photography," explains Pratt, "and taking photographs in a war zone is about as immediate as it gets." Pratt's first experience of war was in central America where, he told me, he froze the first time he came under fire when travelling in a column with Nicaraguan Sandinista guerrillas which drove into a Contra ambush. "That was the point when I had to decide whether I really wanted to do war photography," he says. "There is no point whatever in putting yourself in life-threatening situations if you can't take pictures. That would be insane."

Some photographers are drawn by danger and excitement, others by the idea that their pictures can bring about change. Pratt admits to "getting a buzz" out of taking risks, but argues that pictures can and do make a difference. "The images of Vietnam, particularly those of wounded US soldiers, went a long way to changing public opinion in the States. Photographs of suffering do alert public opinion, even if they don't often change the minds of politicians." Photography is by its nature an intrusive medium: the photographer is a participant rather than just an observer. This is especially true in conflicts where people's homes and families are being destroyed. In a Red Cross hospital in Cambodia, Pratt photographed victims of land mines only a few hundred yards from Khmer Rouge positions. In the fly-infested ward, doctors were amputating limbs with no anaesthetic. One Australian photographer couldn't stand it any more and left the room. Pratt stayed and shot pictures. "These situations do affect you, of course they do, but I felt I had to finish the job," he says. "Then I went back to my room in the Monorom Hotel in Phnom Penh, and I just lay on my bed and cried my heart out."

Apart from witnessing deeply disturbing events, the war correspondent often has a personal price to pay. Not only does he or she take the risks associated with the job, but there can also be tremendous pressure placed on personal relationships. It can be even harder for those left at home. Back in Pakistan, we picked up mail from home: birthday cards for me but, in Pratt's case, an altogether more serious letter.

His long-term girlfriend had had enough of worrying and waiting and had left him. I had never seen him so shaken. Returning to Glasgow, he realised there was nothing he could do, short of giving up photographing wars, but this was too high a price to pay. He threw himself into his work, travelling to the Israeli occupied West Bank and Gaza strip to report on the Intifada. In the former Yugoslavia, he crossed the lines from the Serb to the Croat side and was at the siege of Vukovar. He travelled across the killing fields of Cambodia by bus, and covered the fighting between the government forces and the Khmer Rouge.

How does Pratt reconcile his obvious concern for the victims of war with the fact that he makes his living photographing them? "With difficulty sometimes, but I have never tried to glorify war. It may sound corny, but I just try to show it the way it is, as sympathetically and compassionately as possible." It is easy to accuse photographers like Pratt of being war junkies, and he admits he would be devastated if forced to stay safely at home in Glasgow, running a photo agency. "War photography has become my life. It's what makes me tick."

Review: Units 9–16

Find out

1 Ask other students about an argument or disagreement they've had recently.

Do you think they were in the right or in the wrong?

2 *Why do relationships break down?*

Get opinions from other students. Tell the class the results of your survey.

3 Ask one or two people what their star signs are, and what kind of character they are supposed to have.

Do they believe they really are like that?

4 Answer these questions. Say why / why not.

– Is it worthwhile voting?
– Do you think you will be happier in five years' time than you are now?
– Would you like to be a war correspondent?

Compare answers with other students.

Words

1 What's the similarity between these pairs? What's the difference?

mugging	vandalism
police	vigilantes
astronomy	astrology
global warming	the hole in the ozone layer
acupuncture	hypnotherapy
refugees	casualties

2 Add words to these lists.

– geology, physics …
– health, education, law and order …

3 Give an example of

– a revolutionary
– a peace treaty
– a massacre
– an assassination
– an invasion
– a scandal

Role-play

1 A You're visiting a tropical country for the first time, and you're worried about the risks to your health.

B Reassure your friend, and give him/her some useful advice.

2 Work in threes. Choose one of these topics and act out a short radio or TV discussion.

Darwin got it right
Alternative medicine works
It's possible to foretell the future

A You agree.
B You disagree.
C You're in the chair.

3 Prepare a short conversation which contains one of the following remarks.

– You might have told me
– You needn't have bothered
– It was a complete waste of time
– You had no right to …

Writing

1 Work in groups. How much do you know about what's in today's news?

Share your information and together write a short news broadcast.

2 A You're thinking of visiting B's country for a holiday. Write to him/her, saying what you're interested in, and asking advice about where to go and what to do.

B Write back to A, giving him/her advice about different possibilities.

3 *Giving money to help famine victims just leads to worse problems later on.*

Do you agree with this statement? Write a paragraph giving your opinion.

Find out

1 Revision of language from Unit 13, and also Unit 5
- Tell students about a disagreement you had recently. Get students to ask you more questions about it, and ask them to comment on it.
- Pairwork. Students interview each other about a similar occasion, and discuss who was in the right.
- Round-up. Ask pairs to say what they talked about and what conclusion they came to.

2 Revision of language from Unit 12
- Students move freely round the class, collecting opinions from other students, and noting them down.
- Round-up. Find out the results, and build up a list of ideas on the board. Use this to focus on vocabulary from Unit 12.

3 Revision of language from Units 10 & 12
- Tell students your star sign and find out who else in the class has the same. Discuss what the characteristics of the sign are supposed to be, and which of you is really like that.
- Groupwork. Students find out each other's star signs, and discuss whether the characteristics apply to them.
- Round-up. Ask each group what their conclusions were.

4 Revision of language from Units 9, 11 and 16
- Students note down answers to the questions, and think of reasons why or why not.
- Groupwork. Students compare answers and discuss them.
- Round-up. Find out what answers each group gave. If you like, establish a majority 'class' answer to each question.

Words

1 Revision of language from Units 9, 10, 13, 14 & 16
- Look at the pairs of words, and establish the similarities and differences, e.g.

  mugging/vandalism: both are crimes; mugging = stealing from people in the street; vandalism = damaging property.

2 Revision of language from Units 10 & 16
- Students add as many words to the lists as they can.
- Build up lists on the board.

3 Revision of language from Unit 16
- Students write examples for each category.
- Ask students to read out their examples, and build up lists on the board.

Role-play

1 Revision of language from Units 9 & 14
- Preparation. Build up on the board a list of possible worries (e.g. the water, food, malaria, vaccinations).
- Pairwork. Students improvise a conversation.
- As a round-up, ask people who were about to travel whether their friend answered their questions satisfactorily.

2 Revision of language from Unit 10
- Preparation. Look at the topics, and briefly establish what the issues are (but without going into detail).
- Divide the class into groups of three, and assign roles. Each group chooses a topic to discuss. If you like, give a short preparation time for students to think what they are going to say.
- Groupwork. Students improvise a discussion.
- As a round-up, ask each chairperson what happened in their discussion.

3 Revision of language from Units 11 & 13
- Pairwork preparation. Working together, students choose one of the remarks and and build up a conversation round it. They can make notes, but they shouldn't write out the conversation in full.
- Pairs come to the front of the class in turn and act out their conversation.

Writing

1 Revision of language from Unit 16
- As a preparation, build up a few topics on the board.
- Groupwork. Students brainstorm what they know about each topic, and together write a news broadcast.
- Round-up. Each group presents their news broadcast.

2 Revision of language from Unit 9
- Preparation. Build up possible topics on the board (e.g. *where to go, important sights, what to take with you, safety*). Look again at Unit 9, and focus on useful language.
- Students write letters asking advice.
- Students pass their letters to another student, who writes a reply. They give their replies back to the student who wrote the letter.
- Round-up. Ask a few students to read out their letters and replies.

3 Revision of language from Unit 11
- Elicit useful expressions from Unit 11 and write them on the board.
- Students write paragraphs giving their opinion.
- Ask a few students to read out their paragraphs, or collect them to read yourself.

Talking points

The pictures in this activity take up themes from the following units:

A: Unit 13
B: Unit 14
C: Unit 14
D: Unit 9
E: Unit 9
F: Unit 11
G: Unit 16
H: Unit 14

They can either be used for revision of specific language, or as a springboard for freer activity.

The activity can be done in two ways:

1 Mini-lectures

Preparation: Students choose one of the pictures and prepare a short talk based on the topic, making brief notes if they like (but not writing the talk out).

Activity: Students give their talk in turn to the rest of the class. At the end, other students can ask questions.

2 Game

Preparation: Students prepare to talk about two or three of the pictures, looking back at the appropriate unit to recall things they might say.

Activity: One student chooses a topic and says a sentence or two about it. Another student then continues, adding another sentence, and so on.

Self-study Workbook: Review, Units 9–16

Exercise A: Multiple-choice cloze
Students choose the best words to fill gaps in a text.   *10 items*

B: Cloze
Students fill gaps in a text with appropriate words.   *10 items*

C: Sentence rewriting
Students rewrite sentences, using given words and any other necessary words.   *12 items*

D: Correcting a text
Students identify superfluous words in a text.   *10 items*

E: Word-building
Students fill gaps in a text with words derived from given words.   *8 items*

Talking points

Prepare a short talk (about one minute) using one of these pictures as a starting point.

Additional material

Flat 3
34 Marlborough Road
Birmingham

Global Travel Ltd
110 Edward Street
Birmingham

Dear Sir/Madam,

I have seen your advertisement in the *Evening News*, and I would like to apply to work in your travel agency this summer.

I have some experience of secretarial and office work. After leaving school, I worked for a firm of accountants, where I was given secretarial training and learned how to type and use a computer. I have also worked as an assistant in a department store, so I am used to dealing with customers and helping with problems.

I have visited Spain and Portugal several times, and know many of the main tourist areas in both countries. I speak Spanish fluently, and I have a basic knowledge of Portuguese. I have always been interested in travel and I have a good sense of geography.

I am an outgoing and confident person, and I think I would enjoy working for you.

I am looking forward to hearing from you.

Yours faithfully,

Diana Jarvis

Diana Jarvis

Joseph's Dream,
by Paula Rego

Write a description of
the painting. Include
enough details so that
someone else could
visualise it.

3 Focus on Form Cleft sentences with 'It' *Student A*

Which do you think are the correct choices?
Check your answers with B.

Use this text to check B's answers.

Christopher Columbus

Christopher Columbus was born in *Spain/Portugal/Italy*
in 1451. He believed that he could reach *India/China/
America* by sailing west. *Manuel I of Portugal / Ferdinand of
Spain / Henry VII of England* eventually agreed to pay for
a voyage, and in August *1492 / 1494 / 1496* he set sail on
the *Santa María / Hispaniola / Mayflower* and two other
ships. They reached *the coast of Labrador / the West Indies /
New England* on October 12, and took the news back to
Europe. After three more voyages to America, Columbus
died in poverty in *Spain/Italy/Portugal* in 1506.

Marco Polo

Marco Polo grew up in Venice. In 1271 his father
and uncle left on a trading expedition to China,
and took Marco Polo with them, although he was
only 15 years old. After travelling on horseback
for several months, they eventually reached their
destination, and they were invited to stay at the
court of the Emperor Kublai Khan. Marco Polo
entered the Emperor's service and learned to
speak fluent Mongolian. He returned home 23
years later, and wrote an account of his travels.

3.4 In the frame *Student B*

Snare,
by Paula Rego

Write a description of the painting. Include enough details so that someone else could visualise it.

3 Focus on Form Cleft sentences with 'It' *Student B*

Use this text to check A's answers.

Christopher Columbus

Christopher Columbus was born in Italy in 1451. He believed that he could reach India by sailing west. Ferdinand of Spain eventually agreed to pay for a voyage, and in August 1492 he set sail on the *Santa María* and two other ships. They reached the West Indies on October 12, and took the news back to Europe. After three more voyages to America, Columbus died in poverty in Spain in 1506.

Which do you think are the correct choices?
Check your answers with A.

Marco Polo

Marco Polo grew up in *Venice/Barcelona/Naples*. In *1271 / 1371 / 1471* his father and uncle left on a trading expedition to *India/Persia/China*, and took Marco Polo with them, although he was only 15 years old. After travelling *on foot / by ship / on horseback* for several months, they eventually reached their destination, and they were invited to stay at the court of the Emperor *Genghis Khan / Kublai Khan / Aga Khan*. Marco Polo entered the Emperor's service and learned to speak fluent *Chinese/Persian/Mongolian*. He returned home *three/23/ 43* years later, and wrote an account of his travels.

'Own goal' defender shot dead outside restaurant

A COLOMBIAN footballer was shot dead yesterday by angry fans who blamed him for their side's early exit from the World Cup. Andrés Escobar, a defender who scored an own goal during his side's defeat by the United States team, was confronted by a group of men as he left a restaurant in Medellín, 200 kilometres from Bogotá. After an argument about his poor performance, they fired 12 bullets. One of the gunmen is reported to have said to Escobar before the shooting 'Thank you for the own goal.'

Tennis stars strike it rich on and off the court

There's lots of money in tennis these days – and for the big players, a large proportion of it comes from big business.

Andre Agassi recently signed a contract with Nike worth a reputed $100 million over ten years, in addition to an estimated $8 million in prize money, and Pete Sampras this year became a Wimbledon millionaire by beating Boris Becker. Steffi Graf is generally thought to be worth more than $30 million through winnings and advertising, and Martina Navratilova, nine-time Wimbledon singles champion, has a personal fortune estimated at more than $20 million.

FOOTBALLER FACES SUSPENSION AFTER ATTACK ON SPECTATOR

ERIC CANTONA, the Manchester United striker, will probably be suspended for the rest of the season after he attacked a spectator during the match against Crystal Palace at Selhurst Park last night.

The incident happened moments after Cantona had been sent off for kicking out at another player, his sixth sending off in 16 months.

As he walked off the field, a spectator was seen running down a gangway from some 20 rows back, apparently to shout abuse at Cantona, who suddenly turned, jumped over the wall and kicked out at the man, and then punched him.

World champion swimmer suspended after drugs test

THE CHINESE WORLD CHAMPION, Lu Bin, has been suspended from all competition for two years after a positive drugs test, the International Swimming Federation announced yesterday. Lu returned a positive result for the anabolic steroid, dehydrotestosterone, in a test on September 30, shortly before the Asian Games.

Lu won four gold and two silver medals at the Games and set a world record for the 200 metres individual medley. At the world championships in Rome last September, she won the 200 metres individual medley title plus two relay gold medals.

4.4 Problems, problems …

Here are the clues for Problems 2–8.

Remember that if you look at a clue, you can only score one point for a correct answer.

2 Two boyfriends

Let's say that the trains in Bill's direction leave at 9.00, 9.10, 9.20, and so on.

To find the answer, you just have to decide when the trains leave in Mario's direction.

Supposing, for example, that they leave at 9.05, 9.15, and so on. That way, Annie would end up going to Bill half time and Mario half the time. So that can't be right.

So when do the trains leave in Mario's direction?

Problem 3 An explosive mixture

The problem boxes are D and E – they each touch six other boxes. If 1 goes in D, what goes in E?

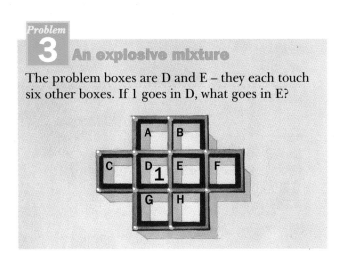

Problem 4 Sweet revenge

There are other things you can do when you move a jar, besides just picking it up and putting it down. What?

Problem 5 One man and his dog

Well, the farmer's going to walk 20 km.
So how long will the dog run in the same time?

Problem 6 On balance

Try dividing the boxes into three groups of three.

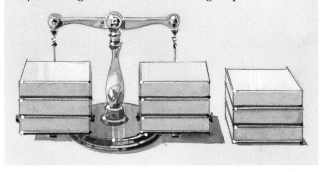

Problem 7 Whodunnit?

Compare what A and B say. Then think about it.

Problem 8 Wrong labels

Try putting your hand in the bag marked 'mixed'.

Life elsewhere?

Douglas Keyworth looks at the evidence for alien forms of life

As we all know, the Earth has everything that is needed for life to develop, which is why we are here.

But four billion years ago, when the Earth was formed, what were the chances that life would emerge? Pretty small, according to biologists – about the same chance that you would have of winning the national lottery five weeks in a row. So we're quite lucky to be here at all.

Elsewhere in the Universe

What about the chances of life forming elsewhere – in our own galaxy, for instance? The Milky Way contains around 400 billion stars. Some (maybe most) of these have planets orbiting around them, and the chances are that many millions – or even billions – of these planets could support life. So it does seem possible that there are some other lottery winners living in the same neighbourhood.

And if you think that there are countless other galaxies out there – many of them far bigger than the Milky Way – then it seems obvious that there must be other forms of life somewhere in the Universe.

Intelligent life

But is it intelligent life, the kind of life that could build space ships and pay us a visit?

Here on Earth there have been billions of species, but only one of them has turned out to be intelligent enough to develop technology and fly into space. And even we're not particularly intelligent: the human race will probably blow itself up long before it learns how to visit other parts of the galaxy.

Alien visits

But let's suppose that there are advanced civilisations, here in our own galaxy, who have developed fast-moving flying saucers. Would they visit the Earth?

First we need to ask: why should they want to? The most likely answer is that their own sun is at the end of its life, and they need to find somewhere else to live.

And the next question is: why here? The diagram shows the part of the Milky Way which probably has the largest number of habitable planets. The oldest ones (and therefore the ones which are most likely to have advanced forms of life) are in the area shaded red. We're towards the edge (marked X).

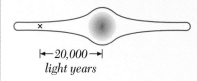

$\leftarrow\!-20,000-\!\rightarrow$
light years

If I were an alien looking for a new home, I think I would try a few million of my neighbouring planets before bothering to travel a hundred thousand trillion miles to visit Earth, on a journey that would take at least 200,000 years.

UFOs

But what about all those UFO sightings that are reported every year? Well, most of them are planes. And whatever the others are, they're not flying saucers. If you were a visiting alien with incredibly powerful technology, what would you do: hide yourself away and keep quiet, or land and take over the Earth? I know what my answer would be.

If there are other forms of life elsewhere in the Universe (and I'm sure there are), that's exactly where they are – elsewhere.

A visiting alien, a trick of the light or a fake?

© 1994 Gabriella Roth

Use these questions to help you talk about the painting.

1 Is there any relationship between the people? If so, what do you think it is?
2 Why is the woman putting her finger to her lips?
3 What are the two men doing?
4 What do you notice about these things?

   – the plant
   – the humming bird
   – the doorway
   – the old woman
   – the dog

5 The painting is called *Sirens Rising*.
   Why do you think the artist gave it this title?

8.1 The right career?

Careers guidance questionnaire

1 Which of these areas can you see yourself working in? Tick the boxes.

- ☐ business
- ☐ arts/entertainment
- ☐ education
- ☐ health and welfare
- ☐ media
- ☐ industry
- ☐ science/technology
- ☐ the environment
- ☐ politics/public life
- ☐ service industries

Other: ....

2 How true are these statements of you? Give yourself a mark out of five.

- ☐ I don't mind hard physical work.
- ☐ I enjoy working with my hands.
- ☐ I enjoy solving problems.
- ☐ I'm a good listener.
- ☐ I'm good with figures.
- ☐ I have a good artistic sense.
- ☐ I'm a good communicator.

3 Do you have any particular skills or leisure interests?

....
....
....
....
....

4 What are/were your favourite subjects at school?

....
....
....

5 What do you expect from a job? Give each of these a mark out of five.

- ☐ prospects for promotion
- ☐ the power to take your own decisions
- ☐ contact with other people
- ☐ a good salary
- ☐ the chance to travel
- ☐ long holidays
- ☐ being able to leave the job behind you when you go home

6 How true are these statements of you? Give each a mark out of 5.

- ☐ I get on with other people.
- ☐ I don't mind taking orders.
- ☐ I need to be my own boss.
- ☐ I go crazy if I do the same thing for too long.
- ☐ I can cope when things get tough.
- ☐ I like to look smart.
- ☐ I can keep smiling – however I'm feeling.
- ☐ I'm punctual.

A

YOU'LL NEVER FORGET THE TASTE

PANTHER LAGER

B

JOIN THE CROWD

20 PALACE Filters CIGARETTES 20

Health warning: cigarettes kill

C

The KG Sportster – it's more than just a bike

Guess who's got the NEW KG Sportster

D

DEATH BEGINS AT 40

Thanks to modern medicine, we live much longer than we used to. So no worries? Not quite. Once you're 40, the risk of serious illnesses like strokes, heart attacks and cancer begins to rise steeply. You'll probably survive – but will your income? You may have to stop working, or get a less strenuous job, or move home. So what will you do for money? It's a worrying thought.

Fortunately, here at the Insurance Union, we've thought of that. Our new Flexilife Policy is designed to protect you and your family while you recover from a serious illness. For a free brochure, phone us free on 000-0000-000 or send in the coupon below.

Insurance Union
We've got your interests at heart

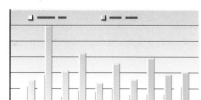

E **STUDY** or **Party?**

You can do both with *Energy Plus* caffeine tablets

Energy Plus WAKES YOU UP KEEPS YOU GOING

F THERE'S MORE TO A SUNCLUB HOLIDAY THAN JUST SEX ...

... BUT WHO NEEDS MORE?

G According to the BBC the world ends just after midnight

12.00 Weather
12.10 Close

MEGASAT TV

News, sport and movies. 24 hours a day, 7 days a week.

H *In just two weeks, YOU could be speaking fluent Italian.*

Sounds incredible? But it's true, thanks to LinguComp's revolutionary LISTEN-AND-SAY method, which brings REAL ITALIAN into your home, your car or your workplace.

It's fun, it's easy, and it works!

For details, fill in this slip

10.2 Science and the environment

For this study, conducted during 1993 and 1994, 25,000 adults in 20 countries were asked 12 true/false questions about science and the environment. The results, by country, are shown in the table.

The items that caused the most problems were:

– Item 8, about the greenhouse effect and the ozone layer (21% correct)
– Item 5, about man-made chemicals and cancer (36% correct)
– Item 3, about the scientific truth of astrology (44% correct).

ENVIRONMENTAL AND SCIENTIFIC KNOWLEDGE AROUND THE WORLD

A study conducted by the National Opinion Research Center at the University of Chicago

Rank	Country	Number correct
1	Canada	7.6
2	New Zealand	7.5
3	Great Britain	7.5
4	Norway	7.2
5	The Netherlands	6.8
6	Northern Ireland	6.7
7	USA	6.6
8	Germany (East)	6.6
9	Czech Republic	6.6
10	Germany (West)	6.4
11	Ireland	6.3
12	Japan	6.2
13	Italy	6.1
14	Israel	5.9
15	Hungary	5.8
16	The Philippines	5.6
17	Slovenia	5.5
18	Spain	5.3
19	Russia	4.8
20	Poland	4.3

14.1 Small but deadly *Aids*

What causes Aids?

Most scientists agree that Aids is caused by the HIV virus. The virus attacks the body's immune system, making the sufferer vulnerable to other diseases. It can be passed on by sexual contact, the use of shared needles for injecting drugs, and (now rarely) by blood transfusions using contaminated blood. It can also be passed on by pregnant women to their unborn children.

Symptoms

A person can be infected with HIV for many years with no symptoms at all, but in around 95% of cases Aids develops eventually. Since Aids sufferers have no defence against diseases in general, the symptoms can vary widely. They may include fever, weight-loss, infections of the mouth and, as the disease progresses, tuberculosis or leukaemia.

How widespread is it?

Aids is a relatively recent disease, but one which has spread rapidly around the world, particularly in Africa and in large cities in many countries. Estimates of the actual numbers involved vary widely.

Prevention

Avoid injecting drugs, particularly with a shared needle, and stick to one sexual partner. The use of condoms is known to reduce the risk of infection.

Cure

There is as yet no cure for Aids, which kills 99% of sufferers. Scientists have produced (and are producing) a number of drugs which slow down the progress of the disease, and there is a huge amount of research into finding out more about the disease. However, no effective vaccine has yet been developed.

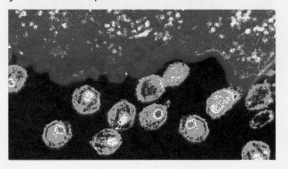

HIV viruses emerging from a blood cell

make it (easier)
enable
prevent
stop
save
encourage
discourage

A

B

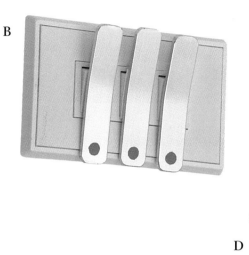

C

D

E

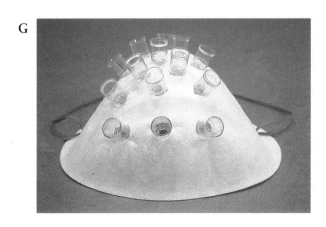

F

ただいま眠っております。
お手数ですが下記の駅で
起こしてください。

西荻窪　多謝

G

H

12.1 The egg test

Inner peace

You're a calm, reflective and thoughtful person, and you're fascinated by hidden meanings and esoteric secrets. That's why you chose the Chinese character *tai*, which is painted on this egg. It symbolises deep inner peace.

What luck!

You have quite a superstitious nature, and you're secretly convinced that your fortune is in the hands of fate. So you naturally respond to the symbols of good fortune shown on this egg. You're optimistic and a positive thinker. Your motto is: if you believe everything will turn out well, then it will.

A quiet life

You're a naturally calm, placid person who longs for harmony and security and loves peace and quiet. You sometimes tend to be too easy-going and amenable, because you'd rather not face the fact that life isn't always quite as peaceful as you'd like it to be.

Lots of fun

You're a naturally cheerful, open and communicative person who likes to be sociable and to have a good time. You have a tendency to be a bit too talkative at times, but other people enjoy your company because you're such fun to be with!

Which way?

You tend to see life as a maze, full of problems and difficult decisions. You're a very sensitive person, sometimes a bit over-sensitive, with a desperate need for warmth and security. Other people sometimes find you difficult to be with, but they also find you fascinating.

What's new?

You're a naturally inquisitive person – you're interested in everything, especially what's going on on the other side of your garden fence! Although you've got an enquiring mind, you don't take things too seriously and you can also see the funny side of things and laugh at yourself. So although people find you a bit nosy, they enjoy your company.

Walking on air

Have you just fallen in love? Or have you just revived an old relationship? Certainly, if you chose this egg, you're feeling very light-hearted. Or maybe you just have a carefree, optimistic personality. Because you like yourself so much, other people find you attractive as well.

Burning with passion

You really throw yourself into life – sometimes a bit too aggressively. You're a natural fighter, dynamic, bold and passionate. You know exactly where you're going in life, and you'll do whatever's necessary to get there. Not surprisingly, you tend to make enemies, but people admire your courage and determination.

Yes, justice was done

I SEEM TO BE ONE of the few people that believe that Mr Newbery was wrong to shoot Mr Revill. As Mr Justice Rougier writes in a letter to today's *Times*, 'Those who believe that a home owner is entitled to shoot a burglar under any circumstances should ask themselves where this principle would end. Is a farmer entitled to shoot a boy stealing apples from his orchard? No? Then we have to strike a balance somewhere.'

Nobody doubts Mr Newbery's anger at the time, but he had planned the shooting, with the gun carefully placed behind a hole in the door. He fired at a range of five feet, which if not attempted murder was certainly extremely reckless.

Consider a similar incident, which took place last January in Houston, Texas. A householder, Jeffrey Agee, shot through the door at two men who were banging on it at four in the morning, killing one of them. In this case, the man was not a burglar but a Scotsman who had got lost and had wandered round the back of a house in search of help. The police did not press charges against Mr Agee. They took the view that his action was justified self-defence, as he could not have known that the men banging on his door were not burglars. As a Houston police spokesman said, 'You hear someone banging on your door like that, what are you going to do?'

The answer seems to be: shoot first and ask questions afterwards. Forget about gun control. An Englishman's allotment, like a Texan's veranda, is his castle. Strangers are guilty until proved innocent, and they had better prove it fast.

There is something seriously wrong about all this. Of course theft is a crime and housebreaking is a menace. But we make life less safe, not safer, by condoning private violence. As the American example shows us, letting people buy guns and use them as they like does not reduce violent crime, it increases it. There is no alternative to a proper police force actively patrolling the streets. There is no substitute for the rule of law. Vigilantes make easy media heroes. But in fact they are a menace to society.

1 What is the judge's point about stealing apples? Is it a fair comparison with what Mr Newbery did?

2 Why does the writer think Mr Newbery was wrong to do what he did?

3 Compare the incident in Texas with the one in England. In what ways
– are they similar? – are they different?

4 What is the writer's opinion of American gun laws?

What causes malaria?
The disease is caused by the bite of the female anopheles mosquito, which passes the malarial parasite from one human to another.

Symptoms
The most obvious symptom is a high fever, but there can be other symptoms such as diarrhoea.

How widespread is it?
Malaria threatens over two billion people in 100 countries in the tropics. More than 100 million people catch the disease each year, and a million die from it, mainly children under five years old and pregnant women. In Africa, malaria kills around one child in 20.

Prevention
One way of preventing malaria is to eradicate the anopheles mosquito, but attempts to do this have not yet been successful. The other is to protect yourself by taking anti-malarial drugs wearing long-sleeved shirts and long trousers, using insect repellents and sleeping under mosquito nets. Unfortunately, in many places the malarial parasite has become resistant to anti-malarial drugs, and the problem is getting worse.

14.1 Small but deadly *Rabies*

What causes rabies?

Rabies is caused by a virus which affects the brain. It can affect all warm-blooded animals, and can be passed to humans through a bite by an infected animal.

Symptoms

At first, victims experience pain on swallowing; later, they become terrified of water, the very sight of which can cause paralysis. The patient eventually dies in a coma.

How widespread is it?

Most countries in the world have rabies, and in some countries it is a serious problem. In Thailand, 100,000 people a year need treatment after animal bites. One country with no rabies is Britain, which has strict controls on the entry of animals from other countries. There are fears that a rabid animal could enter Britain through the Channel Tunnel.

Prevention and cure

People (and their pets) can be vaccinated against rabies, and there have been attempts to vaccinate wild animals by putting out food containing the vaccine.

Once rabies has developed, there is no cure, but there is a treatment for people who have just been bitten. This is very unpleasant, and involves a course of 17 injections in the stomach wall.

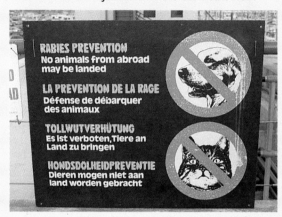

14.1 Small but deadly *Cholera*

What causes cholera?

Cholera is caused by a bacterium, V. cholerae. A person can become infected by drinking water or eating food contaminated by the bacterium.

Symptoms

Diarrhoea and vomiting.

How widespread is it?

There are cholera outbreaks every year in different parts of the world. They are most common in places with unsafe water supplies and poor sanitation.

Prevention

Drink only water that has been boiled or treated with chlorine or iodine. Ice (and ice-cream) made with untreated water can also lead to infection. Only eat food that has been cooked and is still hot when served. Avoid raw seafood and other raw food except fruit and vegetables that you have peeled yourself.

Keep flies off your food – they may have been in contact with infected materials.

Cure

Cholera can be treated by antibiotics, but the real danger is death by dehydration, which can happen in a matter of only a few hours. The most important treatment is therefore rehydration – putting back the water that has been lost. Patients should drink a large amount of water mixed with oral rehydration salts (ORS). In more serious cases, where patients cannot hold down liquid, this can be given via a drip (see illustration). Rehydration treatment will save the lives of nearly all cholera patients.

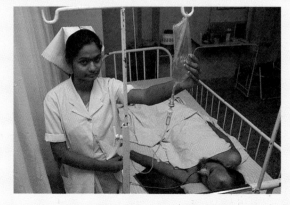

Macbeth – a synopsis

Act 1

RETURNING FROM BATTLE against the King of Norway, two Scottish generals Macbeth and Banquo meet three witches. They greet Macbeth as Thane of Glamis, Thane of Cawdor and King of Scotland. Macbeth is puzzled: he is Thane of Glamis, but the Thane of Cawdor is someone else, and Macbeth's cousin Duncan is King of Scotland.

Shortly afterwards, they find out that the Thane of Cawdor is dead. King Duncan makes Macbeth Thane of Cawdor in his place, and says he will soon be visiting Macbeth at his castle. So the witches were right about one thing. Were they right about the other too? Macbeth sends a message home to his wife, telling her what has happened.

When she gets the news, Lady Macbeth is determined that her husband will become King, and by the time Duncan arrives at the castle with his sons, she has persuaded Macbeth that they must murder him.

Act 2

That night, they drug the guards outside Duncan's bedroom, stab him to death while he is asleep, and smear his blood over the guards. Their hands are covered with blood, and Macbeth is horrified by what they have done. Lady Macbeth calms him down – 'A little water clears us of this deed,' she says – and gets him to bed.

Early next morning, Macduff, the Thane of Fife, arrives to collect Duncan. He finds the King dead, and Macbeth runs into the room and kills the guards. The King's sons, afraid that they will be killed too, run away. Everyone thinks that they arranged the murder of their father, and Macbeth is crowned King of Scotland.

Act 3

Macbeth is worried about Banquo. He is the only other person who knows about the witches – what if he is suspicious? He invites Banquo to a banquet, and has him murdered while he is out riding. At the banquet, Banquo's ghost appears. Only Macbeth can see it, and he is terrified. Lady Macbeth tells the guests her husband is ill, and they all go home.

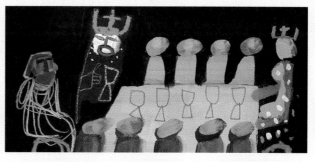

Other people begin to get suspicious. Tormented by guilt and fear, Macbeth visits the witches. They tell him that 'no man born of woman shall harm Macbeth'.

Act 4

Macbeth becomes even more cruel and tyrannical. When he hears that Macduff has gone to England to visit Duncan's elder son Malcolm, he sends soldiers to Macduff's castle to kill all his family and servants. Macduff hears the terrible news, and is determined to take revenge on Macbeth. They raise an army and march to Scotland.

Act 5

[Act Five begins with the sleepwalking scene – see page 75]

As the enemy army approaches the castle, Macbeth prepares for battle. Lady Macbeth kills herself, but Macbeth, sure that he cannot be hurt, rides out to meet the enemy, and finds himself face to face with Macduff.

'Come and fight!' he says. 'No man born of woman can harm me.' But Macduff was not 'born' in the normal way – he was delivered by Caesarian section. The witches have tricked Macbeth. Macduff kills him, and Malcolm becomes King of Scotland.

Tapescripts

1·2 Past experiences

We were in the Arctic. I was with an Inuit guide, and we were a long way above the Arctic Circle. I was taking photographs of seals under water. And the weather had turned bad, so we had decided to spend the night on the ice. So there I was early in the morning, lying in the tent, just waking up, when I felt something moving against my feet. I looked to see what it was, and I could see the shape of a polar bear outside – it was playing with my feet through the wall of the tent. I kept as still as I could, and very quietly woke my Inuit guide and told him what was happening. He said, 'Don't worry. Just stick your head out of the tent and it'll go away.' So I said, 'Well, you stick *your* head out of the tent.' And he did – he stuck his head out of the tent, and sure enough the polar bear went away.

2·3 Learning a language

1 I work in American firm. It is transnationality company. We had, we have had office in Germany because we also a Germany firm. It is, it firm manufactured medical equipment. I work as advi– ... scientist adviser for medicine and sale manager.

2 And they are so really nice family, they are taking well of me at least, and with ... There's also other two people also with this family, they are students. And it's nice, it's nice for living, for managing your life here, so there is no difficulties at all. But especially because it's also the weather everywhere now it's winter time, and it's cold and windy. And, but it's good that it's, there is heat inside the classes, inside the public transportation, inside the home itself. So you feel warm, a little bit.

3 When is Saturday I go to, usually I go to cinema with my friend, my boyfriend, or I, or I go to the restaurant, usually. In the Sunday I don't make, or I make nothing of especial, I stay in my house with my parents, or I stay with my sister, or I study because I am a researcher and study is important for me. I read the article for my job, this, but I don't make a lot of things in the weekend.

4 My family. First my landlady, Fiona, and my landlord, Tony, and they have two children. The one is Carmen, she is five, yes, she is just five years old, and Chloe she just nine, nine month, yeah, old, and very lovely. And Tony is black man, so their skin's black, between black and white and very lovely, pretty, yeah. So I often play with them.

2·4 The truth about lying

1 Sometimes I lie to my husband, normally about the cost of things. This Christmas I bought my grandmother a silver photo frame to frame a picture of her great-grand-children. And the only one that I could find that I really liked happened to be a solid silver one, that was £65, and I told my husband it was silver-plated and it was £6.50. And he didn't notice of course, just looked at it quickly and then it was wrapped up and given to her, and she greatly appreciated it and thought it was wonderful. Of course nobody else knew that I'd spent that much money on it, but I felt that as it could be her last Christmas it was justified.

2 Quite recently I got married and my mother sent me an engraved plate with a little horse and carriage in the Victorian style and I personally hated this plate but I had to pretend that I was thrilled to bits with it, that it was one of the nicest things I could possibly receive, because I knew that my mother would be very hurt if I reacted in any other way.

3 I probably lie mainly to my parents, because they're very over-protective. I find myself lying about school and if I've done my homework. They always want me to be involved in extra activities, and so once I lied and told them I was in orchestra, and I carried this lie on for about six weeks or something. And eventually there was meant to be a concert, and they found out and, you know, it was just all hell broke loose basically, and I got in big trouble.

4 Quite recently somebody showed me a sample of curtain fabric that I thought was really awful, and I just didn't comment too much about it. I said I liked it, I said I thought it would go well in the room, which it would because I didn't like the room either.

5 I'm a teacher and in the course of my work pupils have to produce lots of coursework, and quite often it's necessary for me to lie to those pupils to encourage them to produce work of a better quality. For example, one of my pupils produced a small bike, push-along bike for his baby sister, quite recently. Now the quality of the bike wasn't very good but had I said to him 'That's rubbish' he would have been demoralised and given up. But by encouraging him to think that the work is excellent, he's gone on to produce excellent work.

6 When I was about seven, my sister would have been eleven and my brother was nine, and one Saturday afternoon we were going to be taken to the pictures. We had to have lunch first, and just before lunch I was very hungry, so I stole a banana. And I hid the skin behind a sewing machine in the dining room. My mother found it and asked us who had taken the banana. And I lied and I said it wasn't me. My sister looked terribly guilty for some reason, and my mother kept saying 'It was you, wasn't it? It was you.' And Pam looked more and more guilty, and eventually she got so upset that she couldn't go to the pictures, and I went off and I saw my Walt Disney film with my brother and I had my ice-cream and my popcorn and I have to say I didn't feel guilty at all.

A Double meanings

1 How did the farmer know his pony had a cold? (I don't know.) Because it was a little hoarse.

2 Why couldn't the tennis player light his cigarette? (I don't know.) Because he kept losing his matches.

3 Who won the race, the Malaysian or the Filipino? (Who?) Neither. It was a Thai.

4 Why can't leopards escape from the zoo? (I don't know.) Because they're always spotted.

5 What is the fastest thing in the universe? (I don't know.) Milk, because it's pasteurised before you even see it.

6 What's the difference between a cat and a comma? (I don't know) One's got claws at the end of its paws, and the other's a pause at the end of a clause.

A Intonation and meaning

Part 2

1 A It might be useful to meet and talk about it.
  B Mmm. How about 2 o'clock?
2 A ... and the pains started a few weeks ago?
  B Yes, that's right. About three weeks.
  A Three weeks. Mmm. Right, perhaps you could just lie down now, and I'll examine you ...
3 A I don't suppose you want to go out tonight?
  B Mmm. I'd love to.
4 A So I went to see John ...
  B Mmm.
  A And I told him what I'd decided ...
  B Mmm.
5 A Do you like Thai food?
  B Mmm. As long as it's not too spicy.
6 A Here's a present for you.
  B Mmm. Belgian chocolates!

3·3 Emphasising the point

1 Yeah, weekends are really important to me, because I'm with people all the week, and working very hard, and Sunday's really the only day that I have to myself, and so I really enjoy just getting up late and listening to the radio, wandering round the house. And the thing I really enjoy is reading the Sunday papers in bed. You can just sit there and read and you don't have to get up. Just drink coffee. It's wonderful.

2 I don't think I have any big problems with it and the tenses are no problem and I think I can manage very well but what I find really difficult is phrasal verbs, especially the ones with three words like 'put up with' or 'make up for' something. I think they're really difficult.

3 No it's great, all these fantastic tall skyscrapers, and so busy, people kind of everywhere and lots and lots going on. But the thing that really surprised me about New York was the way the shops stay open all night. You know, any time of the day or night you could go in and buy anything you wanted, four o'clock in the morning, made no difference

4 So I tried ringing the manager quite a few times and was blocked by his secretary each time, which was bad enough, but the thing that really annoyed me was that he never answered my letters, and I found that infuriating.

4·1 Dangerous pastimes

Part 1

A So, Alison, here we are at the airfield. You're about to go and do your first ever parachute jump. (Yes) How're you feeling?
B I'm excited, very very excited, and I'm prepared.
A Glad to hear that. Are you not just a little bit frightened?
B No, not frightened. I am a little nervous, because it's my first time, but I am looking forward to it.
A Good. Tell me, what, what made you decide to do it in the first place?
B Well, some friends of mine have been doing it for a while and they asked me if I'd like to join them and at first I said no but then I decided that, yes, I'm an adventurous type, and they sponsored me to do a jump for charity, so I said 'Fine, why not?' It's a good cause.
A Right. And you know what to do, do you? I mean, have you trained, have you practised?
B Oh yes, yes, yes. They make sure that you're well trained, they wouldn't let you up there if not, and we actually trained for a whole weekend.
A Right, whole weekend. What do you do? I mean, could you take us through it?
B Oh sure. Let's see, you jump, hopefully, and then the parachute's supposed to open, which it does after about four seconds, and if it doesn't you've got a reserve parachute, (Right) and then the second thing is that you have to land properly, so you just bend your knees, roll over when you land, you know.
A And you've learned all that by heart, have you?
B I sure hope so.
A Well don't worry, if you forget, I'll be there to catch you, all right? (Oh thank you) Good luck.
B OK, see you on the ground.

Part 2

A So congratulations. (Oh, thanks) How was it?
B Whew! Well, it was fantastic, really just fantastic.
A And what was it like? What did it feel like jumping out?
B Oh well at first I didn't want to jump out, but I was, I was kind of forced to, which I'm glad, because it was just unlike anything I've ever done before. (I'm sure) You kind of, I don't know, there's this rushing sensation, and then that parachute opens, and then you feel in control because you just slow right down, and that's when,

that's when I kind of enjoyed it, I wasn't at first, but then it was just superb.
A Great. And it all went OK, did it, there were no problems with the parachute?
B No, thank goodness. No problems. Oh – the landing, well, that wasn't so great. I landed OK but I forgot to get up, which they did warn us about, and I was dragged across the ground a little bit, but – no problem.
A The million dollar question. Do you think you'll go again?
B Yes, yes, yes, definitely. (Good) Yes.

4·4 Problems, problems ...

Problem 1: In the post
Clue 1: Well you can't actually make the sword shorter, so you have to make it *seem* shorter.
Clue 2: Supposing she used a box that wasn't too long, but was a bit wider.
Answer: OK, what she did was she got a box 95 centimetres long, but one that was also fairly wide. And then she didn't put the sword in straight, she put it in diagonally.

Problem 2: Two boyfriends
OK, well this is all to do with the times of the trains, and the point is that the train in Bill's direction always comes one minute later than the one in Mario's direction, right? So if you imagine that Mario's train comes at 9 minutes past the hour, and Bill's train comes at 10 past – obviously she's only ever going to see Bill if she happens to get to the station in that one minute between 9 and 10 past.

Problem 3: An explosive mixture
The main problem is with boxes D and E, because they each touch six other boxes. So you start with them, and you put bottles 1 and 8 in D and E. Then you put bottles 7 and 2 in C and F. And once you've done that, the rest of it's easy.

Problem 4: Sweet revenge
Well in fact you only have to move one jar. All you have to do is pick up the second jar, tip all the sweets into the fifth jar, and then put it back again.

Problem 5: One man and his dog
Well after the farmer lets the dog off the lead he walks another 20 km. And since the dog's running three times as fast as the farmer, obviously he'll go three times the distance in the same time. So the answer's 60 km.

Problem 6: On balance
Well in fact he only needs to make two weighings. What he does is, he divides the boxes into three groups, with three boxes in each group, right? Then he

weighs two of the groups together. If one of them's heavier, that's where the diamonds are. If they weigh the same, then the diamonds must be in the group he hasn't weighed yet. OK – now he knows which group the diamonds are in. So all he has to do is take that group and do the same thing again. He takes two of the boxes and weighs them. And that tells him which box the diamonds are in.

Problem 7: Whodunnit?
A and B contradict each other, so one of them must be lying and one must be telling the truth. Now we know there are two liars, so C must be lying as well. So when C says 'I'm innocent' we know he must be lying – so the answer's C.

Problem 8: Wrong labels
Now you have to concentrate a bit on this one – the point is that *all* the labels on the sacks are wrong. So what he should do is take a potato out of the sack marked 'mixed'. OK, let's say it's a white potato. Then that must be the sack with the white potatoes. So what's in the sack marked 'red'? It can't be red (because we know the label's wrong), and it can't be white – so it must be mixed. So that just leaves the sack marked 'white' – and obviously that must contain the red potatoes.

B Conversational remarks

Part 1
1 There, there.
2 See you.
3 Now then.
4 Do you see?
5 Cheers!
6 Come off it.

Part 2
1 A They took my money, my credit cards, my passport, everything.
  B Oh dear. What are you going to do now?
2 They can't just come to me and tell me I can't work for them any more. I mean, it's just not on.
3 A Get on with it. We haven't got all day.
  B OK. I've just got to finish this – I'll be ready in a minute.
4 A But she's got a university degree.
  B So what? You've had more experience – that's what counts.
5 A I'm not really sure if I can come out this evening. I've got so much to do.
  B Well, it's up to you. But let me know what you decide, OK?
6 A What's up? You look up awful.
  B Oh, I've just got a bit of a headache, that's all.

7 A What was his phone number?
  B No idea. Look it up in the book.
8 A Whoops, sorry.
  B Watch where you're going.
  A Sorry. Are you OK?
9 A Phew! That was close.
  B Yeah – maniac.

5·2 Difficult situations

1 I was returning from America, flying into Heathrow Airport, and I was bringing back a diet powder for a friend, and it looked suspiciously like a drug powder. And I was pulled aside by the people at customs, and they found this, and I must confess it did look very suspicious because I had it taped up and it looked very much like drugs. And they took it aside to be tested in a side room and they strip-searched me and went through every item of clothing I had. And they kept accusing me of bringing in what was I mean almost about five pounds of cocaine. Ultimately, they did do a quick test on it and they found that it was just fructose powder, and they released me with a stern warning.

2 I was driving home from work one afternoon down a one-way street to my home, and parked in front of me was a removal van, and it had the back doors of the removal van open so that they could take the furniture and stuff out. And I drove up and tooted my horn, expecting somebody to close one of the doors so that I could drive past. And as I tooted my horn, this huge bloke emerged from behind the door with a crowbar in his hand, and threatened to smash my windscreen unless I backed off. Well, I was in a one-way street, but he was sufficiently threatening for me to actually put the car into reverse and go the wrong way up the one-way street and find another way home.

3 When I was about ten years old I had an argument with a girl in my class. And about a week later the headmistress called me into her office for something, I didn't know what it was. So I went in there, and she told me that I was going to be put in detention for scratching my name in the table. I didn't know anything about this, so I asked her to show me. She took me into the classroom, and sure enough my name was scratched into the table. There was nothing I could do about it. Anyway, the actual girl that I had the argument with finally admitted to me that she'd scratched my name in the table. But there was no way that I

could prove it to the headmistress, so I just had to pay the penalty.

6·2 What needs doing?

1 OK, well I'll have to go and take a look outside because I think there's probably a tile missing from the roof, in which case that will have to be replaced, and it will mean repainting inside on the ceiling.
2 Right, we'll just have to see how big the hole is. We'll be able to repair it if it's not too bad; otherwise we might have to replace the whole inner tube.
3 Right, you'll have to put a new pane of glass in, and part of the frame might have to be replaced as well. All that paint will need scraping off, and then you'll have to repaint it.
4 Right, I'll see if I can get the stain out. It might have to go to the dry cleaner's. I can sew the tear up, that's no problem, and I can sew the button back on, that's easy enough as well.
5 Well, you could try sticking the handle back on again with superglue. But then I wouldn't carry anything too heavy in it or it might come off again.

6·4 They did it themselves

A So Philippe, you're about to open a new restaurant called the Tarte Flambée. Where did you get the idea from?
B The idea comes from Alsace. It's a thin dough of bread which is used to be cooked about 200 years ago by the peasants and they used to roll the bread very thin and put ingredients they had at hand, which was bacon, fromage frais, and they used to put it into the oven and cook it very fast to show them if the oven was hot enough to cook the bread.
A So it was a kind of very old-fashioned fast food, in fact.
B Yes, it was the ancestor of the pizza, really, because originally the pizza was made with bread dough, a peasant dish, which is cheap ingredients, fast to cook, not expensive to eat. And also primarily communal eating, fun, you know, eating as a group of people.
A So your idea is to introduce this as a new kind of restaurant in England, yeah?
B Well, we thought there was a market for sort of good fast food, that it would be a good idea to introduce a simple food, it's not as filling as a pizza is, it's as tasty, moister, and it's cheaper. So as long as we can keep this equation right, then we should

be able to make a success.

A So are you planning to have take-away as well as people eating at the restaurant?

B Yes, eventually we are planning to also put them into little boxes and people can come and have some take-away as well. But primarily we want to make a restaurant which is very characteristic of a cheap bistro-style in France, you know, where you eat around the table, you have the food in the middle, you are cutting it and you have a bit of music around and it's fun and relaxed and not at all like a formal gastronomic restaurant where you have waiters looking at you, you know, in a formal way and filling up your glass of wine every five minutes, you know. This one is much more of a bistro, peasant, I would say, type of eating.

A I mean in England now we've got, if you go to any high street we have pizza parlours and burger places and fried chicken places and baked potatoes. What makes you think that tarte flambée will be as successful as pizza?

B Well the ingredients are fresh and it tastes great I think. And also, primarily you eat it in a group. So you have it in the middle of the table like I was saying, and it's a social occasion, much more than having your own little baked potato or your own little pizza in front of you. This goes in the middle of the table, you cut it in four or six and you're all eating it and when you've finished you have another one. And you don't have to decide, you know, before your meal starts, you don't have to decide how much you want, you can decide that at the time you're eating it, so if you eat one and you feel full, you stop, if you want another one you ask for another one, you know, and it takes two and a half minutes to cook.

A So, when do you open?

B Well we're opening on Friday night, so that's going to be our first night, everybody's very excited about it, so all the staff is eager to start now, and we hope for the best.

A Well, I'll be there. Thank you very much. Good luck.

B Thank you.

C British and US English

Part 1

There's a story of a young Englishman who was staying with a couple in New York. It was his first time in the United States, and on the first night, they had dinner and they were looking forward to going out to see a play on Broadway. After dinner the wife got up and said 'Well, I think I'll just wash up'. Well the Englishman immediately sprang to his feet and said 'Oh let me help'. Well, of course everyone just burst out laughing.

Part 3

Grammar is another area where things can be a little different between American English and British English. One of those areas is with the use of prepositions. For example, we would say *on the weekend* whereas in Britain it's *at the weekend*.

With days of the week we often leave the preposition out altogether. So an American will say *See you Tuesday* rather than the British *See you on Tuesday*.

And then there are some verbs where British people use a preposition but Americans don't. So in Britain people *protest against high taxes*, whereas in America, you simply *protest high taxes*. Likewise, in America you *write someone* and in Britain you *write to someone*.

Another thing I've noticed is that in Britain people say *I like swimming* or *I love watching TV*. Americans prefer to use the infinitive: *I like to swim, I love to watch TV*.

And there's a tense difference too with verbs. Where in Britain people say, for example, *I've already seen him* or *He hasn't come yet*, Americans will often use the Past tense instead: *I already saw him, He didn't come yet*.

And also, in America the past participle of *get* can be *gotten* rather than *got* – so an American will say *I've gotten the tickets* rather than *I've got the tickets*. Those are some of the main differences.

7·3 How do you picture it?

Interpretation 1

There is a girl in the middle sitting at a table. Her face looks open and without any particular expression. She seems to be looking in front of her as if she was waiting for something to happen. Behind her there is a young man. He looks like Andy Warhol. He's also looking in the same direction as the girl as if they were posing for a photograph, saying 'We belong together. We come from the same world.' Behind them there seems to be a screen. There is a third face coming through the screen, with the face of a man who's probably coming from the Third World. He looks hungry and he's looking hungrily at this bowl of soup in front of the girl. Well, I'm not sure what this picture is about. One thing might be a criticism of society, that some people in the Western world have too much of consumer goods and that there are people in the world who are still very hungry.

Interpretation 2

Well, in the centre of this picture there is a young woman, who also I think looks a little bit like a schoolgirl. And the table she's sitting at looks a bit like a school desk. And she seems to be sitting there waiting to be told what to do, or listening to the two people who are behind her. And these two people behind her seem to represent different sides of herself. And on one side there is a man who looks like Andy Warhol, and he looks very sophisticated, very beautiful. And this is the side that she wants to copy, I think. She's got the same hair as he has, they're wearing the same glasses, they're looking in the same direction. And behind her on the other side there is another figure, an older woman, who appears to be pushing her way into the picture from behind. And I think this woman represents another side of herself, a much darker side, she is much more primitive, she's older. And she is not as beautiful as Andy Warhol, of course, but she is much more alive, and she's also much bigger and more powerful in the picture. And perhaps this is the hidden side of herself, which is trying to force its way into her consciousness, and which perhaps she doesn't want to recognise.

8·2 Success story

It's an incredible success story. It was this man Chris Anderson, he was working for a company who produced a home computer magazine. Well, he had a row with his boss and he was sacked, so he decided to launch his own computer magazine. So what he did was, he got together with his wife and a couple of friends, and started a company called *Future Publishing*. Well, they set up an office in his bedroom at home, and they took out a bank loan of about £15,000 and launched their own computer magazine called *Amstrad Action*. Well, the first issue they did, they didn't even sell enough copies to break even, but they kept going and the next issue made a profit and they managed to pay off the original bank loan after just three months. And then after that they just expanded and expanded, they took on more staff and they launched other computer titles, like *PC Plus* for example. They kept adding other magazine titles, on all other sorts of topics like needlework and mountain biking and all kinds of things. Apparently, their turnover now has risen by about 90 per cent a year ever since, and now they've got more than 30 different magazine titles. Eventually Chris Anderson decided to sell the company, and he got something incredible like £50 million for it. He went off to the States and now doing it all over again.

8.4 Dirty money

Part 1

A In the past week, a number of small businesses in Britain have received a fax which promises to make them rich. The fax apparently comes from a top employee in a foreign oil company, who wants to transfer funds out of his country into a British bank account. Alex Clarke, who runs a small software company in London, is one of those who received the fax.

B Well, they claimed that they had 32 million American dollars which they wanted to transfer into my company bank account. According to them all they, I all had to do, rather, was to send them details of the bank account, obviously, and some headed notepaper, headed company notepaper, and that was it basically, the money would be transferred. In return for that we would receive 30 per cent of that money, which comes to a total of very nearly $10 million.

A It sounds like an offer you can't refuse. So was Mr Clarke tempted to do as he was asked?

B I was certainly very much tempted, I mean it's a great deal of money, as you can see, but one of the rules of business is you don't get something for nothing and this really did seem to be too good to be true. And I was a little bit suspicious about a couple of things. Firstly, they did openly and freely admit in the fax that the money was stolen, and secondly, for some reason which they didn't specify, they said they wanted the whole thing kept totally secret.

A So Mr Clarke gave up the chance of a lifetime, and instead sent a copy of the fax to the police. Now I have Inspector John Markham …

Part 2

A … to the police. Now I have Inspector John Markham of the Metropolitan Police with me in the studio. Inspector Markham, good morning.

C Morning, Sue.

A So did Mr Clarke do the right thing, or did he miss out on a fortune?

C No no, he definitely did the right thing. This is actually a fraud, and happens quite a lot. If Mr Clarke had gone ahead, he certainly wouldn't have gained any money, and he would probably have lost a lot.

A So how does the fraud work?

C Well, once they receive your company bank details and your headed notepaper, they can use these to transfer money out of your bank account. Now I'm not going to say how that's done, for obvious reasons. Very likely Mr Clarke would have gone to his bank account one day in a week or two's time and he'd have found it empty.

A Right, so he did do the right thing, then. (Yeah, certainly) But you say this kind of fraud is common. How common?

C Well, there are several cases a year. There was a similar case a few months ago, supposedly from the same oil company, but this time only offering $1.5 million. And before they were caught, these fraudsters had collected around £700,000.

A So is it only small businesses that get approached in this way?

C It is mostly, yes, yes, but it's also happened with charities. What happens is a charity receives a fax saying that somebody's died and has left them a large amount of money. Then later on the charity is asked for £5,000 to pay the death duties and that's the last you hear of them.

A Inspector Markham, thank you very much. (You're welcome) So if you run a small business – or a charity – and you receive a suspicious-looking fax which seems too good to be true, our advice is, sadly, to throw it in the bin or, better still, pass it on to the police.

9.3 Playing it safe

A They say that New York is pretty dangerous now, but are you actually likely to get mugged?

B Oh, you've seen too many movies. No, no. People exaggerate. As long as you're reasonably careful like in any major city of the world, you'll be OK. Of course, it depends upon what part of the city you're walking in.

A Right, that's interesting. Are there certain parts that are more dangerous than others?

B Oh yeah. I wouldn't go walking around in Harlem at the night time, especially if you're white. A stroll through Central Park after dark is not a good idea. Certainly you'll get mugged in there. But in Manhattan, which is really where most tourists go, stick to the main streets and you'll be fine. For instance, 42nd Street is fine. People think if they go to 41st Street or 43rd, because

they're side streets, it'll be safer, but actually there are no police there. So, stick to the main ones, 57th, 34th, 42nd, 14th and so forth.

A Right. So, be confident, be strong, is that the sort of thing?

B Abso–… Look like you belong there. Yeah. You know, tourists, they'll scream 'tourist' by the way they dress, they carry a map, they look at the tops of buildings, they stand on street corners obviously lost, they flash money about, they have too much jewellery. Don't do that. Look like a New Yorker. Walk like a New Yorker. Talk like a New Yorker if you can.

A Difficult. But we'll try. Thank you.

10·2 Science and the environment

This first one is false. We certainly produce some radioactivity, but there's also plenty of natural radiation around – this comes from cosmic rays hitting the Earth, and also from ancient rocks such as granite.

Number two is true. If you've got a cold (which is caused by a virus), it's absolutely no use taking antibiotics.

Three is false. A lot of people believe in astrology, of course – but there's no scientific explanation for how the position of stars or planets at the time of your birth could possibly affect your character. So astrology has no scientific basis.

Four: also true. This hasn't been proved conclusively, but all the evidence we have – fossil remains, and so on – points to evolution rather than any other explanation.

Five is false. Everything on the planet is chemical. Most man-made chemicals are neither more nor less harmful than natural ones.

Number six: false. We all come into contact with radioactivity, but we don't all die from it. On the other hand, radioactivity can certainly be dangerous, and no one really knows what a safe dose is.

Seven: that's true. In fact, some radioactive waste will remain dangerous for hundreds of thousands of years.

Eight: false. The greenhouse effect is caused by greenhouse gases like carbon dioxide, which prevent heat from escaping. The hole in the ozone layer is something completely different – it's the reason you should be careful when you're out in the sun.

Nine is true. Burning them produces carbon dioxide, which is the main greenhouse gas. Coal is the worst, by the way, then oil, and gas is the least harmful.

Number ten: false. Some pesticides are really dangerous, and many of those are now banned. There are some that may cause cancer if they're not used correctly – but certainly not all of them. Eleven true: We're destroying thousands of species a year. Some people believe that we're causing more extinctions than the ones that happened millions of years ago.

And twelve: false. They are one of the major causes of acid rain, and a major source of greenhouse gases – so they certainly do cause air pollution.

10·4 Science fiction

Part 1

The children were always good during the month of August, especially when it began to get near the twenty-third. It was on this day that the great silver spaceship carrying Professor Hugo's Interplanetary Zoo settled down for its annual six-hour visit to the Chicago area.

Before daybreak the crowds would form, long lines of children and adults both, each one clutching his or her dollar, and waiting with wonderment to see what race of strange creatures the Professor had brought this year.

In the past they had sometimes been treated to three-legged creatures from Venus, or tall, thin men from Mars, or even snakelike horrors from somewhere more distant. This year, as the great round ship settled slowly to earth in the huge tri-city parking area just outside of Chicago, they watched with awe as the sides slowly slid up to reveal the familiar barred cages. In them were some wild breed of nightmare – small, horselike animals that moved with quick, jerking motions and constantly chattered in a high-pitched tongue. The citizens of Earth clustered around as Professor Hugo's crew quickly collected the waiting dollars, and soon the good Professor himself made an appearance, wearing his many-coloured rainbow cape and top hat. 'Peoples of Earth,' he called into his microphone.

The crowd's noise died down and he continued. 'Peoples of Earth, this year you see a real treat for your single dollar – the little-known horse-spider people of Kaan – brought to you across a million miles of space at great expense. Gather around, see them, study them, listen to them, tell your friends about them. But hurry! My ship can remain here only six hours!'

And the crowds slowly filed by, at once horrified and fascinated by these strange creatures that looked like horses but ran up the walls of their cages like spiders. 'This is certainly worth a dollar,' one man remarked, hurrying away. 'I'm going home to get the wife.'

All day long it went like that, until ten thousand people had filed by the barred cages set into the side of the spaceship. Then, as the six-hour limit ran out, Professor Hugo once more took microphone in hand. 'We must go now, but we will return next year on this date. And if you enjoyed our zoo this year, phone your friends in other cities about it. We will land in New York tomorrow, and next week on to London, Paris, Rome, Hong Kong and Tokyo. Then on to other worlds!'

He waved farewell to them, and as the ship rose from the ground the Earth peoples agreed that this had been the very best Zoo yet …

Part 2

Some two months and three planets later, the silver ship settled at last onto the familiar jagged rocks of Kaan, and the queer horse-spider creatures filed quickly out of their cages. Professor Hugo was there to say a few parting words, and then they scurried away in a hundred different directions, seeking their homes among the rocks.

In one, the she-creature was happy to see the return of her mate and offspring. She babbled a greeting in their strange tongue and hurried to embrace them. 'It was a long time you were gone. Was it good?'

And the he-creature nodded. 'The little one enjoyed it especially. We visited eight worlds and saw many things.'

The little one ran up the wall of the cave. 'On the place called Earth it was the best. The creatures there wear garments over their skins, and they walk on two legs.'

'But isn't it dangerous?' asked the she-creature.

'No,' her mate answered. 'There are bars to protect us from them. We remain right in the ship. Next time you must come with us. It's well worth the nineteen commocs it costs.'

And the little one nodded. 'It was the very best Zoo ever …'

D Conversational fillers

Part 1

1 Well, I do like it, I mean really I know I shouldn't, but um, you know how it is, if you have one and you want another it's um, it's a bit difficult to stop, really.

2 I think it's a really um disgusting habit, really, and you know, you know if you're um in a restaurant or something and people start smoking, I think it's disgusting, basically, I think it's really awful.

3 Yeah, well I've been smoking now for, ooh I don't know, about 30 years or so I suppose, and I'm kind of smoking one year and kind of giving up the next, and um actually it's been going on like that for ages and um you know when I, when I give up I just put on all this weight. So I kind of give up, and then I get very depressed because I'm overweight, so I kind of um, so I take it up again.

Part 2

A Well, um, let me see, I think it was quite a small room, and um it had yellow wallpaper, I think, as far as I remember, and um yeah with pictures of penguins I think, or something like that.

B Well, you see, the fact is that I've been very very busy recently, and well, to be honest I haven't had time to look at it. And that's how it is really, it just can't be helped.

C Well, I was just thinking um, one possible idea might be um to um organise a sort of fancy dress party, or something like that. I mean, it's just an idea. What do you think?

D Well the fact is, I mean let's face it, the government isn't actually doing anything to improve the health service. In fact, if you ask me all they're really interested in doing is saving money. Well, that's how I see it, anyway.

11·1 For better, for worse

a I think it's more difficult for young people these days. I think that people have to grow up so quickly, it's almost like, you know, your childhood is over and done with before you know it. And schools, you know, they cut back so much on education resources that schools are no longer really a fun place to be. So I find that a bit grim really, I don't see a lot of joy and happiness for young people and teenagers.

b Well I think the streets actually are worse. Any kind of major city that you walk down, the place is completely filthy and there's a lot of homeless people around now and it's actually quite frightening and quite threatening. People are begging all the time. And it's just a nightmare going anywhere these days.

c One area that I think has improved greatly is the variety of fruit and vegetables available in your local supermarket. You can now get about ten different sorts of lettuce and the varieties of tropical fruit that you can now buy are wonderful.

d I think one of the ways things have changed for the worse, and I don't know if this is just me and I'm getting older, but I do think there seems to be a greater sense of lawlessness and a lack of responsibility, especially among some young people, and you see kids doing things that you would never imagine seeing 20 years ago, smashing up trains and things in front of the other passengers, things like that. So I think that's a step backwards.

e The great thing about the nineties for me really is package holidays, because they're so cheap, and you can fly anywhere around the world. Now when I was a kid, well I had one holiday abroad I think, and that wasn't because we were a particularly deprived family, but everything was just much more expensive then, and you didn't get the flights that you have now. Now you can nip down to your travel agent and book a flight for tomorrow and you're half way across the world.

f One of the good things, though, I think about today is that there's a lot more choice around in terms of work and career, especially for women, I think there are more equal opportunities, there are women going into professions that, you know, 20, 30 years ago would be considered solely a male profession. So I think that that's a very encouraging thing about today's society.

g Well, in my mind the way things have moved forwards best really in the last few decades is that in terms of foreigners in this country, people are far more accepting of them. Particularly when it comes to children, you know, in schools people are taught to respect other people's cultures, languages, religions.

h The particular thing that I think has got much worse is overpowering perfumes. You can't walk into a restaurant or a pub or a café without getting attacked by four or five different sorts of stinks, really, and men I'm afraid have also sort of jumped on the bandwagon and this is a trend that I think should definitely be discouraged.

12·2 Relationships

1 I think total honesty with each other, communication – if you can talk about anything and discuss things and you're totally honest about what you want and what you feel, you can't go wrong.

2 I think mutual interests are very important in a relationship. If a couple comes together with mutual interests in something like the theatre and sports and they enjoy the same type of people, then it's a wonderful ground for this couple to make new friends, to laugh together, and through this kind of communication I think a relationship really grows and flowers.

3 One of the important things in a relationship for me is a beautiful partner, because I like to feel proud when I go out, it's nice to have somebody good on your arm, and it rubs off on me. People think 'There's a beautiful couple.'

4 I think a relationship should be about a partnership between close friends and that you should be allowed to lead your own lives within the partnership and have your own friends and your own interests.

5 Well, what I first look for is probably good looks, because at my age it's not going to be such a serious relationship, and so you just like to be with someone who looks good.

6 I think it's very important to be able to admit that you've made a mistake once in a while, and it's also very important I think generally not to take yourself too seriously in relation to the other person.

7 For me the most important thing in a relationship is love. And this means taking the other person as he is and also leaving him the space he wants.

12·4 Skin deep

A You run a tattoo studio in quite a small town. Do you get a lot of business?

B Yes, we do. My clientele basically can come from anywhere from sort of local people up to I get people coming over from Europe, I get visitors from Holland, from all over the place, we do. Yes.

A And what kind of people come for tattoos, I mean, are things changing?

B You could say that. It could be anyone from society, basically; over the last ten years it's become a lot more popular and a lot more acceptable.

A Do you get women, a lot of women coming in?

B I would say probably 50 per cent of the clientele that comes through the studio is female.

A What kind of tattoos do people usually ask for?

B Well, nowadays it can be anything, but the traditional tattoos, the hearts, flowers, roses and daggers, that sort of thing is still quite popular, but we do a lot more of art stuff as well, portrait work and reproduction work.

A Has anybody ever asked you for anything really unusual?

B I think basically if you can think of it we've probably tattooed it at some stage.

A You're talking about parts of the body now, are you?

B Yes and also what can be tattooed on someone. Basically if something can be drawn it can be tattooed, and it really is as simple as that.

A So once you have a tattoo, is that it, you've got your tatoo, or do people come back for more?

B I tend to find that if someone comes in and they have a tattoo done, it can be the first of many. There's a couple of people that that I know, that live in the local area, that have actually become friends, we've got to know each other over the years. I've got a chap who comes in from Devizes and he started off just with a couple of tattoos but now he's wearing a tattoo that is nearly 80 per cent of his body is covered and it's turned into a three-dimensional picture of a castle basically, so as you walk around his body you're looking through the different windows at the scenes that are actually taking place inside. And that, we've been tattooing Winnie for the last five years on a fortnightly basis.

A I see you've got a notice outside warning people that tattoos are permanent and telling them to think about it first. Do you find that's necessary?

B I think so, yes, 'cause someone can come into the studio and there can be a case of 'Oh I like that design, I want that now', spur of the moment, but people do have to realise that it is something that is there for life. Basically the only thing it can be swapped for is a scar. What I tend to do, if I'm not happy that the client is not going to be happy with the tattoo I will not tattoo them, it's as simple as that.

A So you have refused to tattoo people (Yes) who want tattoos?

B Yeah, especially with certain placements, especially with tattoos that are going to be placed on the face or the hands, we just will not do it.

A Now I see a lot more people with tattoos these days than I used to. It's clearly becoming more popular. Do you see a time when tattooing will be a normal thing to do, when you can walk into your local department store, maybe, and there's a tattoo studio in there?

B I don't think so, no. Tattooing has always had a taboo that's sort of gone with it. I think that the idea of walking into somewhere like Debenhams and just getting tattooed I don't think'll happen, somehow.

A So you don't see someone like Princess Diana going out with a tattoo on her arm?

B Well, I mean to be perfectly honest, I mean the Royal Family back in the early 19th century were heavily tattooed themselves. Yes.

E Regional accents

1 I had a very very happy childhood. I was brought up on the coast, in this lovely little seaside town, and you know so there was always plenty to do there, like you know on the weekends or after school. You could go down the beach, and play on the rocks. A really, really lovely place to live, I think.

2 Well, the thing I always remember about the weekend, right, is that my old man had a bit of work on the side, I mean he had the job during the week, you know, but he needed to do something else at the weekend to make ends meet. So he used to a little bit of catering, he used to do, like, weddings and parties, things like that, you know.

3 I grew up on a farm, and one thing about that is you tend not to have many playmates, and so therefore I was sort of limited in that I could only really play with my brother, my sister was too small at the time. And it's a kind of wonderful world for children to grow up when you grow up in the countryside, and all your games are all based out in the fields or down the woods, and you just invent all the time, because obviously I think that you've got these wonderful places to explore, so I mean our woods became the jungle and wonderful rich forests.

4 I always hated my cousin Linda. She was a year younger than me, but she always got me in trouble. And I remember one day we were visiting grandma, and Linda said to me, 'Let's go see Auntie Sal because she's got candy.' And so off we went, and our parents hadn't realised we'd gone missing. And they sent the neighbours out searching for us and all my relatives. And one of our uncles, Uncle George, finally found us, and put us in his car to take us back, and when we got home, I was punished, my mother spanked me.

5 We used to really like going down to the harbour because there was so much going on down there. There was a little bay, and a boat used to be down there. It was tied up, I don't know who owned it, but we used to sort of borrow it, it wasn't stealing, we just borrowed it, you know. And we'd all pile into it, there'd be two or three girls, a couple of dogs, we used to have an oar to row – one oar to row with, and that was it, we used to go heading out on the harbour. And it was pretty deep, it was pretty dangerous I reckon, but you know we used to love it, it was great fun.

6 Well, I was at boarding school when I was a child, all girls. And my best friend was Sarah, Sarah Woolley. And I was thrilled to bits when she invited me for half term to stay with her family. And she lived near the coast, and from her bedroom you could see the sea. And I thought that was just wonderful.

7 I've got two brothers, and they're twins. I remember as children we were always fighting, especially my two brothers over something or nothing. But the three of us, we used to be in a gang. But there was another gang as well, and with these two gangs we used to have rival fights and throwing stones at each other. It was a really roughish neighbourhood, you could say, and you really had to be tough and ready to go.

13·3 Speaking your mind

1 A Oh, by the way, they're not coming after all.
  B What? You could have told me earlier. I've just spent the last three hours getting the place sorted out.

2 Don't you ever run out into the road like that again. You could have been knocked over.

3 A Well, that was awful. What a waste of time. Why did we bother?
  B I don't know. Couldn't believe it. Frozen pizza. I mean, we might just as well have stayed at home and had a take-away.

4 A Everything ready?
  B Yes, no thanks to you.
  A Why, what do you mean?
  B Well, you might have offered to lend a hand, instead of just sitting there reading the paper.

5 *Newsreader:* … in the semi-final of the World Cup, New Zealand defeated England by 45 points to 25.
  Viewer: Oh, I might have known. As soon as we come up against a really good side, we lose.

6 Look, I know they were pretty boring, I know they were going on and on, but you needn't have been quite so rude. I mean, what was I to say? I was so embarrassed.

7 For me? Oh, you needn't have bothered. But they're lovely. Thank you so much.

14·2 ## Medical treatment

1 Will you roll up your sleeve, please. Here you go. Be very quick. There we are. All finished.

2 Right, I'm just going to put this over here. There we are. OK, I'm just going out of the room for a minute. Um, all you've got to do is keep absolutely still. OK?

3 A Mm-hmm. Mm. Oh. Yep. Here's one. One small cavity. Listen, I can fill it right away if you like. You probably want an injection.
  B Oh, no, I don't, thank you. I don't like them.

4 Oh that's a bad cut isn't it. We'll have to do something about that. Right, sit still, I'll just put some cream on it first, it doesn't sting (Ooh) – it's all right. There we are. Now just put this on. There we are. Sit still. There we are.

5 OK, I'm going to make an incision above the left ventricle. Scalpel, please, nurse. Thank you. OK.

6 I'll give you two lots to keep you going. There we are. That's two tablets three times a day, OK? And if that doesn't do the trick, come back next week.

7 OK, open your mouth. Good. Now close your mouth. Keep it under your tongue – Oop, don't bite it. That OK? (Mmm) Good.

14·3 ## Alternative medicine

Well the first teaching job I had I was teaching at a secondary school in West Africa. And this school was way out in the bush, a long long way from the nearest town. And it was a fairly kind of dusty area, the school, and very few of the boys had shoes and most used to walk around with bare feet. And there were scorpions in the area, and almost every day one or other of the students would get a scorpion sting. Now these scorpions weren't fatal but the bite was, the sting was very very painful and if it wasn't treated it would keep you in bed for a week, you wouldn't be able to walk for a week. And the usual thing to do was to go down to the hospital, which was one of the few parts of the town that had electricity, and the hospital would give you an injection and that would help the pain, and after say two or three days you'd be able to get up and walk around again and resume lessons. But many of the students at the school preferred to go to a traditional doctor, and now and again I would be asked to take a student with a scorpion sting down to this doctor on my motorbike. And the treatment that the traditional doctor would give the patient was extraordinary, it was completely different from anything else that I've ever seen. The first thing he used to do was to mix up a very kind of muddy looking liquid which the student would drink. And then there'd be some kind of chanting from the traditional doctor, and he would start with his fingers on the affected foot and would chant all the time and move his fingers gradually up the student's leg, up his body, and then along his arm to the end of his fingers. And apparently what was happening I was told was that he was supposedly moving the poison, or moving the sting, up through the student's body and then out of his fingers, and therefore somehow getting rid of the sting altogether. And the extraordinary thing about this was that it worked, and the moment the sting supposedly left the student's finger he was able to, you know, the pain was gone and he was able to walk, and very often I wouldn't give him a lift back to the school on my motorbike, he'd go and stay and do some shopping and then walk back on his own. So this was somehow or other a far more effective treatment than could be provided by Western medicine at the hospital.

14·4 All the perfumes of Arabia

DOCTOR: I've watched with you for two nights now, but I can't see any truth in what you told me. When was the last time she walked?

GENTLEWOMAN: Since the King went off to war I've seen her get up from her bed, put on a dressing gown, unlock her desk, take out a piece of paper, fold it and write on it. Then she reads it, seals it, and goes back to bed – yet she's fast asleep the whole time.

DOCTOR: There must be something very wrong with her if she's asleep, and yet behaves as if she were awake. Tell me, in this disturbed sleep of hers, as well as walking around and the other things she does, what have you ever heard her say?

GENTLEWOMAN: I'm not telling you that.

DOCTOR: You can tell me – and I think you ought to.

GENTLEWOMAN: I'm not telling you or anyone else, not without a witness to support what I say. Look, here she

comes. This is exactly the way she's been before, and, I swear it, fast asleep. Watch her. Keep hidden.

DOCTOR: Where did she get that candle?

GENTLEWOMAN: It was next to her bed. She has a candle there all the time. She insists on it.

DOCTOR: You see her eyes are open.

GENTLEWOMAN: Yes, but she can't see anything.

DOCTOR: What's she doing now? Look at the way she's rubbing her hands together.

GENTLEWOMAN: She often does that. It's as if she's washing her hands. I've known her keep it up for a quarter of an hour.

F Formal and informal

a They say they're sorry but they can't help you any more.

b He was walking down the High Street when he saw two men trying to break into a parked car.

c The dining car's near the back of the train.

d You aren't allowed to drink alcohol in here.

e He say's he's very glad so many people have come to the meeting.

15·1 Memories

1 & 2: See page 78.

3 … And then when I was about 13 my parents were sent abroad to work. They didn't want to disrupt my education and so they sent me off to boarding school. I really hated it there. The food was terrible and we had to go to bed at 9.30 every evening, and we were never allowed to go out in the evening. But of course we did use to sneak out in the evenings, just to go around the village where the school was, and one night I was caught, and I really thought I was going to be expelled, but in fact in the end all that happened was that the headmistress wrote a letter to my parents.

16·1 War and peace

1 Vietcong guerrillas launched a surprise attack on Wednesday on six towns throughout South Vietnam. They also attacked four US air bases, inflicting heavy damage. This is the largest offensive launched by the communist forces so far in the Vietnam War.

2 A force of nearly 3,000 American troops invaded the Caribbean island of Grenada yesterday. Fierce fighting continued today, as Grenadan and Cuban troops resisted the invasion.

President Reagan, speaking on television last night, said the troops had been sent to the island to protect Americans living there and to restore democracy.

3 The Tanzanian government has closed its borders to tens of thousands of Rwandan refugees who have fled from their camps in Burundi in fear of their lives. More than 200 refugees are believed to have been killed in a massacre at one of the camps two days ago.

4 The Presidents of Serbia, Bosnia and Croatia yesterday signed a peace treaty which it is hoped will end the 43-month-old war in Bosnia. The agreement was reached after three weeks of intensive negotiations, in which Washington put strong pressure on all three parties to accept the peace plan.

5 Russian troops have now begun to arrive in the town of Kizlyar in Dagestan, where a group of heavily armed Chechen guerrillas are holding around 2,000 hostages in the town's hospital. The hospital is now surrounded by tanks, and a government spokesman has warned the guerrillas that the hostages must not be harmed.

16·4 On the front line

A Most people imagine that being a war correspondent is a pretty dangerous job. Is it in fact as dangerous as that?

B No, it probably looks a lot more dangerous on television or on newspaper than it really is, because you do have a lot of restrictions which actually prevent you from getting to the very dangerous areas. Various sides in a conflict quite often don't actually want a journalist to see exactly what's going on, so they do their best to stop you, especially if you're a foreigner. I myself have only on very few occasions actually got to a front line. Far more often, and this is the case with most journalists I think, you're quite a long way back. So the real dangers are probably of making mistakes. You can accidentally come across a dangerous place, and this is what happened to me in particular. I was driving to Sarajevo, and we found ourselves actually crossing one front line, then in no man's land, where there were dead bodies which hadn't even been reclaimed, because it was so dangerous to be there, and finally crossing over to the other side. At one stage we were surrounded by one of the sides who were actively burning down a village that we happened to be passing through, it was still on fire. So it really is often really by accident that you end up in a dangerous place and it doesn't happen that routinely.

A What about the kind of things you see, I mean, the distress of seeing people wounded and seeing victims, innocent people killed, do you find this affects you emotionally, or can you cut yourself off from it?

B Usually, you're so caught up in your own job, the deadlines that you're involved with, the number of things that you have to do and to cover, that it becomes quite technical, which is actually a help, because that means you can keep your distance, you can insulate yourself emotionally from what's going on. But obviously you can't help but be caught up and I find that even though I've done it so often just driving across miles and miles for hours and hours across areas of Bosnia in which every single village has been burnt, the houses have all been torched deliberately, you know, by one side to stop the people of the other side coming back and living there, that still really affects me, makes me feel very angry and emotional. And obviously on occasions you see people, children especially, when you see children who've been victims of it, I ... The worst occasion was when I saw a group of refugees who'd been driven from their homes quite early on in the war, and there was a young woman who after many hours of walking across a front line carried her baby who'd died and she wouldn't let go. And that, you know, I still remember that, I'll never forget it.

A Being in a war zone and reporting war, you're in a place where important events are happening and life is very exciting. What is it like coming back to London, say, to the ordinary world? Does it seem very flat in comparison?

B Yes, there's always this strange culture shock. It takes a while to get used to the culture shock, you walk round in a daze. And also I'm fortunate, I have a family, so I think that helps. I think if I was living by myself it would be more difficult, it's probably more difficult for journalists who are single. But there is this other thing, I mean, yes, life seems slightly flat and dull, it's an awful thing to say but quite often you miss, when just routine things are going on back home, you miss the adrenalin I suppose and I think there is such a phrase as becoming an 'adrenalin junkie', which I was very aware of. But I think if you're aware of this thing that life is going to seem very flat, then that's at least some precaution.

Reference section

1 Present, past and future

Present tenses

Present simple	works
Present continuous	is working
Present perfect simple	has worked
Present perfect continuous	has been working

- We use these tenses when talking from the standpoint of the present – what things are like *now*.

Present simple
This is used for talking 'in general', or about repeated actions:
- He *comes* from Vladivostok.
- She *works* ten hours a day.

Present continuous
This is used for saying what's happening at the moment or 'around now':
- He can't talk to you now – he's *washing* his hair.
- *Are* you still *going* out with Linda?

Note: Both the Present simple and Present continuous are also used to talk about the *future*. See General grammar reference section, page 126.

Present perfect simple
This is used for talking about recent events, or things which happened in the past when we are interested in their relevance to the present:
- I've *stopped* smoking. (= I don't smoke now)
- I've just *started* a new job. (= now I have a job)

We also use the Present perfect simple to talk about *experience* (things you have done at some time in your life):
- I've *travelled* at lot in East Asia and Australia. (= at various times)
- I've never *eaten* raw fish. (= at any time)

Present perfect continuous
This is used for talking about recent activities:
- I've *been working* hard recently.
With *for/since*, it is used to talk about activities which started in the past and are still continuing:
- He's *been working* for 12 hours (and he's still working).

Using Present perfect simple instead of continuous
We use the Present perfect simple instead of the continuous in these cases:
1 with *stative verbs* (see General grammar reference section, page 126):
   - I've *had* a lot to do recently. (*not* been having)
   - We've *known* them for years. (*not* been knowing)
2 to express *negative* duration (to say how long it is since something happened):
   - I *haven't seen* her for years.
   - She *hasn't played* chess since she was a child.

Past tenses

Past simple	worked
Past continuous	was working
Past perfect	had worked

- We use these tenses when talking about things which are *set in the past*.

Past simple
This is used for talking about events or states in the past, and for telling the main events of a story:
- I *studied* zoology at university.
- Suddenly, I *woke* up.

Past continuous
This is used for saying what was going on (the background to a story):
- The sun *was shining*.
- I *was lying* in my tent when I heard a noise outside.

Past perfect simple
This is used for going back from the past to things that had happened earlier:
- When I arrived, everyone *had* already *finished* eating.
- There *had been* heavy snow the day before.

Future tenses

Future simple	will work
Future continuous	will be working
Future perfect	will have worked

- We use these tenses when talking about things which are *set in the future*.

Future simple
This is used for talking about events or states in the future:
- In the future, people *will live* much longer.
- The film *will finish* at 10 o'clock.

Future continuous
This is used for saying what will be happening at a particular point in the future:
- By 2010, some people *will be living* in space.
- I'll *be waiting* for you when you come out.

Future perfect
This is used for talking about things that will already be complete at a point in the future:
- In ten years' time, we *will have discovered* a cure for cancer.
- By the time I'm 60, I *will have stopped* smoking.

(See also General grammar reference section, page 126.)

Knowledge and experience

- To talk about experience, we can use the Present perfect tense (see above):
  - I've been to Los Angeles several times.
  - I've never used an IBM computer.
- Other ways to talk about experience:
  - I have (some) experience of hotel work.
  - I'm used to working with elderly people. (= I've done it before, so I know about it)
- Ways to talk about knowledge and qualifications:
  - I have a good knowledge of Japanese.
  - I'm familiar with Macintosh computers.
  - I'm a trained mechanic.
  - I'm a qualified secretary.
  - I have qualifications in Spanish and Italian.

2 Communicating

Types of written and spoken English

message	leave a message (for someone)
note	write a note (to someone), leave a note (for someone)
notes	take/make notes (e.g. from a lecture)
notice	put up a notice
announcement	make an announcement
speech	make/give a speech
lecture	give a lecture
sermon	give a sermon
contract	write/sign a contract
minutes	take the minutes (of a meeting)

- A note is usually to ask or remind someone to do something (e.g. 'Please buy more milk. Back at 6'). You take or make notes from a book or lecture, or to prepare for a speech. Minutes are notes you take at a meeting, to record what happened.
- A notice gives public information (e.g. 'No smoking', 'Closed until Monday').
- Types of message: an email message, a phone message, an answerphone message, a message in a bottle.

Communicating: Idioms

- If you meet someone regularly, or often phone or write to them, you are in touch with them. Notice these expressions:

be get keep	in	touch with someone
lose be out of		

In more formal English, we say be in contact with, lose contact with, etc. This has the same meaning.

- Other idioms concerned with communicating:
  - we get on well (with each other) = we like each other, and have plenty to talk about

- we're not on speaking terms = we don't speak to each other when we meet (because we're enemies)
- make small talk = talk about unimportant things (e.g. the weather)
- make it up (with someone) = become friends again after having an argument

Learning a language

- Learning a language involves:
  - learning grammar, vocabulary, pronunciation and intonation
  - developing the four skills: reading, writing, listening and speaking
  - being able to use the language fluently (= being able to communicate easily) and accurately (= not making mistakes)

3 Making things clear

Relative clauses

- There are two kinds of relative clause in English:
  - Defining (or identifying) relative clauses tell us which person or thing the speaker is talking about:
    The people who live next door have bought a dog.
    Where's the book that I lent you?
  - Non-defining (or non-identifying) relative clauses just give us more information about the person or thing:
    Mrs Smith, who lives next door, has bought a dog.
    I'm reading 'The Idiot', which is a novel by Dostoyevsky.
  Non-defining relative clauses are dealt with in Unit 5.

Defining relative clauses: pronouns

	Person	Thing
Subject	who/that	which/that
Object	(who/that)	(which/that)
Possessive	whose	–
Place	–	where

- If the relative pronoun is the object of the relative clause, it can be left out:
  - She's the person you met on Saturday. (= who/that you met)
  - Where's the book I lent you? (= which/that I lent you)
- In more formal English, we use whom as an object pronoun to refer to people:
  - He is a man whom I admire greatly.
- If the relative clause contains a preposition, it can be left 'hanging' at the end of the clause:
  - Are you the person I spoke to yesterday?
  - This is the chair I usually sit in.
- In more formal English, the preposition comes before the relative pronoun:
  - Are you the person to whom I spoke yesterday?
  - The village in which I grew up no longer exists.

Cleft sentences

- We use cleft sentences to give emphasis to a particular part of the sentence. Compare:
  The Americans landed on the Moon, not the Russians.
  → It was the Americans who landed on the Moon, not the Russians, or:
  It wasn't the Russians that landed on the Moon. It was the Americans.
  I admire Peter's *honesty*.
  → The thing I admire about Peter is his honesty.

- Cleft sentences with *It*:

It was John	who spoke to you, (who) you met,	not Alex.
It wasn't Alex	that spoke to you. (that) you met.	It was John.

- Cleft sentences with *What* or *The thing (that)*:

What The thing	I really enjoy is eating outside.
What The thing	I hate about Mondays is getting up early.

Participle phrases with *-ing* and *-ed*

- There's a woman. She's sitting on a bench. She's reading a newspaper.
  → There's a woman sitting on a bench reading a newspaper.
- He was lying on the grass. He was stretched out. He had his legs crossed.
  → He was lying stretched out on the grass with his legs crossed.

4 Sports and games

Dangerous sports

- Names of some 'dangerous' sports:

> *In the air:* parachute jumping, skydiving, hang-gliding, ski jumping, bungee jumping
> *On water:* white water rafting/canoeing
> *On land:* mountaineering, rock climbing, off-piste skiing
> *Underground:* potholing
> *Under water:* scuba diving

- People do dangerous sports because they're *exhilarating/thrilling/exciting*. They get a *thrill* out of them.
- You need to be thoroughly *prepared/trained* by a qualified *instructor* or *guide*, and you often need special *equipment* such as *safety helmets*, *ropes* and *axes*.

Sports and games

- Common expressions connected with different sports and games:

Sport/game	Common expressions
tennis, etc.	players, serve, service, hit the ball over the net, in/out, score a point
football, etc.	teams, kick/hit/throw the ball, pass the ball to another player, tackle, score a goal
board games	throw the dice, move a piece, land on a square, take your opponent's piece
card games	shuffle the pack, deal the cards, play a card, win a trick; the four suits: spades, clubs, hearts, diamonds

Issues in sport

- Sportsmen and sportswomen can be either *amateurs* (they play for enjoyment) or *professionals* (they are paid money to take part). In all sports, individuals or teams *compete against* each other, and *matches*, *contests* or *championships* are organised. The winner(s) receive a *prize*, a *medal* or sometimes *prize money*.
- Sometimes *sportsmen* and *sportswomen* (especially *athletes*) take drugs to improve their *performance*. This is illegal, and tests are often carried out before *sports contests*. If the *competitor* is caught, he or she may be *disqualified* or *suspended*.
- *Football matches* attract large numbers of *spectators*. Occasionally there are outbreaks of *violence* between *supporters* (or *fans*) of different *teams*, and so the crowds at major matches are usually tightly *controlled*.

5 Set in the past

Past perfect tenses

- There are two past perfect tenses, Past perfect simple:

I'd She hadn't	seen the film before.

and Past perfect continuous:

I'd He'd	been	talking on the phone. living there for 5 years.

- We use these tenses to *go back* from the past to things that had happened *earlier*.
- We use the Past perfect simple to talk about *previous actions* or *events*:
  - When I returned, the room was empty – everyone *had left*.
  - The restaurant was completely full. Unfortunately, we *hadn't reserved* a table.

- We use the Past perfect continuous to talk about *previous activities*:
  - We were exhausted – we'*d been walking* all day.
  - I was starting to get worried. I'*d been waiting* for over an hour and she still hadn't arrived.
- Past perfect tenses are often used when reporting things people said or thought:
  - He told me his first wife *had died* in a car accident.
  - Later, I discovered that he'*d been lying* to me.

Reporting verbs

Reporting verbs may be followed by several structures:
- verb + *that*
  say admit deny
  - He denied that they'd ever met.
  - She admitted that she had lied.
- verb + object + *that*
  tell remind warn
  - I reminded him that we had to leave at three.
- verb + *to* + infinitive
  offer promise refuse threaten
  - He offered to lend me his bike. (*not* ~~offered me to~~)
- verb + object + *to* + infinitive
  remind warn
  - They warned us not to swim out too far.
- verb + *-ing*
  admit deny accuse someone of
  - She denied stealing the money.
  - They accused him of accepting bribes.

Non-defining relative clauses

- Non-defining relative clauses are used to give additional information. Compare:
  - My best friend Paula has just moved to Kuusamo.
  - My best friend Paula, *who I went to school with*, has just moved to Kuusamo, *which is a town in the north of Finland*.
  They are always separated from the main part of the sentence by commas.
- In non-defining relative clauses we can use *who*, *which*, *whose* or *where*, but not *that*. It is not possible to leave out the pronoun:
  - My grandmother, *who* is 80 next month, has just gone into hospital.
  - My oldest possession is my camera, *which* I was given for my tenth birthday. (*not* ~~that I was given~~)
  - In 1993 Steven Spielberg made 'Schindler's List', *for which* he received an Oscar.
  - The shop at the end of the street, *where* I usually buy my bread, has closed down.
- In more formal English, we can use *whom* as an object pronoun or after prepositions:
  - Professor Johnson, *whom* you may already know, will talk to us about butterflies.
  - Her brother, *to whom* she dedicated her first novel, is still alive.

(See also Defining relative clauses, Unit 3.)

Sequence expressions

- Structures that emphasise that there was a *short interval* between two events:

As soon as The moment	I saw the car, I decided to buy it.

(= I saw the car. Immediately, I decided to buy it.)

- Structures that emphasise that there was a *long interval* between two events:

It was only when It wasn't until	I saw his house that I realised that he was poor.

(= At first I thought he was rich. After some time, I saw his house. Then I realised he was poor.)

6 Do it yourself

Instructions

- Some common expressions found in instructions:
  - Add boiling water.
  - Rinse thoroughly.
  - Apply two coats of paint.
  - Select the desired programme.
  - Wait until surfaces are completely dry.
  - Stir well.
  - Ensure (that) surfaces are free from dirt.
  - Leave to dry overnight.
  - Press the button marked 'Play'.
- Articles and pronouns are often omitted in instructions:
  - Apply paint and leave to dry = Apply *the* paint and leave *it* to dry.
- Notice that instructions often use special verbs:

Instructions	'Normal' English
ensure that	make sure that
apply	put on
insert	put in
position together	put together
depress	press down

Problems and repairs

- Common household problems:
  - The glass is *cracked/broken*.
  - My dress is *torn*.
  - The door's *rotten*.
  - The paint is *peeling (off)*.
  - The pipe is *leaking*.
  - The walls are *damp*.
  - There's a *stain* on the carpet.
  - The tyre has got a *puncture*.
  - My coat has got a button *missing*.

- Some of these words can be used as verbs or nouns:

It's cracked.	There's a crack in it.
It's torn.	There's a tear (/teǝr/) in it.
It's leaking.	There's a leak in it.
It's stained.	There's a stain on it.

- 'Mending' verbs:

mend	(re)paint
repair	stick (on/together)
replace	sew (up/on)

- Notice the structure *needs* + *-ing*:

The door needs	mending. repainting. replacing.

Cooking

- 'Cooking' verbs:

boil	fry	bake
simmer	grill	roast

- To *simmer* is to boil very gently.
- You *bake* bread or cakes in the oven; you *roast* meat in the oven.
- *To cook* is a general word: 'cooked food' means 'not raw' (it could be boiled, baked or fried).

- Other verbs used for preparing food:

chop	mix	melt	pour
slice	add	sprinkle	serve
peel	stir		

You *mix* two or more things together:
- *Mix* the eggs with the flour.
- *Mix* the eggs and the flour together.

You *stir* things round (usually with a spoon):
- *Stir* the sauce slowly.

You *pour* liquids:
- *Pour* the sauce over the fish.

You *sprinkle* sugar, grated cheese, breadcrumbs, etc.:
- *Sprinkle* sugar over the top of the cake.

7 Working it out

must, might and can't

- The model verbs *must, might* and *can't* are used for drawing conclusions or making deductions:

  They must be at home = I'm sure they are at home
  They might be at home = Perhaps they're at home
  They can't be at home = I'm sure they're not at home

- Like other modal verbs, *must, might* and *can't* are followed by the infinitive without *to*. There are four possible forms:

	Simple	Continuous
Present	work	be working
Past	have worked	have been working

  – He *must work* hard – he looks worn out all the time. (= in general, every day)
  – They *can't be working* – there's no light on in the office. (= at the moment)
  – She *must have worked* hard in her life. (= in the past)
  – They *can't have been working* – there was no light on in the office. (= when I went there)

- *Must, might* and *can't* can also be followed by a passive infinitive:
  – It *can't be made* of silk – it's not shiny enough.
  – This picture *might have been taken* during the War.

'Unreal' conditionals

- We use *if* + *Past tense* (2nd conditional) to imagine unreal things in the *present*:
  – If they weren't at home, the door would be locked.

- We use *if* + *Past perfect tense* (3rd conditional) to imagine unreal things in the *past*:
  – If they'd seen us, they would have waved.

- We can also mix the two types of conditional in one sentence. One part can refer to the present, and one part to the past:
  – If they weren't at home, they would have locked the door.
  – If you'd broken your leg, you wouldn't be able to walk.

- Notice how we can combine *must, might* and *can't* with conditional sentences:
  – They must be at home – otherwise the door would be locked.
  – You can't have broken your leg. If you had, you wouldn't be able to walk.

Appearance

'Sense' verbs

look sound smell taste feel	+ adjective like + noun as if + clause

– He *looks* rather young.
– It doesn't *feel like* leather.
– It *sounds as if* there's someone at the door.

• In informal English, people often use *looks like*, etc. before a clause, instead of *as if*: You look like you need a rest; It sounds like there's someone at the door.

General impression: seem *and* appear

He	seems appears	to like classical music to be living alone to have been in the army

• *Seem* is normally followed by *to* + infinitive, but can also be followed by an *adjective*, by a *noun* or by *like* + *noun*:
  – She seems to be rather sad *or* She seems rather sad.
  – They seem to be interesting people *or* They seem (like) interesting people.

Reason and purpose

• We talk about the *reason why/that* people do things:
  – There are various reasons why people keep dogs.
  – One reason that people keep dogs is for protection.

• We can often leave out *why* and *that*:
  – The main reason I went there was to see a friend.
  – One reason people keep dogs is for protection.

• We talk about doing things *for a reason*:
  – People keep dogs for various reasons.
  – I went there for the same reason that you did.

• Structures expressing purpose:

Many people smoke	*to* relax. *in order to* relax. *so as to* relax. *as a way of* relaxing.

8 In the market-place

Careers

• General areas and typical jobs:

business	sales manager, accountant
arts	sculptor, actor, designer
entertainment	comedian, singer
education	lecturer, educational adviser
health	nurse, surgeon, hospital manager
welfare	social worker, welfare officer
media	TV presenter, journalist
industry	factory worker, manager
agriculture	farmer, forestry worker
technology	researcher, engineer
the environment	architect, ecologist
politics	politician, MP, minister
service industries	travel agent, salesperson

• The person in charge of a *company* or *organisation* is the *manager* (in informal English, the *boss*). People who are *employed* in the company are *employees*.

  If you work for yourself, you are *self-employed*.

  People who work in offices are often called *white-collar workers*. People who work with their hands are *manual workers*.

• Talking about ability and skill:
  – She's *good at* communicating with people / making money / designing things.
  – He's *good with* figures / his hands / children.
  – He's *a good* listener/communicator.
  – She's got *a good* business *sense* / artistic *sense* / *sense of* design.

• Things you might be interested in when applying for a job:
  – opportunities for promotion / for travel / to meet people
  – pay, working conditions, working hours, holidays.

Companies

• Expressions for talking about companies and business:
  – She *runs* a small business/company; he *works for* a computer company; we're *setting up* / *starting* a new business; the company is *launching* a new *product*.
  – They *broke even* (= covered their costs) / *made a profit* / *made a loss* / *went bankrupt*.
  – The company *has a turnover of* £100,000 a year (= the total amount of money it takes in).
  – They *took out a bank loan* (= borrowed money from the bank); they *paid off* the loan; they had to *pay 5% interest on* the loan.
  – They *took on* (= employed) more *staff*; they had to *lay staff off* (= ask them to leave); several employees *were made redundant* (= lost their jobs).

Advertising

- Some adjectives to describe advertisements:

appealing	shocking
eye-catching	offensive
persuasive	misleading

- In most countries, there are *rules* or *guidelines* about advertising. If an advertisement breaks these rules, the advertiser may be asked to *withdraw* the advertisement, or it may be *banned*.

9 Possibilities

will and would

- *will* is used for *making predictions*, and for saying what you expect (or don't expect) to happen:
  - I expect it *will* rain tomorrow.
  - Do you think there *will* be another world war in our lifetime?
  - He's taking his driving test tomorrow, but somehow I don't think he'*ll* pass it.
- *would* is used for *imagining* things which you don't see as really going to happen:
  - What *would* you do if you met a polar bear?
  - Why don't you give up smoking? That *would* make your cough better.
- Notice how, in the same context, we can change from *will* (for predicting what will happen) to *would* (for imagining other possibilities):
  - The council's plan to widen the main road *won't* solve the traffic problem – it *will* just encourage more people to use their cars. A better idea *would* be to make the road narrower, then people *would* leave their cars at home and use public transport.

depend on

- *depend on* can be followed by a noun or an indirect question:
  - How long will it take to get there?

It depends on	the traffic.
	how much traffic there is.
	whether we get stuck in a traffic jam.

- Before indirect questions, we can also use *it depends* without *on*:
  - It depends how much traffic there is.
  - It depends whether we get stuck in a traffic jam.
- Notice the expression *It depends*:
  - How long will it take to get there?
  - It depends. (= It depends on various things)

Expressing probability

Two ways of expressing probability:
will/won't + adverb

They	will certainly will probably probably won't certainly won't	reply to your letter.

is certain/likely/unlikely to

They	are certain are likely are unlikely are certain not	to reply to your letter.

- Notice that *likely* and *unlikely* are *adjectives*, so we say:
  - He's *likely* to come today.
  - There *are unlikely* to be many people there.
- In US English *likely* can also be used as an adverb:
  - He *will likely* come today.
- *likely* and *unlikely* can also be used regularly as adjectives:
  - She might phone, but it doesn't seem very *likely*.
  - I think the whole story sounds extremely *unlikely*.

Alternatives

- Expressions for weighing up alternatives:

Either ... or ...
Alternatively ...
..., or else ...
Another possibility ...

- *Either* you could go straight to university, *or* you could wait for a year and earn some money first.
- You could go straight to university, *or else* you could wait for a year and earn some money first.
- You could go straight to university. *Alternatively*, you could wait for a year and earn some money first.
- You could go straight to university. *Another possibility would be to* wait for a year and earn some money first.

10 Life, the universe and everything

Branches of science

- Sciences and scientists:

science	scientist
chemistry	chemist
physics	physicist
mathematics	mathematician
biology	biologist
genetics	geneticist
astronomy	astronomer
zoology	zoologist
geology	geologist

- Some basic scientific ideas:
  - The main *gases* in the air are *oxygen, nitrogen* and *carbon dioxide*. Water consists of two *elements*: *oxygen* and *hydrogen*.
  - *Atoms* combine together to form *molecules*.
  - According to Darwin's theory of *evolution*, different *species* of plants and animals have *evolved* over millions of years by natural selection.
  - When the *surface* of the Earth moves suddenly, it causes *earthquakes*.
  - The Earth and the other *planets* in the *solar system revolve* round the Sun. Our solar system is part of the *galaxy* we call the Milky Way.
  - The main groups of *vertebrates* (animals with backbones) are fish, *reptiles, amphibians*, birds and *mammals*. Many *species* of animals (such as dinosaurs) have become *extinct*.
  - Many *diseases* are caused by *bacteria* or by *viruses*. Diseases caused by bacteria can often be *treated* with *antibiotics*.
  - A *triangle* has three *corners* (or angles) and three *sides*. Some other common *geometrical shapes* are: *square, rectangle* and *circle*.

The environment

- Environmental issues:
  - *Nuclear power stations* use *radioactive* materials, and produce *radioactive waste*. If there is an accident, *radioactivity* can escape into the atmosphere.
  - Gases, such as car *exhaust fumes* and smoke from *power stations*, cause *atmospheric pollution*. They also prevent heat escaping from the Earth's atmosphere, and this causes the '*greenhouse effect*'. It is believed that the greenhouse effect contributes to *global warming*.
  - In modern farming, *crops* are *sprayed* with *chemicals* and *pesticides*. Some people believe that these are *harmful* to people and may cause *cancer*.
  - Because of the destruction of their *habitats* (especially *tropical rain forests*) many species of animals and plants are becoming *extinct*.

'Unscientific' beliefs

Beliefs	What people believe
astrology	The star sign you were born under affects your character.
telepathy	People can communicate directly by thinking.
psychokinesis	People can move objects by concentrating their thoughts on them.
fortune-telling	People can tell the future from cards, coffee cups, etc.
witchcraft	People can influence other people by casting a magic spell.
reincarnation	After they die, people are reborn in another body.
superstition	Particular things (e.g. black cats) bring good or bad luck.
ghosts	Ghosts of dead people sometimes appear in the place where they died.

11 Evaluating

Time comparison

Cities	are noisier than / aren't as pleasant as	they used to be.
Most people	have more free time than / don't work as hard as	they used to.

- Notice that the verb *be* is repeated after *used to*, but other verbs are omitted:
  - He's healthier than he used to *be*.
  - He *looks* healthier than he used to. (*not* ~~used to look~~)
- We can also make comparisons beginning with *used to*:
  - Cities *used not to* be as noisy as *they are now*.
  - Most people *used to* work harder than *they do now*.
- We can also use the Present perfect:
  - Cities *have become* noisier (over the last 50 years).
  - People *have started* having more free time.

Evaluation structures

It's a good idea / It's not a good idea	to go on a diet.

It's worth(while) / It's not worth / There's no point in	going on a diet.

- *It's not worth doing* and *There's no point in doing* both mean that you can do something, but it will achieve nothing:
  - There's *no point in giving* her flowers – she wouldn't notice them.
  - It's *not worth* taking a taxi – you can walk there in five minutes.

- We can say something is *worth doing* or is *worthwhile doing*:
  - It's really *worth*(*while*) visi*ting* Scotland – it's a beautiful country.
- Notice these expressions with *worth* and *worthwhile*:

I'm glad I saw that film.	It was really worth it. It was really worthwhile.

Causative verbs

enable allow force encourage help make it easier for	someone	to + infinitive

stop prevent discourage save	someone	from + -ing

Examples

- Fax machines *enable* people *to* send letters instantly.
- The mist *prevented* us *from* see*ing* clearly.
- Having a job in a factory *forced* him *to* get up early.
- Dishwashers *save* you (*from*) wash*ing* all the dishes by hand.
- The new tax laws *will encourage* people *to* save money.
- They increased parking charges to *discourage* people *from* driv*ing* into the city centre.

Advantages and disadvantages

One The Another (etc.)	advantage of disadvantage of drawback of problem with trouble with (good) thing about	......	is ...

- All these expressions are followed by a noun or an *-ing* form:

One advantage of	old age being old	is that you have lots of time.

- They are used to 'label' what you are talking about as good, bad, difficult, interesting, etc. Compare:

  If you live in the country, it isn't easy to go shopping.
  → *One of the main disadvantages of* living in the country *is that* it isn't easy to go shopping.
  When you're abroad, everything seems slightly unusual.
  → *The most exciting thing about* being abroad *is that* everything seems slightly unusual.

12 Yourself and others

Character adjectives

cheerful	sociable	cautious	vain
optimistic	talkative	fussy	self-centred
light-hearted	inquisitive	sensitive	aggressive
carefree	nosy	insecure	determined

- The following adjectives have a negative meaning:
  talkative = you talk too much
  nosy = you want to know other people's business
  fussy = you worry about every detail
  insecure = you're unsure of yourself
  vain = you admire yourself
  aggressive = you tend to quarrel or fight with people
- *sensitive* can have a positive or a negative meaning:
  - He's a very *sensitive* person who appreciates beauty. (= with fine feelings)
  - Don't be so *sensitive* – I was only joking. (= easily hurt)
  In the negative sense, we can also say *over-sensitive*:
  - Now he won't speak to me – I think he's being a bit *over-sensitive*.
  Notice the word *sensible*, which has quite a different meaning = 'having good sense':
  - She was *sensible* enough not to carry too much money around with her.
- Compare:
  - *self-centred* (negative) = always thinking about yourself and putting yourself first
  - *self-confident* (usually positive) = sure of yourself
  - *self-satisfied* (negative) = too pleased with yourself
- Notice how we use the expressions *tend to* and *have a tendency to* in describing what people are like:
  - She's very sociable, but she *tends to* be rather nosy.
  - He *has a tendency to* worry too much about details.

Relationships

- Some things that people often look for in a relationship with a partner:

honesty	respect for the other person
friendship	ability to communicate
equality	sense of humour
good looks	shared interests

- Other kinds of relationship:
  - *colleagues* (people you work with)
  - *neighbours* (people who live near you)
  - *acquaintances* (people you know but are not very close to)
- You may:
  - know other people well or just know them *by sight*
  - *get acquainted with* or *make friends with* them
  - *get on well* or *badly with* them
  - have *a lot, not much* or *nothing in common with* them
  - *envy* them (or *feel envious of* them) (= you wish you had what they have).

13 Right and wrong

should(n't) have

He	should shouldn't	have + -ed

She	should shouldn't	have been + -ing

- We use *should(n't) have + -ed* for criticising things people *did* or *didn't do*:
  - She should have stopped at the traffic lights (but she didn't).
  - You shouldn't have shouted at him (but you did).
- We use *should(n't) have been + -ing* for criticising things people *were* or *weren't doing*:
  - She shouldn't have been driving so fast. (that's why she couldn't stop)
  - You should have been paying attention. (then you would have heard what I said)
- Other expressions for talking about right and wrong:
  - She was (quite) *right/wrong to* complain about it.
  - People *have a right to* say what they think.
  - The government *has no right to* imprison people without trial.
  - It was *your own fault (that)* you ran out of money – you should have taken more with you.
  - I wasn't *to blame for* the accident – I wasn't even there.

needn't have & could have

He	needn't could	have + -ed

- *needn't have (done)* is used to talk about what someone did that *wasn't necessary*:
  - They *needn't have brought* food to the party (= they brought some food but there was plenty already).
  - I *needn't have got* here on time (= I got here on time, but then I had to wait for everyone else).
- *could have (done)* is used to talk about an *opportunity* to do something, but the person didn't do it:
  - Why did you hire a car? You *could have borrowed* mine.
  - I didn't know you were staying here. We *could have met* for a drink.
- Notice that *needn't have done* and *could have done* can often be used in the same context:
  - You *needn't have hired* a car – you *could have borrowed* mine.
  - I *needn't have got up* early this morning – I *could have stayed* in bed for another hour.

might have & could have

You	might could	have + -ed

- *Might/could have (done)* is used to criticise people for what they *didn't* do. It is milder and less direct than *should have (done)*:
  - You *might/could have told* me you'd be late. (you didn't tell me)
- *Might/could have (done)* is also used in a different sense: to imagine things that didn't in fact happen:
  - He was crazy to go swimming in this weather: he *might/could have drowned*. (luckily, he didn't drown)
- *Might (as well) have (done)* is also used to say that it *wasn't worth* doing something:
  - It wasn't worth taking a taxi – we *might as well have walked*.

Contrasting ideas

- Some common ways of contrasting two ideas:

Mild contrast

It may be true that … To some extent it's true that …	But also … On the other hand, …

Moderate contrast

Many people think that … People often claim that … It's commonly believed that …	But in fact, … However, … In fact, however, …

Strong contrast

Many people think that … People often claim that …	On the contrary, … In fact, …

  - *It may be true that* supermarkets make shopping easier. *On the other hand*, they make it very difficult for smaller shops to survive.
  - *Many people think that* the United Nations has achieved almost nothing at all. *In fact, however*, just providing a place where different nations can talk to each other is itself a sign of progress.
  - *It simply isn't true* that the government is helping poor people. *On the contrary*, their policies are making poor people even poorer.

14 Body and mind

Diseases

- Many diseases are *infectious* (you can catch them from the air, from flies, water, etc.).
  Some diseases are *curable* (= you can cure them), some are *incurable* (= you cannot cure them) or *fatal* (= you die from them).
  An *outbreak* of cholera = many people get it at the same time. A cholera *epidemic* = a very large number of people get it at the same time.
  The *symptoms* of 'flu are a high temperature and aching limbs.

Medical treatment

- Verbs and nouns connected with medical treatment:

Verbs	Nouns
examine	examination
operate	operation
prescribe	prescription
vaccinate	vaccination
inoculate	inoculation
X-ray	X-ray

- If you go to see a doctor, he/she will probably examine you (give you an *examination*). He/She may *prescribe* medicine for you to take (write/give you a *prescription*).

- If you need an *operation*, you *go into hospital*. They will give you an *anaesthetic*, and the operation will be performed by a *surgeon* (he/she will *operate* on you).

- You can be *vaccinated* (or *inoculated*) to protect you against catching certain diseases (e.g. cholera, measles, polio). Babies usually have their first *vaccination* (or *inoculation*) at the age of six months. In everyday conversation, people talk about *having an injection*.

- If you have a *toothache*, you should go to a dentist. He/She will examine your teeth, and may give you a filling.

- You can take your *temperature* by putting a *thermometer* under your tongue. If your temperature is more than 35°, we say '*You've got a temperature*' or '*You've got a fever*'.

- If you think you've broken your leg, you can have it *X-rayed* at the hospital.

- If you cut your finger, you put a *plaster* on it. If you cut your hand badly (or if you sprain your wrist), you may have to put a *bandage* round it.

Alternative medicine

- Some forms of alternative medicine and healing:

Type	What they use
traditional medicine	herbs and traditional remedies
homeopathy	homeopathic medicines
acupuncture	needles
faith healing	religious faith and touch

15 Using the passive

The passive

Active	Someone *stole* his wallet. Terrorists *have kidnapped* them.
Passive	His wallet *was stolen*. They*'ve been kidnapped* by terrorists.

- In forming the passive, the object of the active sentence (*wallet, them*) becomes the *subject* of the passive sentence.

- The passive is formed with *be + past participle*. It can be in any tense: past, present or future.

	Simple	Continuous
Present	is built	is being built
Present perfect	has been built	–
Past	was built	was being built
Past perfect	had been built	–
Future	will be built	–
Present infinitive	be built	–
Past infinitive	have been built	–
-ing form	being built	–

- These days, most houses *are built* of concrete.
- Their house isn't finished yet. It*'s* still *being built*.
- This is where the new airport *will be built*.
- In my opinion, the school shouldn't *have been built* so near the main road.

Notice that the continuous form is normally only used in the present and past tenses.

Using the passive

- We often use the passive when we are interested in *what happened* rather than in who did the action:
  - His wallet *was stolen*. (we don't know who stole it)
  - She's just *been given* a new job. (obviously, by her employers)
  - The airport *will be finished* next spring. (it isn't important who finishes it)

- We also use the passive in order to keep *the same subject* over several sentences:
  - I had a terrible time crossing the border. First I had to wait for two hours, and then I *was interrogated* for an hour by the secret police. (I'm talking about *my experiences*, so I want to keep *I* as the subject)

- Notice that the passive is especially common in scientific writing, especially in describing processes:
  - First the metal *is heated* to a temperature of 500°, then it *is poured* into a large container.

The passive with 'get'

- In conversational English, we often use the passive with *get* instead of *be*, especially with particular verbs describing accidental events, e.g.:

get lost	get killed	get stolen
get stuck	get mugged	get caught

- Take a map, in case you *get lost*.
- He tried to cheat the tax office, but he *got caught*.

- The passive is also commonly used with *get* to talk about things that happen *often* or *repeatedly*:
  - She often *gets invited* to read her poetry, but she doesn't always *get paid*.

The 'have' passive

Active Passive 'Have' passive	They're repairing her car. Her car is being repaired. She's *having* her car *repaired*.
Active Passive 'Have' passive	Someone stole my bike. My bike was stolen. I *had* my bike *stolen*.

- The 'have' passive is formed with *have* (+ object) + *past participle*. Like the normal passive, it can be in any tense:
  - *Present simple*: I usually *have* my hair *cut* on Saturday.
  - *going to*: He's going to *have* his eyes *tested*.
  - *Present perfect*: Help! I've just *had* my handbag *snatched*!
  - *Past continuous*: When I walked in, he *was having* his back *massaged*.
  - *-ing form*: I hate *having* my photograph *taken*.
- The 'have' passive can be used:
  - for things that you *arrange to happen* (have your eyes tested, have your photograph taken, have your house painted)
  - for things that *happen to you without you intending them* (have your face slapped, have your car stolen, have your house broken into)
- Notice the difference between the *'have' passive* and the *Present perfect tense*:
  - I've cut my hair (Present perfect = I've done it myself)
  - I usually *have* my hair *cut* at Toni's ('have' passive, = I usually get them to do it)

Passive reporting verbs

He is They are	known believed said thought assumed reported	to	work for the Mafia. be living in Chicago. have robbed a bank.

- *He is thought to be …* means the same as *People think he is …* Compare:

> *People think* he works for the Mafia.
It is thought that he works for the Mafia.
He is thought to work for the Mafia.

- Passive reporting verbs are especially common in more formal written English (e.g. newspaper reports). In conversational English, active forms are more usual:
  - They say he robbed a bank.
  - Everyone knows he's living in Chicago.

16 World affairs

War and peace

- Some common verb/noun pairs:

Verb	Noun
attack	attack
fight	fighting
invade	invasion
resist	resistance
damage	damage
negotiate	negotiations
agree	agreement

- Examples:
  - Rebel troops *attacked* the capital.
  - Rebel troops *launched an attack on* the capital.
  - The two sides *fought* through the night.
  - *Fighting* continued through the night.
  - American forces *invaded* the island.
  - Local troops *resisted* the *invasion*.
  - Local troops *put up* fierce *resistance to* the invasion.
  - They *damaged* several buildings.
  - They *caused* severe *damage to* several buildings.
  - After *negotiating* for a long time, the two sides *reached agreement*.
  - After long *negotiations*, the two sides *agreed* to end the war.
- Other expressions:
  - *Refugees fled* (past of *flee*) across the border. They found shelter in *refugee camps*.
  - The rebels *took* several *hostages* and held them in a hospital building. Troops *surrounded* the building. After negotiations the rebels agreed to *free* the hostages.
  - The two sides *signed* a *peace treaty* (or *peace agreement*) to end the war.

Political systems

- In a *democracy*, people vote in a *general election*. The *party* that wins forms the *government*. The other parties are *opposition* parties. The leader of the government is the *prime minister* or *president*, and he/she chooses other *ministers* to form the *cabinet*.
- In a *monarchy* (e.g. Britain, Sweden, Thailand), the highest person is the *monarch* (king or queen). In a *republic* (e.g. Russia, the USA, South Africa), the head of state is the *president*.
- Areas of government:

Area	Concerned with
health	hospitals, doctors, health care
education	schools, universities, adult education
defence	army, navy, air force, weapons
economic affairs	the economy, taxation
foreign affairs	relations with other countries
home affairs	police, prisons, housing
employment	jobs, unemployment
transport	roads, public transport
environment	pollution, wildlife
agriculture	farming, forestry

General grammar reference: the English tense system

- There are three 'time frames' in the English tense system: the present, the past and the future. Within each time frame, there are four 'aspects': *simple, continuous, perfect simple* and *perfect continuous*. This gives the twelve main tenses of English.

	Simple	Continuous
Present *Present perfect*	works has worked	is working has been working
Past *Past perfect*	worked had worked	was working had been working
Future *Future perfect*	will work will have worked	will be working will have been working

Simple tenses

- The Present simple is used to talk about things in general, or repeated actions:
  - My sister *speaks* fluent Arabic.
  - I *have* a sauna every Friday evening.
- The Past simple is used to talk about actions or states in the past:
  - They *got* married last Saturday.
  - In the Middle Ages, forests *covered* most of Europe.
- The Future simple is used to talk about events or states in the future:
  - The world *will end* in 2050.
  - *Will* you still *be* here this evening?

Continuous tenses

- Continuous tenses are used to talk about activities *going on* at a particular moment:

Present: He*'s staying* with friends at the moment.
Wait a minute – I*'m* just *changing*.
Past: When I came in, they *were playing* cards.
Future: By next spring, we*'ll be living* in Canada.
I*'ll be waiting* outside (when you arrive).

Perfect tenses

- Perfect simple tenses are used to talk about actions that are *already finished* or *complete* at a particular moment (when they happened is not important, but rather the fact that they are complete):

Present: She*'s been* all over the world. (= she knows a lot of countries)
I*'ve changed* my clothes. (= now I'm wearing new ones)
Past: When I came in, they *had* already *left*. (= they weren't there any more)
Future: By next spring, we*'ll have moved* to Canada. (= we'll be there by then)

- Perfect continuous tenses are used to talk about *activities* going on *just before* or *up to* a particular moment:

Present: I*'ve been washing* the car. (that's why I'm wet)
We*'ve been living* together for a year now.

Past: They*'d been waiting* for over an hour, and they were starting to get impatient.
Future: By next Sunday, I*'ll have been working* here for a year.

Stative verbs

- Some verbs are normally used only with simple tenses. There are four main types:
  - *verbs expressing attitudes*: like, love, hate, prefer, want, wish, need
  - *verbs of knowledge and belief*: know, believe, doubt, mean, remember, forget, understand, think (= believe)
  - *verbs connected with having and being*: be, have (= possess), own, belong to, include, consist of, seem
  - *verbs of the senses*: see, hear, sound, taste, smell (= give out a smell)
- Examples:
  - This cake *tastes* wonderful. (*not* ~~is tasting~~)
  - We*'ve known* each other for years. (*not* ~~been knowing~~)
  - He desperately *needed* help. (*not* ~~was needing~~)

Talking about the future

- We can talk about the future in various ways in English:

will
We use *will* to make predictions:
  - I expect a lot of people *will* come to the lecture.
  - Don't leave the butter out in the sun – it *will* melt.

We also use *will* when *making a decision* to do something:
  - I think I*'ll* have an ice-cream.
  - I know. I*'ll* ask Mary what to do.

Present simple
We use the present simple to talk about future events which are part of a *programme* or *timetable*:
  - My train *gets* in at 6.30 this evening.
  - Don't be late: the concert *starts* at 8 o'clock.

Present continuous
We use the present continuous to talk about things that are *already arranged* for the future:
  - We*'re having* a party on Friday: do you want to come?
  - I*'m playing* table tennis this evening.

going to
We use *going to*:
1 to express *intention*:
  - When I grow up, I*'m going* to be an airline pilot.
  - I*'m going* to have a hot bath and go to bed early.
2 to talk about things that have *already started to happen*:
  - Look out! We*'re going* to crash! (we've already started skidding)
  - She*'s going* to have a baby. (she's pregnant)

Note: We do not use *will* to express intention, so we wouldn't say 'I'll have a hot bath' unless we are *actually deciding* to do that as we speak.

Irregular verbs

Infinitive	Simple past	Past participle
be	was/were	been
beat	beat	beaten
become	became	become
begin	began	begun
bend	bent	bent
bite	bit	bitten
blow	blew	blown
break	broke	broken
bring	brought	brought
burn	burnt	burnt
build	built	built
buy	bought	bought
can	could	(been able)
catch	caught	caught
choose	chose	chosen
come	came	come
cost	cost	cost
cut	cut	cut
do	did	done
draw	drew	drawn
dream	dreamt	dreamt
drink	drank	drunk
drive	drove	driven
eat	ate	eaten
fall	fell	fallen
feed	fed	fed
feel	felt	felt
fight	fought	fought
find	found	found
fly	flew	flown
forget	forgot	forgotten
forgive	forgave	forgiven
freeze	froze	frozen
get	got	got
give	gave	given
go	went	gone (been)
grow	grew	grown
hang	hung	hung
have	had	had
hear	heard	heard
hide	hid	hidden
hit	hit	hit
hold	held	held
hurt	hurt	hurt
keep	kept	kept
know	knew	known
lay	laid	laid
lead	led	led
learn	learnt	learnt
leave	left	left
lend	lent	lent
let	let	let
lie	lay	lain
lose	lost	lost
make	made	made
mean	meant	meant
meet	met	met
pay	paid	paid
put	put	put
read	read	read
ride	rode	ridden
ring	rang	rung
rise	rose	risen
run	ran	run
say	said	said
see	saw	seen
sell	sold	sold
send	sent	sent
set	set	set
shake	shook	shaken
shine	shone	shone
shoot	shot	shot
show	showed	shown
shut	shut	shut
sing	sang	sung
sink	sank	sunk
sit	sat	sat
sleep	slept	slept
smell	smelt	smelt
speak	spoke	spoken
spell	spelt	spelt
spend	spent	spent
spread	spread	spread
stand	stood	stood
steal	stole	stolen
sweep	swept	swept
swim	swam	swum
swing	swung	swung
take	took	taken
teach	taught	taught
tear	tore	torn
tell	told	told
think	thought	thought
throw	threw	thrown
understand	understood	understood
wake	woke	woken
wear	wore	worn
win	won	won
write	wrote	written

Phonetic symbols

Vowels

Symbol	Example
/iː/	tree /triː/
/i/	many /'meni/
/ɪ/	sit /sɪt/
/e/	bed /bed/
/æ/	back /bæk/
/ʌ/	sun /sʌn/
/ɑː/	car /kɑː/
/ɒ/	hot /hɒt/
/ɔː/	horse /hɔːs/
/ʊ/	full /fʊl/
/uː/	moon /muːn/
/ɜː/	girl /ɡɜːl/
/ə/	arrive /ə'raɪv/
	water /'wɔːtə/
/eɪ/	late /leɪt/
/aɪ/	time /taɪm/
/ɔɪ/	boy /bɔɪ/
/əʊ/	home /həʊm/
/aʊ/	out /aʊt/
/ɪə/	hear /hɪə/
/eə/	there /ðeə/
/ʊə/	pure /pjʊə/

Consonants

Symbol	Example
/p/	pull /pʊl/
/b/	bad /bæd/
/t/	take /teɪk/
/d/	dog /dɒɡ/
/k/	cat /kæt/
/g/	go /ɡəʊ/
/tʃ/	church /tʃɜːtʃ/
/dʒ/	age /eɪdʒ/
/f/	for /fɔː/
/v/	love /lʌv/
/θ/	thick /θɪk/
/ð/	this /ðɪs/
/s/	sit /sɪt/
/z/	zoo /zuː/
/ʃ/	shop /ʃɒp/
/ʒ/	leisure /'leʒə/
/h/	house /haʊs/
/m/	make /meɪk/
/n/	name /neɪm/
/ŋ/	bring /brɪŋ/
/l/	look /lʊk/
/r/	road /rəʊd/
/j/	young /jʌŋ/
/w/	wear /weə/

Stress

We show stress by a mark (/'/) before the stressed syllable:
later /'leɪtə/; arrive /ə'raɪv/; information /ɪnfə'meɪʃn/.

truant
a child who stays away from school without getting permission (you *play truant*)

chock
a piece of wood you put under the wheel of a car or lorry to stop it rolling down a hill

milliner
someone who makes or sells women's hats

pew
a seat you sit on in church

Luddite
a person who is opposed to change, especially technological developments

usher
someone who shows guests to their seats in a theatre or cinema

rustler
in the Wild West, someone who steals cows

browser
a computer program that allows you to explore the Internet

cluck
the noise a chicken makes

limpet
a small sea animal with a shell that sticks to rocks, and is hard to get off

cuckold
(old-fashioned word) a man whose wife is unfaithful

a pig in a poke
(idiom) something you buy without being able to see it first (*poke* is an old word for 'bag')

larder
a cool cupboard or room in which food is kept (nowadays, most people use fridges instead)

pipedream
a hope for the future that has no chance of coming true

scaffold
a platform on which people are executed (especially by hanging)

Self-study Workbook: Study skills exercises

Study skills A: Using reference books

A: Using a dictionary
Students look up words on a sample page from an English dictionary.

B: Finding your way around a book
Students look at the contents page of a travel guide and answer questions.

Study skills B: Dealing with vocabulary

A: Guessing unknown words
Students guess the meanings of unfamiliar words in a text.

B: Learning new vocabulary
Students practise noting down new vocabulary with collocations.

Study skills C: Approaching a reading text

A: Predicting what you will read
Students look at the headlines and subheadings of a newspaper article, and guess what it will say.

B: Reading for the main idea
Students skim the article quickly and decide which are the main points.

C: Finding specific information
Students read the article more carefully and note down particular information.

Study skills D: Summarising information

A: Taking notes
Students listen to an interview and compare two sets of written points.

B: Writing a summary
Students study a summary of the interviews, then write a similar summary themselves.

Study skills E: Developing a piece of writing

A: Jotting down ideas
Students compare different ways of making notes for a piece of writing, then try out the one that suits them best.

B: Writing a draft and making improvements
Students study a rough draft of a piece of writing and an improved version, then write their own draft and improve it.

Study skills F: Reading between the lines

A: Understanding implied meaning
Students study the opening paragraphs of four novels, and decide what the novels are about.

B: Reading a poem
Students read and listen to a poem, and focus on implied meanings in it.

Acknowledgements

The authors would like to thank the following for their contributions to *Language in Use* Upper-intermediate:

– for contributing to the listening and reading material: Colin Aitkin, Anginette Barton, Fran Brooks, Nick Brooks, Mark Calland, Sean Connolly, Dawn Coutts, Bryan Cruden, Shiroma da Silva, Mary Drummond, Hazel Jones, Thomas Jones, Anastasia Katsikiotis, Richard Keyworth, Meredith Levy, Steve Mitchell, Stephen Myers, Philip Older, Louisa Preskett, Paula Preskett, Gaby Rado, Paul Roberts, Philippe Roy, Simon Taylor, Diana Thompson, Pam Thompson, Ingrid Williams, Jan Williams, Larissa Williams, Gabriella Zaharias; staff and students of Abon Language School, Bristol, and BPELF, Edinburgh; and all the actors whose voices were recorded in studio sessions.
– for advice and help with the pronunciation exercises: Martin Hewings of The University of Birmingham.
– for designing the course: James Arnold (Gecko Ltd).
– for commissioning artwork: Wendy Homer (Gecko Ltd).
– for the production of the recorded material: Martin Williamson (Prolingua Productions) and Peter and Diana Thompson (Studio AVP).
– for photography: Chris Coggins.
– for picture research: Sandie Huskinson-Rolfe of PHOTOSEEKERS.
– for clearance of permissions: Sophie Dukan.

The authors would also like to thank the following at Cambridge University Press:

– Colin Hayes, for his continuing support and help.
– Peter Donovan for organising the project.
– Joanne Currie for overseeing the design of the course.
– Linda Matthews for control of production.
– Sue Wiseman and Val Grove for general administrative help.

Special thanks go to:

– James Dingle of Cambridge University Press, for his expert management of the various stages of the project, and for his continuing commitment to *Language in Use*.
– Meredith Levy, our Editor, for her professionalism, good judgement and tireless attention to detail.

The authors and publishers would like to thank the following individuals for their help in commenting on the material and for the invaluable feedback which they provided:

Silvia Ronchetti, Buenos Aires, Argentina; Julia Barraco, British Council, Athens, Greece; Richard Rice, Associazione Culturale Delle Lingue Europee, Bologna, Italy; Niall Henderson, Chiuro, Italy; John Eaglesham, British School of Milan, Italy; Jonathan Wright, The Language Project, Bristol, UK; Matthew Wicks, Language Studies International, Cambridge, UK; Brian Cruden, Basil Paterson Edinburgh Language Foundation, UK.

The authors and publishers are grateful to the following copyright owners for permission to reproduce copyright material. Every endeavour has been made to contact copyright owners and apologies are expressed for any omissions.

Süddeutsche Zeitung and Dr. Rudolph Schütz for the quotations on p. 9 from Süddeutsche Zeitung Magazine no. 21/95; New Scientist for the text on p. 15; Boxtree Ltd. for the extracts from *The Fun and Games Puzzle Book* on pp. 24–25; The Guardian for the article by William Mayes **on** p. 34, © The Guardian; Philippe Roy for the Tarte Flambée material on p. 35; Future Publishing Ltd. for the PC Format cover on p. 43, © 1993 Future Publishing Limited. Used by permission. All rights reserved; Toyota (GB) Limited for the advert on p. 43; Benetton for the advert on p. 47 (B), © Benetton; The National Opinion Research Centre at the University of Chicago for the questionnaire on p. 53; Robert E. Rogoff for *Dessert* by Robert E. Rogoff on p. 55, Copyright © 1995 Robert E. Rogoff. All rights reserved; Die Abendzeitung for the text and content of the egg paintings on pp. 62 & 100; Punch Library for the cartoons on p. 63 (A, C, D & F); Private Eye for the cartoons on p. 63 (B & E); The Times for the article on p. 68 by Bill Frost and Kathryn Knight, the articles on p. 91 by Andrew Malone (*tl*) and Jon Ashford (*tr*), the article on p. 101 by Simon Jenkins, and The Sunday Times for the article on p. 91 (*b*), © Times Newspapers Limited, (1994 and 1995); HarperCollins *Publishers* Limited for the story 'Zoo' by Edward D. Koch taken from *Young Extraterrestrials* on p. 109.

The authors and publishers are grateful to the following illustrators, photographers and photographic sources:

Illustrators: Peter Byatt: pp. 24, 25, 92; Paul Davies: p. 23; Paul Dickinson: p. 31; Max Ellis: p. 55; Hilary Evans: pp. 10, 61; Gecko Limited: all DTP illustrations and graphics; Helena Greene: p. 33; Sue Hillwood-Harris: p. 30; Phil Healey: pp. 9, 46, 71; Amanda MacPhail: pp. 18, 51, 81, 96; Michael Ogden: pp. 11, 97 *tr*, 97 *br*; Pantelis Palios: pp. 14, 27, 73, 86; Tracy Rich: pp. 15 *b*, 58; Martin Sanders: pp. 62, 67, 100; Brian Smith: p. 29; Kath Walker: pp. 13, 69; Colin Wheeler: p. 15 *t*; Dan Williams: p. 44; Rosemary Woods: p. 78; Annabel Wright: pp. 53, 63 *t*, 74, 103.

Photographic sources: Ace Photo Agency: p. 12 (9); Allsport/Russell Cheyne: p. 22 (inset); François Gohier/Ardea London: p. 70; Art Directors Photo Library: pp. 64 (B), 65 *r*, 87 (D); John Gilbert/Aspect Picture Library: p. 49 *l*; Portrait of Marco Polo (1254–1324), by Dolfino (litho), Biblioteca Nazionale, Turin/Bridgeman Art Library, London: p. 21 *r*, Portrait of Shakespeare, engraving by Droeshurt, 1623, British Library, London/BAL, London: p. 87 (B), *Self Portrait with Bandaged Ear*, 1889, by Vincent Van Gogh (1853-90), Courtauld Institute Galleries, University of London/BAL London: p. 47 (G), Little Red Riding Hood, by Arthur Rackham (1867–1939), Private Collection/BAL London. 'The Arthur Rackham pictures are reproduced with the kind permission of his family': p. 19 *t*, *The Sick Child*, 1907, by Edvard Munch (1863–1944), Tate Gallery, London/BAL London, © The Munch Museum/The Munch-Ellingsen Group/DACS 1997: p. 20; British Council Collection: p. 90; Britstock/Eric Bach: p. 38 (D), Britstock/R. Schumann: p. 65 *bm*; Camera Press Limited: pp. 28 *t*, 49 *tr*, 87 (G); The J. Allan Cash Photolibrary: p. 101; Chris Coggins: pp. 8, 12 (1, 2, 7 & 8), 33, 35, 42, 45, 62, 64 *b*, 88, 100; Corbis-Bettmann/UPI: p. 82 *tl*; Empics/Presse Sports: p. 47 (F); Mary Evans Picture Library: p. 21 *l*, MEPL/Michael Buhler: p. 38 (B); Chris Fairclough Colour Library: p. 12 (5); David Sillitoe/The Guardian, © The Guardian, p. 34; Robert Harding Picture Library: pp. 40, 49 *br*, RHPL/Nigel Francis: p. 47 (H); Sarah Murray/Hutchison: p. 47 (A); Images Colour Library: pp. 19 *b*, 22 (E & F); John Arthur/Impact Photos: p. 83 *m*, David Reed/Impact: p. 73 *b*, Simon Shepheard/Impact: p. 12 (4); Kenji Kawakami for the photographs taken from 101 *Unuseless Japanese Inventions*: pp. 59, 87 (F) and 99; 'Popeye' reproduced by kind permission of TM & © 1996 King Features Syndicate Inc.: p. 65 *bl*; Universal/Kobal: p. 47 (D); David Heyelin/NHPA: p. 73 *t*, Rod Planck/NHPA: p. 72 (B), Andy Rouse/NHPA: p. 87 (A); 'PA News' Photo Library: p. 28 *b*; Ron Giling/Panos Pictures: pp. 87 (C), 102 *b*, Jeremy Hartley/Panos: p. 72 (D); The Photographers Library: pp. 22 (A), 48; Pictor International: pp. 12 (6), 72 (A), 87 (H); Pictures Colour Library: p. 64 (C); Popperfoto: p. 82 *mr*; Private Collection: p. 89; Raymonds Press Agency, Derby: p. 68; Rex Features Limited: pp. 22 (D), 102 *t*, Rex Features/The Sun: p. 91; *Regarding Soup* and *Sirens Rising* by Gabriella Roth, © 1994 Gabriella Roth: pp. 39 & 94; Roswell Footage Limited: p. 38 (C); Scott Camazine/Science Photo Library: p. 98; Spindrift Photos/David Pratt: p. 85; Frank Spooner Pictures/Gamma: pp. 47 (C), 64 (D), 82 *tr*, 82 *br*; Tony Stone Images/Kevin Kelley: p. 52, TSI/Lester Lefkowitz: p. 38 (A), TSI/David Madison: pp. 22 (B & C), TSI/Joseph McBride: p. 22 *t*, TSI/Marc Pokemprier: p. 60; Georges De Keerle/Sygma: p. 65 *ml*, Brooks Kraft/Sygma: p. 87 (E), Richard Melloul/Sygma: p. 83 *r*, François Poincet/Sygma: p. 80, Mathieu Polak/Sygma: p. 12 (3), P. Le Segretain/Sygma: p. 83 *l*, Randy Taylor/Sygma: p. 82 *bl*; Telegraph Colour Library/FGP: p. 93, TCL/Ian Sanderson: p. 72 (C); Viewfinder Colour Photo Library: p. 47 (E).

We have been unable to trace the copyright holders for the pictures on p. 64 (A), taken from 'Tattoo, The Exotic Art of Skin Decoration', by Michelle Delio and p. 65 *tl* by George Selleck/Bodyworks. We would be grateful for any information that would enable us to do so.

t = top   *m* = middle   *b* = bottom   *r* = right   *l* = left

Picture research by Sandie Huskinson-Rolfe of PHOTOSEEKERS.
Cover design by Dunne & Scully.
Design and production handled by Gecko Limited, Bicester, Oxon.
Colour scanning and reproduction by Goodfellow & Egan, Cambridge.
Permissions cleared by Sophie Dukan.
Sound recordings by Martin Williamson, Prolingua Productions at Studio AVP.
Freelance editorial work by Meredith Levy.